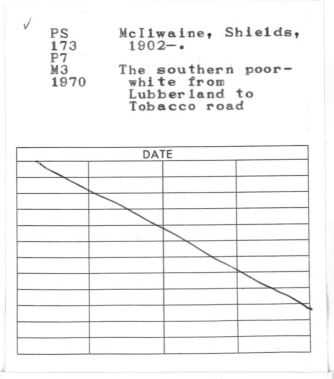

DATE			

THE SOUTHERN POOR-WHITE

FROM LUBBERLAND TO TOBACCO ROAD

THE SOUTHERN Poor-White
FROM LUBBERLAND TO TOBACCO
ROAD ✤ ✤ By SHIELDS McILWAINE

COOPER SQUARE PUBLISHERS, INC.
NEW YORK — 1970

For My Parents
in the Old North State

ACKNOWLEDGMENT

The author gratefully acknowledges the aid given by the following in the preparation of this volume: Professor Percy H. Boynton and Drs. Napier Wilt and Walter Blair of the University of Chicago for guidance and encouragement; Franklin J. Meine of Chicago for the use of his collection of American humor; Professor Samuel H. Monk and Dean A. Theodore Johnson of Southwestern for reading the manuscript; Catherine McIlwaine and Carl Arnault for clerical drudgery; and the General Education Board of New York for a fellowship.

SHIELDS McILWAINE

CONTENTS

INTRODUCTION   xiii

CHAPTER ONE. WILLIAM BYRD OF WESTOVER DIS-
COVERS THE FRONTIER LUBBER   3

    I. THE FIRST LITERARY PORTRAIT OF THE
       POOR-WHITE   9

CHAPTER TWO. LITERATURE INTRODUCES ANTE-
BELLUM AMERICA TO THE POOR-WHITE   16

    I. VIEW FROM THE PLANTATION PORCH:
       GEORGE TUCKER AND WILLIAM A. CAR-
       UTHERS   16

    II. WILLIAM GILMORE SIMMS, THE CHARLES-
       TON IDEAL, AND THE SQUATTER   25

    III. NORTHERN CONCEPTION OF PO' WHITE
       TRASH: JAMES R. GILMORE AND MRS.
       STOWE   32

    IV. SOUTHERN COMIC PORTRAITS OF CRACK-
       ERS, WOOLHATS, AND DIRT-EATERS   40

CHAPTER THREE. THE SOUTH CLAIMS THE POOR-
WHITE FOR WAR AND LITERATURE   75

    I. THE POOR-WHITE IN THE CIVIL WAR AND
       RECONSTRUCTION   75

    II. POST-WAR NORTHERN REPORT ON THE
       POOR-WHITE: ALBION W. TOURGEE AND
       JOHN W. DEFOREST   87

    III. YANKEE INTEREST IN THE NEW SOUTH
       AND THE POOR-WHITE   100

    IV. SENTIMENTAL AND HEROIC POOR-WHITE:
       JOEL CHANDLER HARRIS AND THOMAS
       NELSON PAGE   110

    V. OLD-SOUTH HUMOR WITH NEW-SOUTH
       SENTIMENT: RICHARD MALCOLM JOHN-
       STON AND OTHERS   128

Contents

VI. PICTURESQUE BACKGROUNDS AND LOUISIANA CAJUNS: GEORGE W. CABLE AND KATE CHOPIN   134

VII. NATURALISTIC MATERIAL AND LOCAL-COLOR METHOD: ALICE FRENCH AND HER ARKANSAS REDNECKS   153

CHAPTER FOUR. AMERICA MAKES THE POOR-WHITE A CAUSE AND A LITERARY VOGUE   163

I. TENANT AND SHARECROPPER: THE CONTEMPORARY POOR-WHITE   163

II. POOR-WHITE AND THE SECOND LITERARY REVIVAL IN THE SOUTH   169

III. LOCAL COLOR ONCE MORE: MARJORIE RAWLINGS' RE-DISCOVERY OF THE FLORIDA CRACKER   174

IV. CRITICISM AND PROPAGANDA: ELLEN GLASGOW TO T. S. STRIBLING   184

V. SENSIBILITY AND REALISM: EDITH S. KELLEY, ELIZABETH MADOX ROBERTS, AND PAUL GREEN   199

VI. NATURALISTIC MODES: THE GOTHIC, THE RIBALD, AND THE TRAGIC: WILLIAM FAULKNER AND ERSKINE CALDWELL   217

CONCLUSION: BACKWARD GLANCE OVER THE POOR-WHITE'S STORY   241

BIBLIOGRAPHY   249

INDEX   271

ILLUSTRATIONS

FACING PAGE

PINEYWOODS FOLK OF NORTH CAROLINA   118

CAJUN FATHERS AT THE SCHOOLHOUSE   150

HENRY HULL AS JEETER LESTER IN "TOBACCO ROAD"   230

INTRODUCTION

I N THE SOUTH, "POOR-WHITE" MEANS CONTEMPT; *poor-white trash* may start fists flying. *No 'count* and *po' buckra* likewise connote scorn for the lowest Southern farmers. And *peckerwood* is "like nigger, or swear words, or certain small mono-syllables of vulgarity."[1] To nineteenth-century Northern writers these folk were also *mean whites* and *low-downers*.[2]

Undoubtedly Negroes originated some of these words. On the lower Atlantic seaboard and the islands off the coasts of South Carolina and Georgia, Gullah slaves added an African word to American English. To them, in their native land, the feared and hated white slave-hunters were "encompassing power"—*m'bakara*. In the States, pronunciation and meaning shifted after the Gullahs learned to brag like Thomas Nelson Page's Uncle Gabe:

> *My folks war'n none o' yo' po' white trash:*
> *No, sah, dey was ob high degree,—*
> *Dis heah nigger am quality.*[3]

Then they muttered their old West African term with new meaning, "po' buckra."[4]

Such childish condescension of house slaves toward

---

1. H. H. Kroll, *Cabin in the Cotton*, 121.
2. J. W. DeForest, "Drawing Bureau Rations," *Harper's Magazine*, XXXVI (May, 1868), 794.
3. "Uncle Gabe's White Folks," *Library of Southern Literature*, IX, 3883-85.
4. Its first appearance was about 1825. This information was supplied by M. M. Matthews from the laboratory of the *Dictionary of American English on Historical Principles*, University of Chicago. Hereafter referred to as *DAE*. See also G. M. Shelby and S. G. Stoney, *Po' Buckra*, preface.

the poorer whites must have amused the planters. At any rate, the terms stuck; for the Southern "darkie" as a namer of things is a very Adam whom his "white folks" have always quoted with delight. Certainly, in view of the universal currency of *poor-white trash*, to argue, as Erskine Caldwell has done, that "no white Southerner would apply the term to another of his own race, unless perhaps, he were a remnant of last century's landowners,"[5] is to blink the facts. The Southern vocabulary was formed before the war when an elegant planter minority lent class emphasis to thinking. Then, a "Tuckahoe" with his plantation on the Virginia Tidewater or seaboard was many notches above the plain "Cohee," a Scotch-Irish farmer across the mountains in the western valley of the state. Here were nicknames indicating a social cleavage—one that split the Old Dominion when the Civil War broke out. Nor were the tags for poor-whites, despite their origin in disdain or humor, any less valid. There was and is a poor-white class in the South.

Furthermore, names were given to these people by Southerners which did not necessarily imply contempt and which compassed several levels of humble life: for example, *Cracker*, *tar-heel*, and *Cajun*. Joel Chandler Harris was proud to call himself a Cracker.[6] "A native Georgian," writes a journalist, "does not mind being called a Cracker, but over in Mississippi we object to it, for it's a term Negroes apply to white trash."[7] North Carolinians of all classes have enjoyed singing:

5. *God's Little Acre*, viii.
6. R. L. Wiggins, *Life of Joel Chandler Harris*, 181-82.
7. J. H. Street, *Look Away!* 150.

Introduction

I'm a tar-heel born, and a tar-heel bred,
And when I die, I'll be a tar-heel dead.

And the Cajuns—Louisiana French of Canadian origin—while always aware of the lifted noses of the
Creoles, have often been most worthy of respect. Nevertheless, these terms were and are used to indicate the
poor-white class. A Georgia contemporary of Harris and
a careful local-colorist wrote of "that class of people,
who in Georgia are usually called Crackers . . . 'white
trash' or 'taller-face po' buckra' " and of an overseer
as a "lower-middle class Southern white man, a grade
or two above the Cracker in knowledge and sagacity."[8]
Cajun—a word that was once *Acadian* and suggested
Longfellow's *Evangeline*—is now applied to "the illiterate, lower-class French of Louisiana."[9]

And names reveal much about poor-whites. Since
usually they have either been pushed back into the
sandy pine barrens, for example, in South Carolina and
Georgia, by the planters, or have settled there to escape
malaria, they became "sand-hillers" and "pineywoods
tackies"; in Alabama and Mississippi, they have found
themselves crowded onto the uplands and have become
"hill-billies."[10] At least one standard piece of clothing
became their sign and symbol: a black, wool hat with
wide, drooping brim was utility itself—a good sun-shade,
fan, or dipper at branch or spring. In South Carolina,

8. Louis Pendleton, *In the Wire-grass*, 24, 122.
9. A. J. Carver, preface to "Cajun," in *American Scene*, 503. The difference between
Creole and Cajun has not been understood by many critics. See two theses: R. C. Beale,
Development of the Short Story in the South, 60; and M. C. Harrison, *Social Types in Southern
Prose Fiction*, 84.

10. Later origin; *ca.* 1900 to Alabamians (*DAE*). Recently it has become a popular
misnomer for mountaineers. Another term, *red neck*, probably belongs to Gulf Region
(U. B. Phillips, *Life and Labor in the Old South*, 350).

The Southern Poor-White

Ben Tillman gave these "woolhats" his especial political care. Naturally enough, their habits, mannerisms and occupations fastened certain tags to them. In North Carolina pineywoods gangs working in naval stores were soon "tar-heels";[11] while Georgia, as early as 1766, began to obtain state's rights to the term, "Cracker," which, most likely, backcountry Georgia bumpkins brought upon themselves by showing-off in town, boasting and cracking their long snake-whips to attract attention. Apparently, Charles H. Smith, the Georgia humorist, who knew his Crackers, was close to the truth when he said that the term, a Gaelic word meaning boaster, was applied by the Scotch settlers to the idle "no 'counts" of Georgia.[12] Along the coast a local nickname was given to sorry folk who were content to live largely on conchs (mollusks or shellfish) picked up on the beach. "The North Carolina Conch," wrote a Yankee surveyor in 1870, "is unquestionably the lowest specimen of the race known."[13] But the besetting sin and final proof of their trashiness, especially to Northern and British travelers, was the habit of clay-eating.[14] "Dirt-eaters," "clay-eaters" were living illustrations of the Southern saying, "common as dirt."

Indicative as such nicknames or tags are, they do not tell enough about these folk. The poor-white class must be defined and limited, first, by some negative distinctions. Abject poverty is not a necessary criterion: in one

11. First evidence, *ca.* 1864 (*DAE*).

12. Other suggested origins are the practice of cracking corn for eating; and a British nickname for expert Georgia long rifles with Gen. Francis Marion's partisans (theory of R. M. Johnston; unlikely).

13. J. S. Bradford, "Crackers," *Lippincott's Magazine*, VI (Nov., 1870), 458.

14. Southern publication concerning this habit began at least as early as 1808.

respect, poor-white poverty is relative to that of its dominant neighbors: placed next to the opulent South Carolina rice-planters, much of the state of Arkansas would have been poor-white. Yet most poor Arkansans did not consider themselves "trash." Thus the poverty of poor-whites is partly psychological, partly material. But how poor is a poor-white? Suffice it to say, that the cabin life of the frontier, stripped of its exhaustless resources of game, fish, forest fruits, and land, is that of the poor-white today. A poor backwoods existence reduces itself to much the same common denominators anywhere, anytime. In the Indiana backcountry about 1816, Abraham Lincoln and his parents were eking out the same flea-bitten existence of ignorance, filth, and sickness that William Byrd recorded in 1728 during his surveying tour among the Virginia and North Carolina outlanders. As Rupert B. Vance has said, "The ebb of the frontier remained in the 'poor white.' "[15] His way of life today might be called that of his ancestors—much lowered by two centuries of hardscrabbling and increasing economic pressure.

Nor does the manner of landholding invariably denote the class, in spite of the fact that squatters, shanty-boaters, sharecroppers, and tenants are ordinarily poor-whites. Many tenant farmers in the South today show the industry and morality of their well-living neighbors; and the thousands of poor-whites in the Florida scrub, the Louisiana pine flats, the Georgia pine barrens, and elsewhere, own their miserable hovels and patches.

Certainly the popular conception that all Southern

15. *Human Geography in the South,* 75.

poor-whites are as degenerate[16] as Erskine Caldwell's
Jeeter Lester in *Tobacco Road* (1932) is, to say the least,
myopic. The dregs of this class in the great cotton sections have been underfed victims of malaria, hookworm,
and anemia; these live on the dog-level in every respect.
Yet a far greater number regard bastardy with horror
and live with the mournfulness so whiningly expressed
in the Sacred Harp "sings." Nor are they *all* utterly
worthless; no census returns will ever show the host
of them who have worked hard for a life-time, to no
avail, against an agricultural system and outside forces
beyond their control.

These are the poor-whites as a class. But what were
their origins? Or stated otherwise, what conditions
before the Civil War produced them?

For over two hundred years the myth has persisted
that all Southern poor-whites derive from indentured
servants shipped to the colonies by England. Yet these
servants, called kids, represent only one source of colonial labor. To Virginia, for example, came convicts and
wage-workers on contract. True, the whole servant class
was described by Hugh Jones, historian of the Old
Dominion, as "the poorest idlest and worst of mankind,
the Refuse of Great Britain and Ireland."[17] Yet he admitted that some of these bound servants became industrious freemen. And poor people of good blood indentured themselves to doctors and lawyers to learn a
profession; other kids were probably harmless paupers,
the victims of English debtor laws. No single class or
nationality of immigrants may be called the "only be-

16. By degeneracy is meant whatever isolates poor-whites from "decent" people of
the countryside: for example, disease, filth, promiscuity, shiftlessness, thievery, etc.
17. *Present State of Virginia*, 115.

Introduction

getter" of the poor-whites. The po' buckra descend from the same plain people that settled much of the South—English, Scotch-Irish, Germans, and French.

The making of poor-whites from these various strains is a story that unwinds from two interlocked factors: first, the living conditions of the frontiersman or settler, and second, the plantation and slavery.

Before the establishment of industry in the North and of the planter system in the South, the forefathers of the poor-whites all over America were much the same: sluggards in the backlands or on the fringe of settlement. Early in the nineteenth century, Timothy Dwight, preacher and president of Yale, described the professional settlers of the North: "Under the pressure of poverty, fear of a gaol, and the consciousness of public contempt, they leave their native places and betake themselves to the wilderness . . . because they love this irregular, adventurous, half-working and half-lounging life, and hate the sober industry and prudent economy, by which . . . a . . . bush pasture might be changed into a farm . . . The forester quits his house, to build another like it . . . to girdle trees, hunt, and saunter in another place . . . In the meantime he becomes less and less a civilized man."[18]

Thus despite Frederick Jackson Turner's rhapsodies on the blessings of the frontier, the evils also weighed heavily in the scales—evils that made poor-whites of the weaker settlers. Isolation bred ignorance; the loss of social standards destroyed domestic pride, so that the log cabin with a stick-and-dirt chimney and a dirt or puncheon floor seemed good enough to folk who had no

18. *Travels in New England and New York*, II, 459-60.

outside stimulus to improvement. The dirty cabin-life of the frontier simply remained after it should have passed.

Nor did frontier slovens have any more ambition for their tables than for their cabins. The woods supplied game, fruits, and honey. Why should they wear themselves out farming more than a corn patch and a few rows of sorghum? Like the Negro of a later day they probably thought that

> *Cawn bread en de black molasses*
> *Is better dan honey en hash*
> *Fer de fahm-han' coon*
> *En de light quadroon*
> *Along wid de po' white trash.*[19]

Several half-wild, razor-backed hogs completed the staples of the cabin—staples that remain those of the sharecropper hut of today. And pork ruled the settlers' boards. "That ar Jake'll never make a man, cap'n," said a Florida Cracker to a surveyor of his boy. "He don't take kindly to hog and hominy, but ketches them no 'count birds and eats 'em."[20] But corn pone, hog, and 'lasses, hymned by historians as the food of the pioneers, was just the steady diet to ruin the less stalwart.

The Southern climate, perhaps no less than improper food, accentuated laziness, for in the forest clearing settlers "went native." Unlike their fellow laggards in the North, they did not need to prepare very much for winter. And as nature grew more prodigal in the Deep

19. J. C. McNeil, *Lyrics from Cotton Land*, 98.
20. Bradford, "Crackers," *loc. cit.*, 461.

Introduction

South the sluggards became more listless and sorry. A Georgia family en route to Texas thought the people in a newly settled part of Alabama "more like hogs and dogs than . . . folks."[21] As English travelers of the early nineteenth century went South on the Atlantic seaboard they noticed the increasing shabbiness and unkemptness of all farms.[22] The backwoods folk were merely out-loafing other Southerners.

But the Southern climate, despite the theory that its enervating effect is a popular illusion, did justify some listlessness. The unhealthfulness common to settlers' "deadnins" in nearly all American regions was accentuated in the South. Swamplands, rotting logs and stumps afflicted the cabin-dwellers with "malary" or the "Virginia sickness." Then chills and fever wracked their bones and yellowed their faces. Mild weather and poverty led to their going without shoes; bare feet then picked up hookworm. To cure these "miseries," they swallowed monstrous quantities of calomel, quinine, and corn whiskey; and some of them took to chewing resin and eating clay.

The lazy woods-folk, however, were not trifling solely because of "complaints" and isolation; they had energy enough for what they liked to do. While there were woods and game for the squatter, "white Indians" might be found. Ten years after the Civil War in the South Carolina pinelands lived a sandhiller, Jack Williams, "long of limb and gaunt of frame, keen-eyed and sallow-faced." Jack despised work heartily, but with his long, loping stride he would plunge through canebrakes

21. Phillips, *op. cit.*, 340-41.
22. J. L. Mesick, *English Traveller in America, 1785-1835*, 142-43.

and follow the baying of his hound all night after a deer that he could turn into whiskey at the store. Like an Indian, he regarded his wife as a squaw and spent his days smoking in the doorway. On being reproached by a summer visitor for taking his ease while his wife dug out the well, Jack drawled, "Wy wot's a 'oman good fer but to work? It's a pleasure to her to help her husband when he's wore'd out wid a long mawnin's hunt."[23]

Ignorant, dirty, lazy, badly nourished, Indian-like, content—many of these slovenly outlanders, by the time parts of the South became somewhat closely settled and the planter economy established, were too much set in their lolling way to adapt themselves to any ordered society. They did not wish to be town laborers; few cared for an overseer's job because of the slaves' contempt for po' buckra and because of the overseer's embarrassing relation to the planter's hall. In 1860, a Southerner spoke what was the general planter opinion of the poor-whites. "There is no longer any possible method by which they can be weaned from leading the lives of vagrom-men, idlers, squatters, useless to themselves and the rest of mankind."[24]

And the writer unwittingly inferred the second factor in the making of poor-whites, the labor monopoly of the plantation which did render most of the Crackers useless. Any system of controlled labor—white, red, or yellow—would have had the same evil effect upon poor workers. "Any man who is an observer of things," wrote William Gregg, the Southern industrial pioneer, in 1851, "could hardly pass through our country, with-

23. Robert Wilson, "In the Pineland," *Lippincott's Magazine*, XVI (Oct., 1875), 446-47.
24. D. R. Hundley, *Social Relations in Our Southern States, 119.*

Introduction

out being struck with the fact that all the capital, enter-
prize, and intelligence is employed in directing slave
labor; and the consequence is that a large portion of our
poor white people are wholly neglected and are suffered
to while away an existence in a state but one step in
advance of the Indian of the forest."[25] The South had
not heeded the advice of the wise Virginia historian,
Hugh Jones, who in 1724 had urged his colony to stop
importing slaves, to employ the poor then on the dole,
and thereby "advance the Good of the Publick."

Another evil of slavery, proclaimed by the abolitionists
and denied by Southerners after the early 1830's, was the
stigma placed on lowly tasks by slavery. Undoubtedly
the laziest Crackers welcomed an excuse to loaf. But
as early as 1736, the more general truth was plain to the
Virginia aristocrat, William Byrd of Westover: "I am
sensible of many bad consequences of multiplying the
Ethiopians among us. They blow up the pride and ruin
the industry of our white people, who, seeing a rank of
poor creatures below them, detest work for fear it should
make them look like slaves."[26] The jobs that poor-
whites could hold, for example, those in domestic
service, were thus closed to them. They knew the
feeling of Southern housewives about servants—a feeling
which Mrs. Jones of Georgia expressed in no uncertain
terms when it was proposed that she hire a white nurse
during a visit in New York. "It may do well enuff for
people who don't know the difference between niggers
and white folks; but I could never bear to see a white
gal toatin' my child about and waitin' on me like a

25. Quoted by G. M. Weston, *Poor Whites of the South*, 3.
26. *Virginia Magazine of History and Biography*, XXXVI (1928), 220-21.

nigger."[27] It may be significant that today in the South
to do a hard, dirty job is to "work like a nigger."

These matters of origin suggest the query: what is
especially distinctive about *Southern* poor-whites since
there were and are such people all over America? The
answer is that only in the South have these folk been set
apart so much as a class. In other sections, nicknames—
for examples, the pikes of Missouri and California, the
buckeyes of Ohio, and the Hoosiers of Indiana—which
were at first applied to rough poor people, were soon
generally adopted by natives of each state. Not so with
poor-white and its many synonyms. The scorn or indifference of the planters, the ridicule and scoffing of the
slaves, the lack of adequate outlet for humble labor—
all these created the Southern poor-white class in the
popular mind and made the sandhillers feel trashy.

In these pages, only poor-whites in rural districts will
be considered, for there the class originated; there all
but their recent history has occurred; there only operates
their peculiar, historic psychology. The urban chapter
of the Southern poor-white is being enacted in the
cotton mills, where actually he is no longer a poor-white
in the old country sense, but a "lint-head," an industrial pawn, hardly differentiated from his Northern
brothers. Mountaineers, so often confused with poor-
whites by critics, but never by Southern country people
or informed natives, have an entirely different group-
feeling and social matrix. Their Union sympathy in the
Civil War, even the literary treatment of them, should
indicate their uniqueness. In Joel Chandler Harris'

27. W. T. Thompson, in Henry Watterson's *Oddities in Southern Life and Character*,
181-82.

Introduction

Civil War story of Hog Mountain, "At Teague Poteet's," the comment of the Unionist hero on a neighbor's news that "Sou' Ca'liny done plum gone out and
Georgy a-gwine" may stand for the sentiment of all
loyal mountaineers in fiction. "Them air Restercrats,"
said Teague Poteet, "kin go wher' they dang please;
I'm a-gwine to stay right slam-bang in the Nunited
States."[28]

In this volume, the author tries to tell the social story
of the poor-whites and then to show its literary treatment in different periods. Thus the method employed
is social interpretation in narrative form rather than the
conventional argument and analysis of literary history.
Literary considerations have been limited to the
changes and additions in period-handlings which cum-
ulate in the complete social portraiture of the po'
buckra in literature.

These, then, are the poor-whites—Crackers, peckerwoods, woolhats or what you will—that herein may be
seen moving down to our time from the eighteenth-
century backcountry of the Virginia-North-Carolina
borderline in William Byrd's colonial world to the
Georgia Tobacco Road of Erskine Caldwell only yes-
terday.

28. *Mingo and Other Sketches*, 48-49.

CHAPTER ONE

WILLIAM BYRD OF WESTOVER DISCOVERS THE FRONTIER LUBBER

I
T WAS HIGHLY INCONGRUOUS THAT THE LITERARY discovery of the poor-white should have been made by William Byrd of Westover (1674-1744), whose epitaph justly described him as "a well-bred gentleman and polite companion," distinguished by "a happy proficiency in polite and various learning," and "a great elegance in taste and life." Born to position and a rich Virginia estate, educated privately in England after 1684 and during 1692 at the Middle Temple in London, he became the brilliant associate of William Wycherly, Charles Boyle, and others, developing at the same time a penchant for the petty gossip of elegant indecencies so beloved by the Age of Pope.

But since William Byrd was as capable as he was often frivolous, the circumstance which caused him to write of the poor-whites came about naturally enough. After entering the Council of State in 1709, he had been reckoned a great man in the colony. In 1728, when the long-standing boundary dispute between Virginia and North Carolina was to be settled by a survey, Colonel Byrd seemed a logical choice as one of his government's commissioners. And so it happened that he left splendid Westover for the backwoods where he discovered those trashy frontiersmen whom he called lubbers. That they should have inspired one of the most charming authors in early American literature to expend his wit upon them in the *History of the Dividing Line*[1] was indeed a happy coincidence. In this account of his adventures during the survey, Byrd left the first vivid picture of the poor-whites. With playful contempt and humor, he portrayed them as a group of runaways from Virginia, lazy, irreligious, filthy, and diseased.

For nearly a hundred years critics have stressed the maliciousness of his portrait. That it is severe there is no denying. Nevertheless, a thorough study of the factors conditioning his description will prove that it was neither so malicious nor so one-sided as critics have assumed.

His depiction of the lubbers was conditioned, for example, by the contemptuous attitude of Virginia toward North Carolina, which was well-established before Byrd put pen to paper. It dated back to the setting in 1665 of a new boundary that created, as the Reverend Hugh Jones said in 1724, "a very long list of land fifteen miles broad between both colonies (called the Disputed Bounds) in due subjection to neither, which is an Asylum for the Runagates of both Countries."[2] Thus four years before Byrd's first notes, the tradition of North Carolina as the refuge of runaways was fixed in print.

Consequently, when Byrd wrote the *History of the Dividing Line*, he had only to report well-established generalizations and cite examples. Andrew Dukes had run away from Maryland to the Disputed Bounds "thro a strong antipathy he had for work and paying

---

1. W. K. Boyd (ed.), *William Byrd's Histories of the Dividing Line.* Herein are the second form, *Secret History of the Line*, hereafter referred to as *SH*, and *History of the Dividing Line*, as *HDL.*

2. *Present State of Virginia*, 11.

his debts";[3] in the deep woods, a family of escaped mulatto slaves was raising stock "for a mean and inconsiderable share, well knowing their condition makes it necessary for them to submit to any terms." Not only debtors but criminals were sheltered by North Carolina laws.[4] As irreligion among such folk would seem to follow naturally enough, Byrd echoes Hugh Jones's opinion: "As for churches there are but very few; and I know of but one minister in the whole Government and he is lately removed hence."[5]

Byrd was following the usual ruts of reaction of an older culture toward a cruder one. Witness the English tradition of Virginia as the "haven of the criminal and the indentured servant" from Massinger's *City Madam* (1632) to Defoe's *Moll Flanders* (1722). Yet this older condescension and that of Virginia toward North Carolina were grounded in fact. For, as a result of the influx of slaves into Virginia at the end of the seventeenth century, in the period from 1660 to 1725, there was an exodus of poor-whites from the Old Dominion. And they were pouring into western North Carolina as late as 1730.

But Byrd was influenced not only by the Virginia attitude toward her neighbor colony as expressed in previous writings about lubberland, but also by certain personal matters. He wrote as he did of the poor-whites because he was an aristocrat, a dabbler in science, a land exploiter, and a gentleman with literary ambitions.

Thus his religious criticism may be taken as a representative part of his general aristocratic attitude which

3. *HDL*, 40.
4. *HDL*, 56, 58.
5. *Op. cit.*, 78.

caused him to pose as the sponsor of Anglican ritual to the heathen, white and red, along the dividing line. Like an early Spanish explorer, he joyed in the presence of chaplain Fontaine, attached to the surveying party by the Virginia government "for our Edification and to Christen all the Gentiles on the Frontiers of Carolina where they have no minister."[6]

Colonel Byrd's famous jesting at the expense of back-slidden religion among the lubbers, with "the kind of wit which," so Bishop Meade lamented, "'disfigures and injures the writings of Shakespeare,'"[7] has blinded most commentators to the implications of more pedestrian passages. The number and size of the Rev. Mr. Fontaine's congregations in a sparsely settled country, the numerous instances of parents' waylaying the commissioners with their children to be christened do not support the Colonel's gleeful jibes at backwoodsmen, "content [that] their Offspring should remain as Arrant Pagans as themselves."[8]

As a member of the Royal Society, Byrd was the typical amateur scientist, meddling with curative herbs, noting freaks of nature, and—what concerns us here—generalizing about races and states of man according to universal laws. This naïve beginning in anthropology had centered on primitive people,[9] especially the American Indian, after the visit of the four Indian Kings to London in 1710. Hence, the wonder and curiosity about these savages, expressed by John Smith at the first of

6. *Virginia Mag. of Hist. and Biog.*, XXXVI (1928), 115.
7. Quoted by A. Q. Holladay, *Social Conditions in Colonial North Carolina*, 20.
8. *HDL*, 88, 100, 112, 148, 158.
9. Byrd's library had many primitivistic volumes, especially travel accounts by the Jesuits and Cooke's *Voyages* and literary works such as Shaftesbury's *Characteristics*.

the seventeenth century, became in Byrd a tolerant theoretical approach, in marked contrast with his discussion of the somewhat primitive whites. After hearing the religious belief of his hunter, Bearskin, the Colonel thought it as much as could be expected from "a Meer State of Nature. . . .": "It contained, however, the three Great Articles of Natural Religion: The Belief of a God; the Moral Distinction betwixt Good and Evil; and the Expectation of Rewards and Punishments in Another World."[10]

Here the eclectic virtuoso found handy the Latitudinarianism of the British curate, John Tillotson, whose sermons were used exclusively by Anglican lay readers in Virginia. The "scientist" for the moment took such a long view as to suggest that the "one way of Converting these poor Infidels" is "Charitably to intermarry with them"; for, since "all nations have the same natural Dignity," a dark skin was of no consequence, especially as a second generation would blanch it.[11] This, in spite of their stupid idleness, dirt, and want.

But, turning to the whites who had fallen into the Indian way of life, the "scientist" of Westover held up to ridicule "the hermit" and his "wanton female" for subsisting on fish and living in a bark house. "Thus did these Wretches live in a dirty State of Nature, and were

10. *HDL,* 202.

11. *HDL,* 122. Mrs. Lucy L. Hazard is certainly wrong in stating that "The Virginians with chivalrous naïvete accepted the Indian civilization as one entitled to an equal footing" (*Frontier in American Literature,* 58). And that "In Eighteenth-century America, it was the Southerner and not the Northerner who was free from race prejudice" (*ibid.,* 59). For the colonial answer to "equal footing" see V. W. Crane, "A Lost Utopia of the American Frontier," *Sewanee Review* (Jan.-March, 1919), 48-61. Byrd himself admits that the early planters refused to marry Indians (*HDL,* 122), and his whole discussion of the Indian is one of condescension. John Lawson of North Carolina also recommended miscegenation, but for workers on tobacco farms (*History of Carolina,* 143).

7

mere Adamites, Innocence only excepted."[12]This callousness to the welfare of his own race was derived not only from the milieu-habit of "universal thinking," but from the typical governing theory of colonial officials, who according to Byrd himself: "are more intent to represent the King's authority and making their fortunes than to . . . study the Good of the People of the Country."[13] By "the people," however, Byrd hardly meant the backcountry folk; they were simply resources to be exploited by the land hunger of the Tidewater planters. From his own class, and especially from his father,[14] who cared nothing for America except to reap her rich harvests, William Byrd inherited the will to obtain a vast domain of rich frontier. At the Dismal Swamp, he very likely evolved his scheme to drain it for hemp culture; beyond the settlers toward the mountains, the land fever beset him mightily, so that be bought twenty thousand acres—"the Land of Eden"—from the Carolina Commissioners, whose fees had been paid in land. In his lifetime he added 153,209 acres to the original Byrd estate of 28,231.

As an exploiter of frontier lands, Colonel Byrd was obviously not impelled by humanitarian motives; hence he had no sympathetic understanding of the cultural backsliders along the Dividing Line. He never thought of them as future neighbors. His few gifts to the lubbers while on the survey were the humor of a great person and indicated no concern for the poor lubber class. He criticized the English for not pushing westward; he planned to settle a colony on his vast lands as a "Guard

12. *HDL*, 46.
13. *Virginia Mag. of Hist. and Biog.*, XXXVI (1928), 216-17.
14. P. A. Bruce, *Virginia Plutarch*, 140.

to the frontiers"; and yet he ridiculed the lubbers who were serving as such a guard. The truth is that back of Byrd's striving was his desire to become an absentee landlord in London, enjoying social amenities paid for by a rich colonial estate. In contrast, Hugh Jones, who had no land barony in mind, evolved detailed schemes[15] for ameliorating Virginia's poverty class.

I. THE FIRST LITERARY PORTRAIT OF THE POOR-WHITE

BESIDES these general factors conditioning his observation, there was his immediate and primary purpose in writing the *History of the Dividing Line*. This was the desire to win acclaim among his British and Virginia acquaintance for wit and scientific knowledge. "'Tis a great misfortune," he wrote in 1735 to My Dear Cousen Taylor, "for an Epistolizer not to live near some great city like London or Paris, where people play the fool in a well bred way, and furnish their neighbors with much discourse. In such places, stories rowle about like snowballs, and gather a variety of pretty circumstances in their way until at last they tell very well, and serve as a good entertainment for a country cousen."[16] And the finesse of the naughty story for which this is the prelude gives credence to his boast that "I have one infirmity—never to venture anything unfinished out of my hands."[17]

Nor was his pride in his "scientific" knowledge less cocksure. "We vertuosos," he liked to say, remembering his corresponding membership in the Royal Society. No doubt, he hoped that his largest padding of the

15. *Op. cit.*, Appendix, Scheme III.
16. J. S. Bassett (ed.), *Writings of Col. Byrd William*, 394.
17. *Virginia Mag. of Hist. and Biog.*, XXXVI (1928), 355.

Secret History—old wives' herb-lore and descriptions of wild life—would enhance his standing as a colonial member of the London scientific body.

As it happened, his scientific and literary ambitions precluded any concern for a sober and carefully balanced view of North Carolina folk.

These various personal attitudes colored the picture of the poor-whites limned by this not exactly disinterested historian. As an aristocrat and a land exploiter he had too much at stake to be impartial or humanitarian. And more than anything, his wit, though it made his book delightful reading, led to a misleading emphasis. For, as the best comic material in the *Disputed Bounds*, the poor outlanders suited his wit so perfectly that to our day his jests have stung tar heels into somewhat misdirected rebuttals. And because Byrd's comedy of lubber life eclipsed the rest of his book and because his humorous ridicule was often generally phrased, they have thought that the whole North State had been damned.

Yet Byrd was more accurate than these critics believe. As a matter of fact, the homes of neatness and industry noted by Byrd far exceed in number the dirty shanties of the sluggard. Earlier Hugh Jones had admitted "some good living" in North Carolina, but Byrd's pleasant reflections on "that Hospitable Roof" of Andrew Mead; Mr. Kinchen, who "lives in much affluence"; Timothy Ivy's household in which "everyone looked tidy and clean"; and a number of others alter somewhat the traditional opinion of Byrd's commentary. Nor did he claim that only his neighbor state was cursed with indolence and its evils: "I am sorry to say it, but Idleness is the general character of the men of the Southern parts of this Colony [Virginia] as well as in North Carolina."[18] This shows that Byrd was depicting, playfully at that, the marginal existence of poor-whites on any Southeastern frontier. Nevertheless, his brilliant group-portrait of the lubbers was accurate and is still largely true on the lowest level. Moreover, it should be noted that the conditions and traits of poor-whites stressed by Byrd have remained constants in travel literature to the present, a fact which indicates that as a class these people are both a part and a backwash of the advancing frontier.

What most impressed Byrd was their laziness. "These indolent wretches" let their hogs and cattle run in marshes and drown.[19] In the pines beyond Dismal Swamp, they "like the Wild Irish, find more pleasure in Laziness than Luxury."[20] Here, while three days passed heavily for the Colonel, ensconced at Thomas Speight's, he "had nothing to do, but make the best observations we cou'd upon that Part of the Country." The result was the famous account of lubberland:

"Surely there is no place in the world where the Inhabitants live with less Labour than in North Carolina. It approaches nearer to the Description of Lubberland than any other. . . .

"Indian Corn is of so great increase that a little Pains will subsist a very large Family with Bread, and then they may have meat without any pains at all, by the help of the Low Grounds, and the great variety of Mast that grows on the High-Land. The Men, for their Parts,

18. *HDL*, 304.
19. *HDL*, 54.
20. *HDL*, 102.

just like the Indians, impose all the Work upon the Poor Women. They make their Wives rise out of their Beds early in the Morning at the same time that they lye and Snore, till the Sun has run one third of his course, and dispersed all the unwholesome Damps. Then, after Stretching and Yawning for half an Hour, they light their Pipes, and, under the Protection of a cloud of Smoak, venture out into the open Air; tho', if it happens to be never so little cold, they quickly return Shivering into the Chimny corner. When the weather is mild, they stand leaning with both their arms upon the corn-field fence, and gravely consider whether they had best go and take a Small Heat at the Hough, but generally find reasons to put it off until another time.

"Thus they loiter away their Lives, like Solomon's Sluggard, with their Arms across, and at the Winding up of the Year Scarcely have Bread to Eat."[21]

But this account, instead of being unique, is merely the most amusing sketch of the "big lazy among folks in the sticks." In Virginia, as early as 1705, Robert Beverley was "ashamed to publish this Slothful Indolence of my Countrymen. . . . They sponge upon the Blessings of a warm sun and a Fruitful Soil, and almost grutch the pains of gatherings in the Bounties of the Earth."[22] And only four years before Colonel Byrd observed the lubbers—supposedly of North Carolina— Hugh Jones was worried about their Virginia cousins: "The common Planters leading easy Lives don't much admire Labour, or any Manly Exercise, except Horse-Racing, nor Diversion except Cockfighting. . . . This

21. *HDL*, 90-91.
22. Robert Beverley, *History of Virginia*, 283-84.

easy Way of Living, and the Heat of Summer makes some very Lazy, who are then said to be Climate-Struck."[23]

But that Byrd actually saw his sluggards one must concede, for fourteen years earlier, John Lawson, Surveyor-General of North Carolina, lyricizing about his "delicious country . . . placed in that Girdle of the World," admitted that while some of its people were industrious, he dared "hardly give 'em the Character in General. The easy way of living in that Plentiful Country makes a great many Planters very negligent."

The traditional explanations of this lethargy: mild climate and fruitful soil, Byrd merely copied; yet he suggested others, notably malaria, perhaps to this day the greatest plague of the Southern poor-white. Around Dismal Swamp, he declared: "They are devoured by musketas all summer and have Agues every Spring and Fall, which corrupt all the Juices of their Bodies, give them a cadaverous complexion, and besides a lazy, creeping Habit, which they never get rid of." Having a "custard complexion," they "looked no better than ghosts,"[24] had to saturate themselves with "the bark" (quinine) or "end their Lives with a Dropsy, Consumption, the Jaundice, or some such Illness."[25]

Worse still, the constant eating of pork without enough salt produced "the Country distemper," "apt to improve into the Yaws,"[26] causing the "downfall of

23. *Op. cit.*, 48.
24. *HDL*, 54, 74, 84.
25. Hugh Jones, *op. cit.*, 50.
26. *HDL*, 54. This disease, the yaws, is properly a dietary disease. But the destruction of the nose and hard palate indicates syphilis. For a traveler and physician who considered yaws a venereal disease caught from Negroes, see John Brickell, *Natural History of North Carolina*, 48.

their Noses"—a calamity so general that a good nose was a claim to beauty! Indeed, the tar heels became "extremely hoggish in Temper, and many of them seem to Grunt rather than Speak."[27]

Such people had no house-pride. Byrd with his party should have expected to lie at Andrew Duke's "in Bulk upon a very dirty Floor, that was quite alive with Fleas and Chinches." Neither should their ignorance of Dismal Swamp have surprised him: its damps and "long-tailed gnats" had shaken their bones with chills and fever.[28]

Yet in spite of everything, the friend of William Wycherley could not help enjoying the comedy of these lolling bumpkins. Their gawking at the surveyors delighted him: "Some of more curiosity than others rose out of their sick Beds to come and stare at us." The sight of Cornelius Keith, who lived in a roofless pen with his wife and six children, taking refuge in a fodder stock when it rained, seemed so ridiculous to the master of Westover that he supplied the nails for a roof. Even their reputed indifference to the church amused rather than distressed him. Moreover, all of this comedy was the necessary substitute for the principal source of amusement in the *Secret History:* the sexual adventures of the surveyors. Such Restoration antics as the following required spicy replacement: "In the Gaiety of their Hearts, they invited a tallow-faced Wench that had sprained her Wrist to drink with them, and when they had rais'd her in Good Humour, they examined all her hidden Charms. . . ."[29] Drunk again, the surveyors

27. *SH*, 55.
28. *HDL*, 41, 60.
29. SH, 59.

attacked a kitchen wench, who "wou'd certainly have been ravish't if her timely consent had not prevented Violence." She left early the next morning "and so carry'd off the Evidence" which "would have call'd for some severe Discipline."

Thus William Byrd, finding an equally diverting—yet printable—substitute for sex comedy in the lubbers, made a double contribution to the history of the Southern poor-whites: first, by giving them rare comic depiction over a century before Southern humor took them up, and, second, by leaving a valuable social commentary on the lubber or colonial poor-white who had slipped into Indian ways—ways which will have additional meaning on the Tennessee frontier of David Crockett.

CHAPTER TWO

LITERATURE INTRODUCES ANTE-BELLUM AMERICA TO THE POOR-WHITE

NEARLY A HUNDRED YEARS PASSED AFTER William Byrd, before any writer considered the poor-white worthy of literary treatment. The publication of the *History of the Dividing Line* in the eighteenth century rather than in 1841 might have produced imitators to bridge this gap, but that seems most unlikely. Putting aside speculation, one need only say that the South had no Crèvecoeurs to follow the master of Westover, no novelists until the 1820's. Then, however, the poor-white began to emerge in Southern writing and after various handlings, North and South, by 1870 he had become a character generally familiar to American readers.

I. VIEW FROM THE PLANTATION PORCH: GEORGE TUCKER AND WILLIAM A. CARUTHERS

THE social ideal of the ante-bellum writing class in the South with its resultant literary criteria precluded any sympathy with the poor-whites. To maintain the planter-aristocracy, plain folk had to be kept in place; to ignore the peasant was the ancient manner of the highborn. The most degenerate of the poor-whites had become illicit traders with slaves in liquor and stolen goods, or, being too anemic for such risks, had chosen the Indian existence of squatterdom. If these people

16

happened to own land and shacks, they were soon a nuisance, an obstacle in the way of the ever-expanding plantation in need of new soil. To poor-whites, the usual reaction of the planters was either anger or derision; humor was mostly supplied for them by their comical slaves. Even the master raconteurs of the plantation porch and lawyer's quarters, who reveled in yarns of Dutchmen, Irishmen, Yankees, and Negroes, seemed to avoid their "trashy" neighbors as subjects, except in the more democratic areas like parts of Georgia, Arkansas, and Alabama. Moreover, the planter did not consider the poor-white his especial Lazarus; the proper "brother's keeper," fresh land to the west, was always available and frequently used by the planter himself.

Such an attitude would indicate that there were few, if any, readers among cultivated Southerners of literature about plain country folk or piney-woods tackies; their literary ideal was another barrier to the appreciation of such writings. The primary fact in Southern literary taste and writing before the Civil War is its divorcement from the soil; it was an air-plant. Until about the 1830's, the planters, living the part of English country gentlemen, tolerated only the established classics: Horace, Addison, and Pope. Nor did the succeeding romantic exoticism of Scott, Byron, and Moore bring them nearer Southern ground. Worse, it infected every penholder with elegantiasis and melody madness. Mrs. L. V. S. French brought forth a tragedy of Mexico, *Iztalixo, or The Lady of Tula* (1859); Richard Dabney, a poem, *Rhododaphne; or The Thessalian Spell* (1843); at least two esteemed singers further honored Tennyson's brigade: A. B. Meek with "Balaklava" and J. B.

Hope with "The Charge at Balaklava." Philip P. Cooke's "Florence Vane," the official love song, celebrated Poe's favorite theme, for Florence lies where "the pansies love to dally." Without much caricature, the poetizing lawyer, Mr. Swansdown, in John P. Kennedy's plantation novel, *Swallow Barn* (1834), who had been guilty of a fugitive pamphlet of verses holding "a delicate effusion of super-fine sentiment, woven into a plaintive tale," may pass for a symbol of poetry in the Old South. "The Land Where We Were Dreaming" (1865) carries for Southern verse some ironical implications. Only once, when William J. Grayson wrote *The Hireling and the Slave* (1854), did a Southern poet seize upon surrounding realities—even with controversial purpose.

And yet, the popularity of Goldsmith, Burns, and Scott should have pointed to literary material among the lowly Southerners. At least, Alexander H. Stephens, who loved to tell jokes in Cracker dialect, could write to his half-brother Linton: "Scott's best characters—that is, the best drawn—are his lowest."[1] In 1856, a Southern writer emphatically qualified George W. Curtis' opinion that Scott's women characters were failures by praising Effie and Jeanie Deans. In Scott, however, the feudal parallels were those most earnestly to be desired; the obvious one between Scottish highlanders and our mountaineers may have produced a slight dribble of titles[2] before Miss Murfree; that between the peasants and poor-whites apparently none at all. Ellen Glasgow dramatizes literary history in *The Battleground* when

1. Quoted by Grace W. Landrum, *American Literature*, II (Nov., 1930), 268.
2. H. J. Nott, "The Counterfeiters" in *Novelettes of a Traveller*; John B. Lamar, "The Blacksmith of the Mountain Pass" in T. A. Burke (ed.), *Polly Peablossom's Wedding*.

she shows Major Lightfoot abusing his wife's taste in reading Dickens' novels about low characters.

The motive behind all ante-bellum, Southern fiction of the plantation was that of glorifying the amenities and virtues of genteel country life. Such a purpose could not countenance the poor—often sordid—lives on the fringe of the great estates or in the woods far back of them. John P. Kennedy, who, with the Sir Roger de Coverley papers and *Bracebridge Hall* well in mind, drew the masterly "set of pictures from still life," *Swallow Barn*, did not allow a playful notice of one lone poor-white to blur the genteel pattern of Squire Meriwether's estate; after all, the writer's job was not concerned with "Mr. Absalom Bulrush, a spare, ague-feverish husbandman who occupies a muddy strip of marsh land, on one of the river bottoms, which is now under mortgage to Meriwether."[3]

After the middle thirties, Southern depictors of plantation life, stirred to defense by the violence of abolitionist attacks, lost the genial grace and moderation of Kennedy, surrendered to distortion and bad taste. More than ever, any unsavory element in the Southern economy was suppressed. "The Two Country Houses" (1848) by Philip P. Cooke[4] and "Chronicles of a Planter's Hall" (1854),[5] anonymous, are typical results. When poor-whites entered momentarily into such books, their appearances were given the proper program notes. Mrs. Maria Milward in "Country Annals" (1841) avers that "a piney-woods girl *à cheval* may be picturesque,

3. *Swallow Barn*, 75. Hafen, a tinker, trapper, and fiddler, who, as a Hessian mercenary, had deserted the British, because of his foreign origin, is not regarded as poor-white (see chap. xxviii).
4. *Southern Literary Messenger*, XIV (May-July, 1848).
5. *Ibid.*, XX (Oct.-Nov., 1854).

but . . . certainly not elegant."[6] Into *The Old Planta-tion* (1859), James Hungerford inserted Mr. Pantry, a poor drunken man, who "often hired himself to do a day's work or more to 'some one or other' of his more fortunate neighbors," as an excuse to tell another dull yarn; some oyster and fish thieves are caught and let off to illustrate planter generosity.[7] No characterization of humble people could come out of such writing.

However, a few novels, if they did not dramatize the problem of the poor-whites, introduced and discussed it. In each case, special circumstances made the exceptional treatment possible. While a member of Congress in 1824, George Tucker, a Virginia planter and future professor of moral philosophy at Mr. Jefferson's university, received from the publishers his novel, *The Valley of the Shenandoah*. Into it by inference and frank statement, he packed a wealth of social truth. The entire story indirectly condemned the decay of morality in the commercial North, since the downfall of the gentle Grayson family in Virginia was caused by a New Yorker, who not only violated hospitality by seducing Louisa Grayson, but killed her brother when he demanded satisfaction. More important is the fact that in 1824, it was still possible for a slaveholder like Tucker to discuss dispassionately "the peculiar institution," as did his elder kinsman, St. George Tucker, and Thomas Jefferson.[8] And he could comment wisely on the social virtues and vices of the Dutch, the Scotch-Irish, and the English in Virginia.[9] In addition, he presented

6. *Ibid.*, VII (Jan.-Feb., 1841).
7. *Old Plantation*, 29, 80-81.
8. St. George Tucker, *A Dissertation Upon Slavery*; Jefferson, *Notes on the State of Virginia*.
9. *The Valley of the Shenandoah*, I, chap. iv.

two classes of poor-whites: the tough wagoners who insolently blocked roads, upset carriages, and fore-gathered at "Battletown" for "many a fierce ren-contre";[10] some "indigent beings," a tenant with his family of eight children, the oldest not fourteen, moving to Kentucky. "He had been for many years a tenant on a piece of poor land and finding it hard after paying his rent to support himself with so large a family, and alarmed at the prospect of a crop for the present year, he had sold out . . . and with the proceeds purchased the little cart, and retained enough money with economy to carry him to the West."[11] These, however, are only suggestive social glimpses.

A decade later, another Virginian, William A. Caru-thers, who had moved down into the new Cotton King-dom where large-scale exploitation of slavery accentu-ated its evils, set down in *The Kentuckian in New York* (1834) the most valuable commentary on the poor-whites to be found in the Southern novel until long after the Civil War. The epistolary form of this North-South romance of sectional conciliation enabled Caruthers to comment easily on both sections, for Southern young men court New York ladies and write to other lovers in South Carolina. Yet in following the lovers' travels below and above the Line, the novelist, long before he had his five assorted couples engaged or married, was able to speak his mind on social matters. In the valley of Virginia and Maryland, he asserted, society had fairly "regular gradations"; on the lower seaboard, there was "one immense chasm from the rich to the abject

10. *Ibid.*, I, 141, 178.
11. *Ibid.*, II, 12.

poor."[12] In North Carolina, he found William Byrd's lubber—much the same after a century—but to Caruthers abject poverty was no joking matter; indeed, his tragic sketch compares favorably with Byrd's comic masterpiece:

"See him . . . standing within the door of his pine-log cabin, his hands in his pockets, his head leaning against the door in melancholy mood. Some half-dozen pale and swollen-faced children are sitting on a bench against the side of the hut, endeavoring to warm away the ague in the sunbeams. The wife lies sick in bed. The little fields are barely marked out with a rotten and broken-down pole-fence, and overgrown with broom, or Bermuda-grass, and blackberry bushes. A miserable horse stands beyond the fence, doubtful whether there is better grazing within or without. A little short-cotton or sweet-potato patch, planted by an acre of scrubby Indian corn; and, added to these, five poor sheep, two goats, and a lean cow, complete the inventory of his goods and chattels. You have all his cause for *hope!* You have, too, his causes for fear. He has in his pocket a summons for debt, contracted for sugar and tea, and other needful comforts for his sick wife and children.

"Had he any cause for hope? God knows he had none in the world."[13]

In the Georgia lubberland, back of Savannah, "the dreariness of the eternal pine-barrens or the fever-and-ague appearance of the poor" weighed heavily upon the novelist. But observation carried him on to social remedy: "I would have your lowest class of whites elevated

12. *The Kentuckian in New York*, I, 76.
13. *Ibid.*, I, 78-79.

View from the Plantation Porch

to the dignity of intelligent and independent yeomen."
He would have Southerners study industrious, non-
slaveholding communities like that of the Moravians at
Winston-Salem, N. C.; visit New York, that sectional
prejudices might be allayed and a war averted—a war
that would prevent the South from working out her own
social re-ordering. Brilliant and prophetic, Caruthers'
analysis is also generally accurate for the Cotton King-
dom; however, the size of the yeoman or small farmer
class he greatly underestimated.

During the twenty years after Caruthers' novel appeared, only an occasional unimportant poor-white got
into fiction. For example, in *George Balcombe* (1836) by
the Virginia scholar, Nathaniel Beverley Tucker, somehow Jim Porter, a "long-legged, parrot-toed fellow,"
who lived in the pine woods, found a way into a wild
melodrama of a false will, seduction, Indian adventure
in Missouri, and final justice for all.

Then Thomas B. Thorpe, a Massachusetts man who
had been living in Louisiana for eighteen years, wrote
The Master's House and dedicated it to the "lovers of
mankind" who wish "the evils of society exposed" in
order to initiate "the necessary reform."[14] Like George
Tucker, who called slavery "an evil, both moral and
political [which] admits of no remedy not worse than
the disease" and Caruthers, who expressed the same
opinion, Thorpe was essentially the early anti-slavery
man of the Old South: he admitted the evils of slavery,
but pleaded that "the remedies are . . . neither instant
nor revolutionary"; only bring the South to the admission of the need for reform; "then the manner of its

14. *The Master's House*, 7.

23

accomplishment will readily suggest itself."[15] Yet this is not to say that his novel is exactly like those of the earlier Virginians. His sympathy with and admiration for Southern planters, combined with the new abolitionist, fictional technique, produced a queer novel. Of course, in it, rascally poor-whites operate grog shops and assist at lynchings. Again, as in *The Valley of the Shenandoah*, we meet a sallow-faced, poor-white, "with hair as stiff and colorless as hay," taking his family by ox-wagon from the malarious swamplands of North Carolina to the healthful pineywoods of Alabama.[16] Thorpe's most notable observation on the poor-whites is found in the political battle between the planter, Moreton, and Duff White of Possum Hollow, "the father of a large family, miserably poor and ignorant, but self-conceited, and . . . from the habit of using large words . . . considered a great man in his region."[17] Class prejudice was aroused by circulars, broadcasted in the pineywoods, in which Moreton was accused of making the tackies stand with hat in hand at his gate like Negroes, refusing them admission to his table, and declining to shake hands with such trash for fear of catching the itch.[18] Naturally, all the pineywoods folk voted for Duff, who, with the slush fund of a gambling ring, went to the Louisiana legislature. The social point here is that the planters, even those like Moreton, who

15. In the face of much evidence, two critics have called *The Master's House* a proslavery novel. See Gaines, *The Southern Plantation*, 49; Jeanette Tandy, "Pro-Slavery Propaganda in American Fiction of the Fifties," *South Atlantic Quarterly*, XXI (Jan., 1922), 48-49. The preface alone forbids such classification: the novel contains "many morals" for the guidance in the future (p. 5); prostitution of the Southern pulpit (p. 6); the ironically given sermon by a Southern preacher; and the implied attacks of the story on duelling, chivalric hauteur, etc.

16. *The Master's House*, 77.

17. *Ibid.*, 328.

18. *Ibid.*, 338.

were opposed to giving "the poor white man political, or even legal, equality," were forced to reckon with the poverty vote. Thorpe missed a grand opportunity, however, by not dramatizing Duff White, who instead, is more an illustration than a character.

The contribution of this plantation literature, then, to the interpretation of the poor-whites took the form of illustration and discussion. The grandiloquent Southern literary ideal, which usually ignored the poor folk, caused even the open-minded novelists like Tucker, Caruthers, and Thorpe to use impossible love stories for major themes. With his great personal concern for and understanding of the poor-whites, Caruthers discussed them in a novel of absurd romance and evidently did not consider them suitable for active characters in fiction.

II. WILLIAM GILMORE SIMMS, THE CHARLESTON IDEAL, AND THE SQUATTER

LIKE the foregoing novelists, William Gilmore Simms (1806-1870) always held the plantation view, and for a time at Woodlands, his second wife's estate near Barnwell, S. C., he lived the graceful life of the country gentleman. As a novelist, however, he wrote work which largely belongs to historical and border romance rather than to plantation fiction. And while, in spite of the conventions of the lurid *genre* which he used, he made a definite contribution to the literature of the poor-white, his true talent was thwarted by the aristocratic position that he tried to maintain, both in literature and in life.

Judging solely by the natural bent of his talent and

by his theory of fiction, one would have expected Simms to leave masterly creations of low life and broad comedy. He insisted that writing come out of one's native ground: "To be *national* in literature, one must needs be *sectional*";[1] no single author could understand all of America. His aim as an historical novelist was not "to dilate on great events" or "the Hero rising to the Myth," but to record the unwritten history of the "moving impulses of men" and "the humblest walks of life."[2] When a critic attacked his novels[3] for "their low and vulgar personages," Simms contemptuously styled him a "romanticist . . . who will not look at the material, that make the million, but who picks out from their number the man who should *rule*, not the man who should *represent*." His own practice, he declared, was to adhere to "real life" in presenting "man in all his phases."[4]

Such a literary creed was the natural expression of a courageous, robust man, whose generosities and crotchets were probably much like those of his character, Porgy.[5] Yet both nature and theory were thwarted, first, by the current romance vogue, and, next, by his worship of the Charleston ideal, in which—ironically enough—this middle-class author was never made to feel at home; he might well have been thinking of himself when he wrote in "The Western Emigrants":

> . . . *simple change of place*
> *Is seldom exile* . . .

1. *Wigwam and Cabin*, iv.
2. *The Partisan*, vii.
3. Rufus Griswold (ed.), *Prose Writers of America*, 504.
4. *Mellichampe*, 5, 6.
5. W. P. Trent, *William Gilmore Simms*, 109.

William Gilmore Simms

. . . there's a truer banishment.
'Tis to be
An exile on the spot where you were born;
A stranger on the hearth which saw your youth,
Banished from hearts to which your heart is turned.[6]

The ready market for romance seduced him into wasting his fine energy in lurid border tales little better than dime novels; whereas his desire for home approval partially dictated his use of aristocrats for major rôles, although even his contemporaries knew his true forte to be "the rough-hewn and the half-polished specimens of backwoods humanity."[7] Therefore, seeing the poorwhites from a Charleston pinnacle, he made nearly all of them villains and represented their treatment by the planters as satisfactory and proper. Large landholders such as Capt. Porgy and Mrs. Eveleigh in *The Sword and the Distaff* (1852) displayed toward the squatter Bostwick's family the dignified yet familiar charity of Tudor nobles, not the contemptuous cruelty of Stuart cavaliers. Yet Simms left a record of class feeling even in Revolutionary times. When General Marion's ragged, ignorant partisans marched into the camp of General Gates' continentals, they were jeered as "the crow squad" and sent away by Gates to prevent rioting and insubordination.[8] Only an occasional highborn rascal used a convenient poor-white for evil purposes, but from such instances the author drew no social morals. Yet he made Mrs. Pickett, the wife of a poor-white thus

6. *Poems*, II, 165.
7. Anon., "Mr. Simms' Sword and Distaff," *New York Literary World*, XI (Dec. 4, 1852), 358.
8. *The Partisan*, 439, 445.

victimized in *The Partisan*, the voice of a Tory caste-formula for social happiness: "There's always two paths in the world, the one's for the big people; let them have it to themselves, and let us keep off it"; "poking into the wrong path" causes all the trouble. Granting Simms' aristocratic bias, one must concede his general accuracy, for Revolutionary South Carolina and frontier Georgia, Alabama, and Mississippi had not settled rigidly into that economy which created an acute planter-poor-white problem.

In *Guy Rivers* (1834), Simms first touched the subject of the poor-white by showing some ancestors of the Georgia Cracker: the lawless, brawling squatters of the gold rush into the Cherokee hills.[9] The next year in *The Partisan*, besides a general characterization of Marion's lubber-like guerillas and the charge that the Tory troops of South Carolina were miserably poor desperates and outcasts who "had no sympathy with the more influential classes,"[10] he created Mother Blonay, a poor-white and a villainous, Scott-like hag. A passing visit from a Catawba Indian had given to her a "blear-eyed" bastard, nicknamed Goggle by the countryside. Her "miserable clay and log hovel," "in no respects better than those of the commonest Negro houses," sat in a broom-sedge field, and "a few cheerless pines rose around it." About the hut, a cur barked; while inside, by the fireplace, two great cats kept up "a drowsy hum," and overhead, herbs, gourds, and calabashes hung from the rafters. Before the low fire, Mother Blonay rocked and smoked her pipe. The Ne-

9. *Guy Rivers*, Bk. I, chaps. xiii-xiv.
10. P. 185.

28

William Gilmore Simms

groes and "the whites of the lower class in the same region" thought she had witching powers, and they had her word for it. "I can put the staggering weakness into the bones and sinews of the strong man," she vowed.

Although Simms obviously created Mother Blonay as a plot-devil, he must have warmed to writing the forced interview in the hag's cabin between her and the partisans, for excepting Porgy's antics, it is the best part of the novel. Typical though she is, her cabin, its location, and occasionally her speech are true poor-white. When she threatens to put her "bad mouth" on someone, or resents "having every dirty field-tackey whickering" about Goggle, Simms' bombast seems to be breaking down into folk-talk.

When, however, in *Richard Hurdis* (1838), he presented his next poor-white villain, the result was almost entirely different; in fact, Ben Pickett is the typical abolitionist figure, minus the footnotes of propaganda. Ben, "a sullen, sour, bad-minded wretch," hunted, and stole his corn from the Hurdis' plantation. In his "miserable cabin," he rested his indolent bones, while "his rifle and mangy cur slept in the fireplace," but more often he was wandering about to no purpose. His wife, whose looks were either dark or blank, and his idiot daughter[11] completed the sorry household. Finally, the laborious rationalizing by which Ben's stolid mind sold him as a hired murderer, his stupid blunder in killing the wrong man, and his descent into outlawry and death reveal a notable descriptive and psycho-

11. In an abolitionist novel, this idiot would mean degeneracy; but in Simms it probably means romantic clap-trap. Examples: Frampton, maniac (*Border Beagles*); Chub Williams, half-wit (*Guy Rivers*); Acker, epileptic ("The Giant's Coffin" in *Wigwam and Cabin*); Barnacle Sam, madman ("Sergt. Barnacle," *ibid.*).

logical advance in Simms' treatment of the poor-white.

Always with a natural tendency to the lusty and comic, the South Carolina novelist had written a few earlier tales of surprising frankness, like, for example, that of the sexually potent Negro, Mingo, in "Caloya; or, The Loves of the Driver."[12] But 1853 is the *annus mirabilis* of his career in that so many works are departures from the matter and style of his romances. *The Golden Christmas* satirizes Charleston oddities produced by six generations of intermarriage between first cousins;[13] *As Good as a Comedy*, featuring a Georgia race track, is told in dialect by a Tennessean;[14] "Home Sketches" contains a rare ghost yarn told by a drunken raftsman of the Edisto River;[15] and *The Sword and the Distaff; or, Fair, Fat, and Forty*, obviously a comedy, subordinates romance absurdities to the advantage of character; certainly, no other novel by Simms can show five believable, alive people like Capt. Porgy, Mrs. Eveleigh, Lieutenant Millhouse, Bostwick, and Tom. It is natural, therefore, that in this character novel, Simms should have made his valuable study of the squatter Bostwick.

"Sinewy, lean, elastic," Bostwick had "low swarthy features" and a "sidelong gait"; he "could outwind a horse in a day's journey." During and just after the Revolution, bad company had made him a thief and "fence" for a Tory ring which was relieving the Patriots of their Negroes. Illiterate and despised by the reprobates he served, Bostwick hated the decency of

12. *Wigwam and Cabin*, 361-429. First published in *The Magnolia* between 1841 and 1843, this tale "got Simms talked about" (Trent, *op. cit.*, 181).
13. Trent, *op. cit.*, 195.
14. *Ibid.*, 200-1.
15. *New York Literary World*, X (Feb. 7, 1852), 107-10.

William Gilmore Simms

his family and the great rich folk "who were all as mean as h-ll," even though his squatter family remained unmolested in the swamp corner of Mrs. Eveleigh's land. At last, he secured incriminating papers against the ring leader and came to his death in attempting blackmail.

His social significance is two-fold: first, that his Indian cunning and shiftiness show him to be a degenerate version of the frontier scout,[16] and second, that he illustrates one use made of poor-whites in an earlier Southern "reconstruction."

In the literary history of poor-whites, Bostwick is of considerable importance as the first one to enact a major, novelistic rôle; in one sense, as the key which unlocks the entire plot, he is the hero. And for the first time in fiction, one can know an early Southern squatter intimately: how he feels, eats, walks, and talks. To hear this drunken wretch mouthing insolently over a bottle and cards before being shanghaied by his partners[17] is to realize how much Simms had improved since writing the unnatural speeches of Mother Blonay and Mrs. Pickett.

Yet Simms could not be expected to forego romance devices entirely.[18] Therefore, like a Bret Harte gambler, Bostwick, at the very close of his rotten career, lays down his life to assure the future of his daughter. But the family of Bostwick is entirely romanticized. His

16. To Simms the frontier meant degeneracy: "the license of the wilderness" sank folk to an Indian level; even second-generation wealth came to children "ignorant of its proper uses" (*Richard Hurdis*, 67). This almost inevitable barbarism very likely caused him as a youth to reject his father's offer of wealth and power in Mississippi.
17. *Woodcraft*, chap. xi.
18. In 1869, he tried to write realistic mountain stories, but lapsed into his old manner (Trent, *op. cit.*, 314-15).

31

wife is "a thin, pale-faced body with fair complexion,
still and soft, sad eyes . . ." who keeps her homespun
"scrupulously neat" and the cabin floor "tidily clean."[19]
Constant industry, Bible reading, and pious teaching of
her brood have already borne fruit in the model maid,
Dory, aged twelve. Again, as with Mrs. Pickett, Simms
was averse to presenting a Southern wife as a typical
poor-white slattern, especially in South Carolina; besides, he naïvely wished contrast for the degraded
husband.

III. NORTHERN CONCEPTION OF PO' WHITE TRASH: JAMES R. GILMORE AND MRS. STOWE

No such important role as Bostwick's was given to
the poor-white by Northern writers, but as a
minor character in their novels, he was less melo-
dramatic, more pathetic, and, at times, somewhat
tragic. For Simms' villainous poor-white one feels scant
pity.

Perhaps, for this reason, Simms could continue to use
him as a scoundrel of the past, while other native
Southerners, after the appearance of the *Kentuckian in
New York* (1834), had dropped him as a controversial
subject. When this happened, abolitionist fiction, beginning with Richard Hildreth's *Archy Moore* (1836), took
him up and carried forward with great improvement
the illustration and discussion of his economic plight, so
ably initiated by Caruthers.

In spite of some distortion and exaggeration, the

19. *Woodcraft*, 216. Cf. the "miserable hovel," "foul as a sty," of the squatter in *Richard Hurdis*, 71.

Northern Conception of Po' White

Northern abolitionist novels contain the most valuable economic commentary on the poor-whites to be found in American fiction before the twentieth century. This came about as naturally as the Southern silence, for while the Northerners made the Negro the especial object[1] of their zeal, they did not overlook in the general assault upon slavery a second-best target: the poor-white. Consequently, this second-line attack, repeated with slight variance, in time became both a standard portrait and a surprisingly comprehensive view of the lowest whites in the Old South. And, in 1836, with abolition in full cry, Richard Hildreth, the historian, after a winter's convalescence in Florida, set the pattern for his successors in his novel, *Archy Moore:*

"The poor whites are extremely rude and ignorant, and acquainted with but few of the comforts of civilized life. They are idle, dissipated, and vicious; with all that vulgar brutality of vice, which poverty and ignorance render so conspicuous and disgusting. Without land, or at best, possessing some little tract of barren and exhausted soil, which they have neither the skill nor the industry to render productive; without any trade or handicraft art, and looking upon manual labor as degrading to freemen, and fit only for a state of servitude,—these poor white men have become the jest of the slaves, and are at once feared and hated by the select aristocracy of rich planters. It is only the right of suffrage which they possess, that preserves to them

1. By 1852, a reviewer complained of "that surfeit of 'nigger' literature, which now sickens the popular taste" (*So. Lit. Mess.*, XVIII, Nov., 1852, 703). For the welter of novelistic replies to *Uncle Tom's Cabin* and its kind which took the form of·comparisons of slaves with Northern industrial laborers, see Gaines, *op. cit.*, 46. The more fruitful comparison of Northern factory workers and Southern poor-whites—both victims of giant organizations —was overlooked in the heat of the argument.

the show of consideration and respect with which they are yet treated."[2]

From several Northern novels about the South, one may construct the rest of the Yankee view of the worst poor-whites or "mean whites" as one writer called them.[3] This view presupposed the ability to see the South as a land

Where aristocracy shall batten
Upon the poor man's bones and fatten;[4]

that "the chivalry" by upholding slavery were solely responsible for the existence of "mean whites," who were illiterate—because planters, supporting private tutors and academies, opposed public education, who were shiftless—because the self-sustaining plantation had denied them the opportunities for work and because they were ashamed to do humble jobs that had become "nigger work," and who were degenerate—because poverty had made decent living impossible.[5] Most irritating to the antislavery novelist was the fact that these white victims not only supported the planters, but longed to emulate them: to own a Negro, Mrs. Stowe thought, was "the first point to which the aspiration of the poor-white of the South generally tends."[6] They followed aristocratic firebrands in mob-outrages on liberals,[7] sold their votes to the ruling class "for the

2. Richard Hildreth, *The Slave; or, Memoirs of Archy Moore*, II, 61.
3. J. R. Gilmore, *Among the Guerillas*, Appendix: "The Sum of the Whole."
4. Anon., *Southern Chivalry*, Bk. IV, 42.
5. H. B. Stowe, *Key to Uncle Tom's Cabin*, 184. See also Stowe, *Dred*, 110, 158, 229; J. T. Trowbridge, *Cudjo's Cave*, 25, 29-30; Gilmore, *op. cit.*, 119, 267, 268; Epes Sargent, *Peculiar*, 240-41.
6. Stowe, *Dred*, 424; Trowbridge, *op. cit.*, 212; Sargent, *op. cit.*, 99.
7. *Dred*, 512, 566.

wretched privilege of living in some miserable hut,"[8] and joined the Confederate Army at their landlords' harangues about white supremacy, but probably deserted from bewilderment and cowardice.[9]

In this society, there could be only a few occupations open to the "mean whites." A small number who were not too unhealthy or stupid might become overseers, but fewer still had the courage to face down the scorn of the slaves and command obedience. Hildreth's Jemmy Gordon, "one of those careless, easy, good-natured, indolent sort of men, who are generally pronounced good-for-nothing," soon made a failure at overseeing and turned to criminal ways of dealing with slaves in his lonely, crossroads whiskey shop after dark.[10] This sort of business seemed to Northern novelists especially appropriate for the worst whites; all of Hildreth's are so engaged; in *Dred* (1856), Mrs. Stowe represents the grog-seller, Obijah Skinflint, as a Yankee scoundrel who had married a poor-white and sunk to her level. About these trading shacks on Saturdays, the trash made merry with turkey-shootings and fights, chicken, dog, and human.[11]

If a swamp tacky like Mrs. Stowe's Ben Dakin in *Dred* retained enough frontier hankerings, he lived a hunter-fisher existence, trained fierce dogs to track slaves and took to "nigger catching," the most barbarous and degrading of all the contacts of poor-whites with slaves. All of these occupations seeming too stren-

8. Gilmore, *op. cit.*, 267.
9. Gilmore, *op. cit.*, 114; see also Gilmore's *Among the Pines*, 68-83. Listed as travel; obviously partly fiction.
10. *Archy Moore*, I, 49.
11. J. R. Gilmore, *My Southern Friends*, 55-57.

uous, difficult, or dangerous, the "mean white" resigned himself to a squatter's life, perhaps near enough the planter's porch to make the fear of expulsion always imminent.

As always, the animus of propaganda both simplified and distorted the view, giving wider currency to that persistent myth: a tri-partite Old South of planters, Negroes, and poor-whites. In Mrs. Stowe's *Dred*, North Carolina has not one middle-class yeoman farmer, yet North Carolina was made of such countrymen. This error—wilful or not—led to the exaggeration of the number of the lowest class,[12] and the omission of the largest element of the Southern population: the middle-class and small farmers. For the exciting contrasts of what Mrs. Stowe termed "the vivid lights, gloomy shadows, and grotesque groupings,"[13] only the trashiest of the poor-white-trash were exhibited.

Conceived in violence, such representation, nevertheless, had the broad outlines of truth, and what is more pertinent here, emphatically placed the character and problem of the Southern poor-white in fiction, not in major rôles, but as an actual and ever-present unfortunate. In *Cudjo's Cave* (1864) by the journalist, John T. Trowbridge, Dan Pepperill, "a weak, degraded, kind-hearted man," whose home was near enough the Tennessee mountains to give him Union leanings, was flogged and ridden on a rail for ministering to "a beaten and bleeding slave." Amid "third-degree" threats and outrages, this very real, vacillating nincompoop had

12. Sargent, *op. cit.*, 99; "five millions of mean, non-slave holding whites;" *contra*, however, and exceptional, Gilmore, *Among the Guerillas*, 269: "The class is not large;" no data for computing the number; best opinion, that "it cannot exceed a million."
13. *Dred*, preface, i.

served a Union family nobly, but when offered escape to the free states, he let home instincts prevail over wobbly principles and joined the C. S. A. More penetrating psychologically is Richard Hildreth's analysis of Jemmy Gordon, the Virginia grog-shop keeper, who, although he had been saved from drowning by Archy Moore, the runaway slave, betrayed the Negro for a reward of five hundred dollars. Jemmy's rationalization of his treachery is convincing. And although a minor character Jemmy Gordon lingers in the mind. But in 1863 appeared an exception to the usual pathetic types in the rare comic study of Mr. Bonaparte Mullock by James R. Gilmore, a sort of specialist in Southern poorwhites who deserves separate notice.

In spite of being an abolitionist editor and hysterical hater of "the chivalry," Gilmore tried to see all of the strata of Southern life. On the basis of "sixteen years of intimate business and social intercourse with the planters and merchants of the South,"[14] and the travel thus involved, he published in 1864 an article, "Poor Whites of the South,"[15] which he later incorporated in a general survey of all classes, appended to his novel, *Among the Guerrillas* (1866); in fact, he stated that the purpose of the book was to "depict the different classes of Southern society,—the 'mean whites,' the 'poor whites,' the 'chivalry,' the 'negroes,' and the mixed race. . . ."[16] This gradation is correct, but the use of "poor whites" to mean "yeoman or small farmers," who he rightly declares are "the real hope of the South" and "comprise the great mass of the Southern

14. *My Southern Friends,* 305.
15. *Harper's Magazine,* XXIX (June, 1864), 115-24.
16. *Among the Guerillas,* 266.

people," is obviously an erroneous use of the term. In describing the "mean white" class, Gilmore followed the standard pattern already outlined but stressed their depravity and their political helplessness as fatal to Southern democracy: "They are totally destitute of morals and religion and live in open violation of almost all laws, human and divine. Fathers cohabit with daughters, brothers with sisters, and husbands sell or barter away their wives, just as they would their jack-knives or their rusty rifles."[17] Exaggerated as a general-ization, this charge of promiscuity has significance in fixing the literary tradition of degeneracy and also con-stitutes a perfect introduction to Mrs. Bony Mulock and her conjugal trouble in *My Southern Friends* (1863).

Nine years before we meet this clay-eating wife from "nigh on ter Chalk Level" in North Carolina, Bona-parte, her tall, raw-boned husband with dull, cold eyes, had left her and married a quadroon. His whereabouts having been discovered, Mrs. Bony took a stagecoach on blackmail bent. Oblivious of the disgust of her fellow passengers, "every now and then she wetted a short piece of wood with saliva, and dipping it into a snuff-bottle, mopped her teeth and gums with the savory powder." Tired of dipping, she bluntly asked for tobacco, vowing that: "I durned sight d'ruther chaw." At her destination, she fell into the scheme of Mr. Gaston, a young planter with a weakness for practical jokes, who made Bony confront his sullen wife and hear her demand of one hundred dollars for a quit-claim. Nor would she haggle over the amount: "No, stranger; nary dime under that. I'm gol-durned ef I does." The delighted Mr.

17. *Ibid.*, 268.

38

Northern Conception of Po' White

Gaston paid her, and poor Bony agreed to repay the planter in work. Later, after a sad career involving rails, tar, feathers, and jail, Bony returned to Chalk Level, where his mate offered him fifty dollars to share 'her bed and board.' But she paid him only twenty-five, and Bony complained bitterly over such fraud; but that was soon unimportant: for sundry sorts of dark-dealing, a mob sent Bony away from Chalk Level forever.

For several reasons, the foregoing episode deserves notice: anti-slavery novelists nearly always used men for poor-white rôles which required any action; Mrs. Mulock is no still-life sketch such as Mrs. Dakin in *Dred*. Nor is she an illustrative victim of slavery or of anything else except herself. Her torpid body existed only for ease and sensation, be it from snuff or sex, and to secure both, she barred nothing. Yet to Gilmore, this sordid slattern and her quit-claim appeared broadly comic; certainly Colonel Byrd never laughed at a worse lubber. Nor can one fail to see that the dead-alive manner and the bartering about sex with utter gravity suggest and anticipate Erskine Caldwell's sexual comedies over sixty years later.

Besides the unusual comic departure in creating Mrs. Mulock, the Northern view made three other notable advances in the literary treatment of poor-whites: the dramatization instead of discussion of their social relations, the use of them for minor action-rôles rather than for illustration, and the establishment, or perhaps more accurately, the popularization, of the tradition of their depravity.

39

The Southern Poor-White

IV. SOUTHERN COMIC PORTRAITS OF CRACKERS, WOOL-HATS, AND DIRT-EATERS

THE most important literature about the poor-whites in the nineteenth century was not written by Southern aristocrats, by William Gilmore Simms, or by the Northern writers; it was written by the Southern humorists who, between 1830 and the end of the century, made these shiftless folk come alive in their pages.

To explain why Southerners created the comic portrait of the poor-whites by citing Horace Walpole's dictum to the effect that life is a comedy to the man who thinks, a tragedy to the man who feels, would, doubtless, be too flattering; nevertheless, the laughter produced by their trashy comedians was a heady, sane corrective for the three versions of the tackies already examined. It pointed to the low yet amusing life of the trash as a democratic contrast to the elegant plantation view into which the low-down people seldom entered; it shows them leading an uneventful, harmless, and often joyous existence, instead of following the spectacular and fatal career of a Simms villain; it added to the Northern interpretation some economic footnotes from the actual scene which no amount of logical theorizing could have discovered. But valuable as such corrective implications were, they formed no broad social commentary to match that of Northern novelists, because Southern humorists in depicting the tackies rarely satirized, but wrote from a two-fold impulse: to record types and manners and to amuse. Both of these they succeeded in doing so well that their writings remain the

Crackers, Woolhats, and Dirt-eaters

most important contributions before 1870 to the literary history of the poor-white.

Below what Governor Bob Taylor of Tennessee called "the dividing line between cold bread and hot biscuit," there was, before 1860, only one version of poor-whites generally acceptable: the comic. Above all, such people were not suitable for the polite reading of Southern gentlemen, much less that of the ladies. But no one should forget that all but the most refined planters had one literary standard for books read in the family circle and anecdotes related to guests on the veranda, another for the yarns swapped on the courthouse square, at the livery stable, in the oak grove of the church when there was "all-day preaching and dinner on the ground." The Southern country squire had time and plenty of places for man's talk and stories: these were the *fabliaux* of the Old South. The most sanitary ones of this type now and then appeared in local newspapers or the *Spirit of the Times* with a vague ascription. "Life and Manners in Arkansas. By an ex-Governor of a cotton-growing State"[1] is a typical example. And just in proportion as their home sections were democratic, these amateur authors[2] seemed to release their skits and sketches to the press. In 1882, Henry Watterson was puzzled by one such instance: "Why it is I know not, but certain it is that Georgia, which is made the scene of so much humor of the South, has furnished a large proportion of the humorists them-

1. W. T. Porter (ed.), *Big Bear of Arkansas*, 154-58.
2. Miss Tandy notes these anonymous gentlemen-writers, but not the point of their democratic locale (*Crackerbox Philosophers. . .* 71, 74). Her assertion that the writers of Southern humor "were in general young fortune-hunters from an older more cultured scene" is supported by Baldwin, Hooper, W. T. Thompson and Thorpe; but not by Longstreet, Harris, Crockett, John B. Lamar, Bagby, Taliaferro ("Skitt"), J. B. Cobb.

selves."³ The explanation is that such regions as middle
Georgia, the northern parts of Alabama and Mississippi, and most of Arkansas were the haunts of plain
people.⁴ There the squires very likely possessed the
rough forthrightness of a certain mythical Senator
Jones of Arkansas who, in beginning his harangue about
changing the name of his state, stormed at the presiding
officer: "Mr. Speakeh, God damn you, Sah, I been
tryin' for half an hour to get yo' eye. . . ." Such men
enjoyed, not the exclusiveness of great estates, but the
"oddities of Southern life and character"—especially on
the lower levels.

Certain literary trends were also favorable to humor
about low-class whites. The Southern defence against
the Northern anti-slavery attack had the natural result
of reviving Dixie's hitherto neglected authors. In 1851,
the second edition of *Swallow Barn* was strongly recommended for Southern bookshelves.⁵ By 1852, a Charleston
publishing house, "mainly devoted to the encouragement of Southern authors and the dissemination of
Southern books," had issued a number of volumes, and
at last, *De Bow's Review* felt contrite about Simms:
"Though a Southern writer, Mr. Simms is perhaps more
known at the North than at home. This is wrong and
should be corrected."⁶ When a new edition of that
author's *Sword and Distaff* appeared in 1854, the
Southern Literary Messenger rejoiced in this revival of
such "standard works in Southern Literature," and
declared "that every Southerner should own a complete

3. Watterson, *Oddities in Southern Life and Character*, 329.
4. R. M. Johnston, "Middle Georgia Rural Life," XLIII, *Century Magazine* (March, 1892), 737-42.
5. *So. Lit. Mess.*, XVII (Dec., 1851), 764.
6. *De Bow's Review*, XIII (Aug., 1852), 211.

set"[7] of Simms' writings. Thus, in the general puffing and reviving, Southerners discovered that their humor was superior. Rufus Griswold had told them as much several years earlier: "We have," he said, "the promise of a rich and peculiar literature in the Southwest and South."[8] But when *Flush Times* appeared in 1853, they were emphatic: "In the department of humor we think it can not be questioned that Southern writers have excelled."[9] Then state pride laid claim to humor. In 1859, a proud native declared to the State Historical Society that "Mississippi has a literature, too" and that humor like J. B. Cobb's *Mississippi Scenes* and other "mirth provoking effusions" proved his boast.[10] The next year, a North Carolinian smarting under the traditional Virginia jokes about tar heel poverty, retorted that the Old North State was not poverty-stricken either in life or in literature; witness the superb humorous sketches in *Fisher's River* by "Skitt" (H. E. Taliaferro).[11]

Equally indicative was the reversal of editorial policy on the South's leading magazine. Even in Richmond by 1859, George W. Bagby had read enough of the chief glorifier of the Old Dominion, John Eston Cooke, to say: "Mr. Cooke's eyes are not only in the back of his head, but they are also afflicted with a pair of rose-colored goggles of enormous magnifying powers."[12] In June, 1860, on assuming the editorship of the *Southern*

7. *So. Lit. Mess.,* XX (Oct., 1854), 639.
8. *Prose Writers of America,* 546.
9. *So. Lit. Mess.,* XIX (Dec. 1853), 778-79. It is worth noting that five editions of Longstreet's *Georgia Scenes* appeared in 1850-60.
10. W. C. Crane, "The History of Mississippi," *So. Lit. Mess.,* IX (Feb., 1860), 89.
11. *So. Lit. Mess.,* IX (Aug., 1860), 105-10.
12. *Richmond Whig, ca.* 1859, as quoted by J. O. Beaty, in *John Eston Cooke, Virginian,* 70.

Literary Messenger, he sent out a call for another sort of writing: "We desire especially to obtain home-made purely Southern articles—tales, stories, sketches, poems that smack of the soil." The response was encouraging: several humorous sketches appeared,[13] one of merit, "Parson Squint,"[14] by "Skitt." But by December, Bagby was screaming for secession, and thereafter filled the magazine with diatribes, bad war verse, and silly romance.

Moreover, this recognition by the South of its richness in the literature of crude life has especial significance when considered with its political counterpart. Jacksonian democracy had supposedly put the bottom rail on top, and Northern policy had forced the Southern Whigs into Old Hickory's party. Rustic political wits had flourished in the newspapers, North and South. It remained for Davy Crockett to glorify the Common Man as politician. Nor was Simms behindhand in defending the ignorant frontier judge.[15] As a result, from the thirties to the fifties in the South there was an interest steadily converging upon the Common Man and the humorous writings about him which to a considerable extent dealt with the poor-white. To show how this was done, three general, and necessarily overlapping, poor-white types will be described.

The life of David Crockett (1786-1836) might be called the heroic version of the poor-white,[16] or rather,

13. "Klutz," "The Widow and Her Son," "Love in the Country," "Tom Johnson's Country Courting," which appeared in the July, August, and November, 1860, issues.
14. *So. Lit. Mess.,* XXXII (Jan., 1861), 50-52.
15. *Border Beagles,* 424.
16. The "great-hunter" tradition probably led to the error of regarding him as a mountaineer: "the first contribution of the Southern mountains to the folk epic of American History." Lucy L. Hazard, *Frontier in American Literature,* 48.

incipient poor-white. His prowess as hunter and Indian fighter, as yarn-spinner and practical joker, made him the political ancestor of many Southern champions of the clodhoppers.[17] But in spite of Davy's valorous side, there were the elements of decay in him, which, after the frontier age, would have turned the Gamecock of the Wilderness into a rather typical poor-white, not unlike Thomas Nelson Page's Little Darby.

His Irish ancestors had always been poor,[18] ever moving beyond the fringe of society, ever remaining ignorant. Davy's father was apparently a chronic maker of notes, two of which his famous son worked a year to pay. But before doing that filial chore, the boy had taken to cattle-driving and later bound himself to a Virginia hatter. Thus he began life on a humble level, strongly reminiscent of that Colonial underdog, the indentured servant.[19]

When he had married a lively Irish girl, reality became painful: "Now having a wife, I wanted everything else; and worse than all, I had nothing to give for it." Naturally, Davy became a renter with fifteen dollars' worth of cabin furnishings, secured on a Quaker friend's store-order. The usual poor-white tenant's troubles began—rent was too high. "I found," said Crockett, "I was better at increasing my family than my fortune."[20] He had not learned industry and

17. For a needed and brilliant rehabilitation of Crockett as legislator, see Constance Rourke, *Davy Crockett*, 130-33, *passim*.

18. David Crockett, *Autobiography*, ed. Hamlin Garland, 19. All references to this volume are from "A Narrative of the Life of David Crockett of the State of Tennessee," 13-136, unless otherwise noted.

19. *Ibid.*, 34. Some indentured servants very probably became poor-whites after the rise of slavery in the colonies (*ca.* 1700), though as a general origin of the poor-white class the indentured-servant theory has been discredited (T. J. Wertenbaker, *Patrician and Plebeian in Virginia*, 146, 163).

20. Crockett, *Autobiography*, 49.

frugality while working for the Quakers and the Dutch; it was much easier and more glorifying to win a beef at a shooting-match than to raise one. The remedy for his plight was at hand: only follow the ancestral, Crockett habit—move deeper into the back-country. And the Great Hunter of the West moved no less than six times before his fatal wandering to Texas. Nor was there apparently an excuse for any of these removals except the first. For example, his second wife, a widow, "owned a snug little farm and lived quite comfortable"; yet Davy soon called it unhealthy, dragged her off to the Chickasaw Purchase, where he came down with ague and fever! But he was no worse than most frontier husbands; they usually buried several "squaws." The point is that, in contrast with Davy's usual quarters, the original home of the widow and those of the Quakers and the Dutch indicated husbands who were interested in more than creature comforts for their families. The bear-hunter was not; the cabin life of a poor-white sufficed.

In one light, Davy's consuming purpose seems to have been the boyish avoidance of domestic toil—the ideal of the Indian, the long hunter, the poor-white. The Creek War was one escape. When his young wife begged him not to leave her in a strange country with little children, he gave heroic excuses, but in *The Narrative* he admits the real motive: "The truth is my dander was up." So Mrs. Crockett could only "cry a little and turn about her work." He would risk his life wading through winter sloughs to get powder for sup-plying his family with meat in the heroic way, rather than keep hogs as his neighbors did.[21] While election-eering, he had to "go a-wolfing" to keep his bottle and quid on the hip for voters; his children were enlisted for coon-hunting until midnight to supply the candidate with campaign funds. The politician's life was after Davy's own heart. A two-day squirrel hunt, culminating in a big barbecue, speeches, bouts with the bottle, and a "tiptop country frolic"—that was more than escape.

But this was, indeed, the heroic Crockett, so pat for the legend-makers, political and literary. Inevitably Davy became a part of that burlesque heroic convention: the bully, which, by 1833, when *Sketches and Eccentricities* appeared, was so hackneyed that its author after inveighing against making "every backwoodsman rant and rave in uncouth ways,"[22] shows Davy bullying and fighting a Kentucky boatman like any ring-tailed screamer.[23] Such a formula is of little or no value as portraiture. Only occasionally in such tall tale collections as *Major Thorpe's Scenes in Arkansas* (1858) do we find glimpses of a squatter's shack or a swamp tacky like Lanty Oliphant whose wife had ever one complaint: "always a-drinkin' and talkin' politics when you orter be at work, and there's never nothin' to eat in the house."[24]

The career of Davy, then, has especial value as a footnote to the abolitionist charge that the poor-white vices of slip-shod, lazy farming, roving habits, and

21. *Ibid.*, 116. For a satirical sketch of such "white Indians" as Davy, see T. C. Haliburton (ed.), "Above Work, But Not Beyond Want," in *Americans at Home*, III, 214-26.
22. *Sketches and Eccentricities of Colonel David Crockett of West Tennessee*, 176, and the preface, v-vi.
23. *Ibid.*, 144-45.
24. W. T. Porter (ed.), *Major Thorp's Scenes in Arkansas*, 39, 133.

poverty were caused entirely by slavery. In Crockett, as in most backwoodsmen of his day, these failings already inhered, only to be accentuated and thrown into strong relief by denser and more civilized settlement. And the rapidity with which newly opened lands moved toward this state can be illustrated by Davy's noble fight in Congress against land speculators who were dispossessing his fellow squatters and settlers in West Tennessee and using Jackson's pet banks to finance their chicanery.[25]

Simon Suggs, the hero of *Simon Suggs' Adventures* (1846), written by Johnson J. Hooper, is, unlike Davy, an entirely fictional character. Appropriately enough, he was created in the picaro or rogue tradition, used in Southern humor at least since 1834,[26] for Hooper himself had wandered the South from North Carolina to the Gulf working on newspapers. At times, the traditional Crockett had become the picaresque bad boy in episodes like that of selling the same coonskin for drink after drink. But Suggs is the "simon pure" rogue, unheroic and prideless; he is the swindler errant at cards, land deals, or camp meetings. In 1812, when Davy went forth to war against the Creeks, he was a valiant; in 1836, when Simon, as self-appointed officer, herded the poor-whites of Tallapoosa County fleeing from the same redskin tribe, he became a mock-hero and made war a farce.[27] Thus, in creating Simon Suggs, Hooper turned the earlier glorification of the heroism and humor of such figures as Davy into satire.

Yet, like Crockett, Simon Suggs, the arch-rogue, was

25. Rourke, *op. cit.*, 131.
26. H. J. Nott, *op. cit.* See character of Thomas Singularity.
27. J. J. Hooper, *Simon Suggs' Adventures*, 61.

more poor-white than anything else. His father, a "hard-shell" Baptist preacher in Middle Georgia, was a near-poor-white. At fifty, his ingenious son looked like any trashy Cracker: a long nose hung above a mouth stained by the filthy weed; "a long, but muscular neck . . . inserted after the ordinary fashion in the upper part of a frame, long and sinewy, clad in Kentucky jeans, a trifle worn." And while Simon wandered and swindled, his family existed in true, woolhat poverty. Let his wife bear witness: "Mrs. Suggs informed him that 'the sugar and coffee was nigh about out,' and that there were not 'a dozen jints and middlins,' *all put together*, in the smoke-house."[28]

But it was not in *Simon Suggs' Adventures*, but in *Taking the Census*, that Hooper did with incomparable skill the sketches of Alabama poor-whites which will be noted later.

The third comic type of the Southern poor-white may be termed the Cracker or Longstreet version. Without the distorting political propaganda of the Crockett portrait, or the conventionalized bully-heroics of the Big-Bear humor, and without the fantastic adventures of Suggs, the Longstreet depiction was more homely, more actual, because like *Swallow Barn* and nearly all that is now readable in ante-bellum Southern literature, *Georgia Scenes* (1835) sprang primarily from an historical, not a literary impulse. This was to leave sketches of manners in early Georgia, which would be brought "to light, when time would give them an interest."[29] And, since Longstreet felt compelled to make this record

28. *Ibid.*, 12, 13, 19, 21, 83.
29. A. B. Longstreet, *Georgia Scenes, Characters, Incidents, etc., in the First Half Century of the Republic*, preface, iii. The last two phrases of the title illustrate my point.

a true one, he apologized for "the minuteness of detail," and "for the introduction of some things, which would have been excluded, were they merely creations of the fancy." This "founded-on-fact" subterfuge, well-worn since Defoe's time and frequently used in early American fiction, provided exactly the license which Longstreet needed to depict low, tough Crackers. "Coarse, inelegant, and sometimes ungrammatical language," Longstreet justified, because "it is language accommodated to the capacity of the person."[30] In "Georgia Theatrics," the ultra-moral author appears to have been shocked at Cracker profanity and summarizes it as "countless oaths interspersed, which I dare not even hint at." When the Savannah Innkeeper shouts anent Ned Brace, "Well, d—n the man," Longstreet added a footnote: "I should certainly omit such expressions as this, could I do so with historic fidelity; but the peculiaries of the times of which I am writing, cannot be faithfully represented without them. In recording things *as they are*, truth requires me sometimes to put profane language into the mouths of my characters."[31]

Yet he sometimes dropped this pious, historical pose; then he could allow the winner in "The Gander Pulling" to yell over his prize money: "Oh, you little shining sons o' bitches! walk into your Mas' Johnny's pocket and gingle. . . ." That such talk got into print is highly important here: it meant that poor-whites could now speak their minds in believable fashion. They needed no longer to be mute illustrations.

But the comic poor-white needed to live, move, and

30. *Ibid.*, iv.
31. *Ibid.*, 44.

have his being, grotesque and filthy as it often was. And, indeed, such creation was to Longstreet's liking, for his nature had in it the coarse, humorous strain of any Georgia squire. In "The Horse-Swap," one can see that he enjoyed describing the saddle sore on Bullet's backbone which "measured six full inches in length and four in breadth and had as many features as Bullet had emotions," or enumerating the tearing or loss of ears, eyes, fingers, cheeks, and noses in "The Fight." Moreover, the Georgia writer could hoodwink his neighbors and readers—perhaps himself—by claiming that *Georgia Scenes* "contain nothing more than fanciful *combinations* of *real* incidents and characters,"[32] or that the vulgarities in them were to be viewed as lessons in reform. Thus, in the sketch, "An Interesting Interview," before relating, with obvious delight, the annual meeting in town of two ancient Crackers, he took first his absolution: "I hope the day is not far distant when drunkeness will be unknown. . . ."[33] Hence, it was possible for Longstreet to add the most pathetic and degenerate of poor-whites, the clay-eater, to the gallery of *comic* Southerners. Once this had been done by a Southerner, the way was open to a wide, humorous survey of poor-white life and types to which, among others, "Skitt" (H. E. Taliaferro) and "Bill Arp" (Chas. H. Smith) contributed works of varying distinction.

Using the three general paths—heroic, picaresque, and Cracker—Southern humorists explored the pineywoods and sandhills to discover knots of tackies, so long isolated or ignored that their queer ways made striking

32. P. iii.
33. See also the apologies in "The Fight" and "Georgia Theatrics."

peasant comedy. For, as the Canadian humorist, Thomas C. Haliburton, wrote in 1854, the American folk could not be known by following the main travel routes: "The peculiarities of the people, their modes of thinking, living, and acting, are principally to be sought for in the rural districts, where unrestrained freedom of action, and the incidents and requirements of a forest life, encourage and give room for the development of character in its fullest extent."[34] As a result, while plantation novelists ignored or discussed them, and Simms, the border romancer, used them as villains, Southern humorists first gave to the poor-whites important, literary existence of remarkable range and variety.

The typical poor-white haunt in the pineywoods, which to Northerners represented the land monopoly of the planters and to Southern apologists, the law of like seeking like, was turned to good use by Southern humorists. On the Tallapoosa River in Alabama, whose "banks are generally large irregular hills, that look as if they were struggling to pitch themselves with their huge pines, into the stream," one might see "the cabin of a squatter, stuck to the side of a hill, like a fungus against a wall" and "a little way out from the river, on either side, among the 'hollows'. . . a people half-agricultural, half-piscatory,—a sinewy, yellow headed, whiskey-loving set."[35] Over in Georgia, humor hit off the dilemma of a Cracker who is hard put to give a reason for his remaining in the pineywoods, which had been stripped of so many earlier resources. The nub

34. Haliburton, *op. cit.*, I, v-vi.
35. Haliburton (ed.), *Traits of American Humor*, II, 126.

of the joke hinges upon the backwoods use of lightwood knots (that is, pitchy pine wood) for candles.

"A traveller came one day upon a most desolate-looking location in the sandy pine woods of Georgia, the most prominent features of which were a small field of excessively small corn, over which a thousand trunks of deadened pine trees stood sentry—a very black log cabin, with about half a chimney, doorless, floorless, windowless. . . . Thrusting their long noses through a surrounding rail fence, stood half a dozen miserable long-nosed, land pike breed of hogs, looking anxiously upon an equal number of half-starved, half-hound curs, that were looking enviously at an equal number of white-headed, white-faced children, who were disputing over a half supply of half-roasted sweet potatoes; while 'Lord of all I survey' sat the owner upon the fence, looking the very picture of happy contentment."

Traveller: "Stranger, I'll thank you for a gourd of water."
"Got none—spring's dry. Hogs been in the brook."
"Why, I don't know how you live without water."
"All in use. Roast taters better'n bil'd one—have one, stranger?"
"No, I thank you. You have poor land here. Your corn is very small."
"Yes. Not worth planting."
"Is it good for potatoes?"
"No! nor nothing else!"
"Poor for hogs, too, I should think?"
"Yes, till pine mast falls."
"Is your range good for stock?"
"Not worth a curse."

53

"How's game? . . . that's good I reckon."

"No tain't. Them infernal camp hunters . . . have drove all the deer out. . . ."

"Well, then I hope you have plenty of fish. . . .?"

"What, in that stinking black swamp? No, sir, none but mud fish and alligators. . . ."

"Will you tell me what in the world there is to induce you to locate here. . . .?"

He lifted his long legs from the fence, looked over his field, so as to take in the whole view of dead pines and waving his majestic right hand in the same direction . . .replied . . . "Sir! don't you see that light-wood is tolerable handy?"[36]

The range of Southern comic types presented from the early thirties until shortly after the Civil War was fairly wide, but writers largely followed conventional humorous patterns, for example, ultimately Will Wimble in *The Spectator*, but immediately those of Irving. The bad boy or practical joker, Ned Brace (no poor-white), in *Georgia Scenes* was preceded by Brom Bones in "The Legend of Sleepy Hollow" (1819); and in *Mississippi Scenes* (1850), Joseph B. Cobb, friend and imitator of Longstreet, declared his Bob Bagshot, the poor-white "cut-up" of "The Legend of Black Creek," to be "the very counterpart of Brom Bones." "A roaring, rattle-brained, rumpussing character," he kept his Mississippi community "in a constant stew" by his pranks, fiddled best at "all the barn dances," and "loved a tidy, bright-eyed wench better than all things else." His "most luscious eye" for

36. Haliburton, *Americans at Home*, I, 86-89.

"plump limbs" was so well known that when he was an overnight guest, mothers locked up their "romps at bedtime." This light-o'-love in Bob is his creator's only addition to the Irving type; the story, used by Cobb, like several pieces of the Knickerbocker writer, evolves from a superstition that every year the ghost of a murdered man re-enacts the tragedy.

But there were also stock figures, used only as conventional mouthpieces for set humor. The bully or braggart—already noted—created to give an outlandish "spiel" and a more outlandish cavorting, was usually, with reference to poor-white farmers, an exaggerated convention for recording their strutting in town. "The Yellow Blossom from Jasper" in "The Horse-Swap" of Longstreet, excellent as he is, tells us nothing about the trashy Cracker except his use of trading ruses common to all ignorant countrymen. The bane of formula-writing also renders nearly worthless for this study types like Tom Owen, the Bee-Hunter,[37] who "in a clear day" could "see a bee over a mile away"; the narrator of "The Big Bear of Arkansas," the squatter-hunter, whose gun was "a perfect epidemic among bar"; and burlesque sermonizers like Parson Squint or the preacher of "The Harp with a Thousand Strings."[38] Such narrators have little or no existence before or after their "spiels"; hence one cannot surely determine their social class except to say that it is a low one.

At least two more local sorts of poor-whites appeared that should have been exploited fully by Southern humorists. These were the wagoners and the clay-eaters.

37. T. B. Thorpe, *Mysteries of the Backwoods.*
38. F. J. Meine (ed.), *Tall Tales of the Southwest.*

Before the era of railroads in the South, the carriers were as rough as their job, as violent as they were merry. George Tucker in *The Valley of the Shenandoah* had been mildly amused by them. In his early teens, Davy Crockett followed the big wheels of several teamsters whom he found to be a jolly, good-hearted lot.[39] But their reputation all over the South was a tough one. A Northern traveler in 1835 thought the eastern Mississippi variety "destitute of intelligence" and certainly not amusing:

"They are in general uneducated, and their apparel consists of a coarse linsey-woolsey of a dingy yellow or blue, with broad-brimmed hats; though they usually follow their teams bare-footed and bare-headed, with their long locks hanging over their eyes and shoulders, giving them a wild appearance. Accost them as they pass you, one after another, in long lines, cracking their whips, ... and their replies will generally be sullen or insulting. . . . They will seldom allow carriages to pass them, unless attended by gentlemen, who often have to do battle for the highway. . . . They have a decided aversion to a broad-cloth coat. . . ."[40]

Yet the wagoner was an excellent, though neglected, comic subject. "Skitt" has preserved for us a glimpse of them in Alabama about 1845. Some teamsters pulled up by a man's well, watered their horses without permission, and filled the air with oaths. "Then they commenced popping their whips about in the yard" and asked the farmer's wife to sell them chickens. "We hain't bin eatin' nothin' but dried beef so long we've

39. Crockett, *op. cit.*, 26, 30-31, 33-34.
40. J. H. Ingraham, *The Southwest*, II, 170-72.

wore ur corn-grinders down to the gums. . . ." Later
they camped in a lane nearby, making the night loud
with drunken brawling and finally with "the intonations
of a Hard-Shell Baptist Preacher. . . [which] . . . had
the suck-in and the blow-out of the breath, the *uh!* and
the *ah!*" They were mocking a rascal evangelist who
had "converted" them! Such men deserved the old
doggerel couplet:

Oh, the wagoner was a mighty man, a mighty man was he:
He'd pop his whip, and stretch his chains, and holler 'woe
[gee.'

And the clay-eater, to whom Longstreet gave literary
being in 1833, begot few descendants in Southern
humor.[41] Very likely, Ransy Sniffle's love of the soil was
a whit too complete for comic senses more queasy than
his creator's: and, naturally, Southerners did not care to
have the local perversion of dirt-eating noised abroad,
especially after it became the mark of poor-white
depravity most dwelt upon by Northern and foreign
observers. But Longstreet himself made no use of this
habit beyond the famous one-paragraph portrait in
"The Fight": "Now there happened to reside in the
county just alluded to a little fellow by the name of
Ransy Sniffle: a sprout of Richmond, who, in his earlier
days, had fed copiously upon red clay and blackberries.
This diet had given to Ransy a complexion that a
corpse would have disdained to own, and an abdominal

41. Ransy Sniffle in "The Fight," *Georgia Scenes,* 53-66. Thus far the earliest account
discovered of dirt-eating is the article by Joseph Pitt in 1808, no title (cited by R. B. Vance,
op. cit., 380). Whether this habit was the result of hunger, made excessive by hookworm
and malaria, is hard to say (Stiles, *op. cit.*). In a North Carolina town twenty years ago,
I saw Negroes making balls of clay, mixed with snuff and the ashes of a black-gum tree,
to put in the lower-lip.

rotundity that was quite unprepossessing. Long spells
of fever and ague, too, in Ransy's youth, had conspired
with clay and blackberries to throw him quite out of
the order of nature. His shoulders were fleshless and
elevated; his head large and flat; his neck slim and
translucent; and his arms, hands, fingers, and feet were
lengthened out of all proportion to the rest of his frame.
His joints were large and his limbs small; and as for
flesh, he could not, with propriety, be said to have any.
Those parts which nature usually supplies with the most
of this article—the calves of the legs, for example—
presented in him the appearance of so many well-drawn
blisters. His height was just five feet nothing, and his
average weight, in blackberry season, ninety-five."[42]

Here, with all exaggerations admitted, is the most
complete literary account of the poor-white's physical
debility which forced him to "poke along easy." It is
also a standard list of his ills: malaria, malnutrition,
and hookworm, even though Longstreet could not have
known the last named "germ of laziness."

But what is the function of this description? Apparently that of contrast between Ransy's dead-alive
manner and the sudden energy by which he brought
on a bloody fight. "I have been thus particular in
describing him," says Longstreet, "for the purpose of
showing what a great matter a little fire sometimes
kindleth. There was nothing on this earth which
delighted Ransy so much as a fight. He never seemed
fairly alive except when he was witnessing, or talking
about a fight."[43] Longstreet's comic insight caught the

42. *Georgia Scenes*, 55.
43. *Ibid.*, 55-56.

humor in a social fact which Byrd had overlooked: namely, the incongruity between the listlessness of the trash and the violence of their diversions.

And as surely as there is a humor of the sordid and the grotesque, this habit of geophagy, as old medical books called it, has comic possibilities which writers of the Old South ignored. Travelers, for example, were amazed by the poor-white's appetite for a "sweetish kind of clay" and reported "mere infants . . . with their mouths filled with dirt" and also "children sitting on an old-fashioned hearth picking out the clay or mortar between the bricks." Verily, in such a poor-white Land of Cockayne, other parts of the cabin served as both food and shelter, with the result that "the mud with which they daub the interstices between the logs of their rude domiciles must be frequently renewed. . . ." From such hints as these,[44] imagine a sketch of Ransy, descanting on the best times and places for digging clay and later berating his tow-headed "younguns" for making his hut chinkless! In doing this, one may recall that William Byrd in the eighteenth century scored some of his funniest hits on the subject of lubber diseases; but ante-bellum Southern humorists, restrained by political and literary considerations, lost therein a comic opportunity.

In humor, Ransy begot no literary progeny of clay-eaters, but after his appearance we catch a glimpse now and then of the Sniffle breed, such, for example, as that by William Tappan Thompson, an adopted Georgian and follower of Longstreet. In the country crowd in

44. Charles Lyell, *Second Visit to the United States of America*, II, 7; J. S. Buckingham, *Slave States of America*, I, 551.

town, wrote Thompson, "might be seen the torpid
clay-eater, his bloated, watery countenance illuminated
by the exhilerating qualities of rum, as he closed on his
antagonist, and showed by his performances that he
could eat clay as well in its animate as in its inanimate
form."[45] Ransy, however, must be regarded as the most
plausible ancestor of Ham Rachel of Alabama and Bill
Arp of Georgia, neither of whom took his dirt straight.
And we know their lives much better than that of their
forebear, Mr. Sniffle. Certainly, when "Skitt" (H. E.
Taliaferro), a North Carolinian who moved to Alabama,
in *Fisher's River* (1859),[46] created the woolhat, Ham
Rachel, he enabled readers to know intimately for the
first time not only the poor-white in his comic moments,
but to some extent the easy-going world in which he
lived.

About 1845, Ham lived in Barbour County, one of
the poor "cow counties," with Eufaula as his trading
town. His neighbors, like himself, were poor, plain, and
largely illiterate. "All they cared for was 'to make
buckle and tongue meet' by raising stock, a few bales
of cotton, and a little corn bread." When their bit of
"cotting" was baled and placed on an ox-cart, the
family made for Eufaula, the husband flogging the oxen,
the good wife riding atop the cart-load, and the "child-
ering" footing it as best they could. In town, the wife
disposed of "several extra matters"—the usual "poor-
white money": chickens, butter, and eggs—so that she
could buy knick-knacks and a jug of the "good critter"

45. W. T. Thompson, *Chronicles of Pineville*, 41.
46. All references are taken from chap. xxiii: "Ham Rachel of Alabama"; the other
sketches in the volume deal with the North Carolina mountains. For Longstreet's influence
on *Fisher's River*, see review, *So. Lit. Mess.*, IX (Jan., 1860), 78.

for ailments. There, fortified with two such jugs, swung on a long strap over his shoulder, Ham Rachel met Old John, his dram-loving neighbor, whom later he dropped on his doorstep a sodden lump.

At the supper which Ham wheedled out of Old John's wife for bringing her man home, the sandhiller's curiosity fastened on the narrator, an overnight guest. To disguise his prying intention, he prattled about the food, vowing that "We'd look like the peaked end uv nothin' . . . . if it warn't fur milk, butter, cowpeas, and yam 'tators." Assuming the stranger's innocence of Barbour County etiquette, Ham warned him that the rule was "every man for himself." But after the snatching and gobbling, he abandoned indirection and made a frontal attack: "Ham Rachel loves fur a man to be . . . as thick as cowpeas in thar hull. I've got to know suthin' about yer."

Toward midnight when nausea doubled Old John, the sandhiller ran into the guest's room yelling: "Stranger! Stranger! do yer hear that ole devil pukin' out his innards? I wouldn't keer a dried-apple durn ef he would puke himself outurds. . . . ." But not even such excitement opened the tight-mouthed man. In disgust, Ham joined some wagoners, camped nearby, and howled till sunup, when he was again at the departing guest's elbow with a final scheme: "Stranger, give out yer Eufauly trip today, and go home with Ham Rachel, and a stay a long week. He can treat yer like a king on the best these deadnins affords. Do you see these jugs? Then thar's plenty more in Eufauly. Thar's plenty ov fiddles, gals, and boys about here. I don't know whether ye'r married ur not: no odds; yer wife won't know it, and the gals won't keer a durn. You may sing, pray, dance, drink; ur do anything else at Ham Rachel's." In order to postpone failure to the last, he walked by the stranger's horse, until his home-road branched off into the pineywoods, and soon his slouch-hat, high-hitched copperas breeches, and swinging jugs passed from sight.

But like his probable forebear, Ransy Sniffle, he does not readily pass out of the mind. His morality is as loose as his breeches, his talk as dirty as his shirt, his life in a "cow county" as relaxed and droopy as his old wool hat. Ham Rachel, a definite poor-white in a definite place, seems more actual than Ransy. Indeed, only one convention: that of country curiosity, most often associated with "The Arkansas Traveller," allies him with genre stuff.

Compared with Ransy and Ham, the third member of this comic line showed several acquired characteristics. When Bill Arp appeared in Georgia some twenty-five years after his Alabama forerunner, he was a composite of several comic predecessors: bully, bad boy, loafer, and drunkard. But that apparently indicated neither myth nor convention: Bill Arp was a real person whose life Charles H. Smith (1826-1903) simply recorded in two sketches, "The Original Bill Arp"[47] and "The Georgia Cracker and the Gander Pulling."[48] Whether Smith always held to facts or occasionally strayed into

47. Three versions published in volumes: *Bill Arp's Scrap Book*, 7-19, with much bully stuff; *Farm and the Fireside*, 18-24, most complete; *From the Uncivil War to Date*, 58-64, a posthumous form, cut and cleansed. These books fall beyond 1870, the approximate limit of this chapter; however, in subjects and modes Smith's work belongs to earlier humor. Moreover, all of his books were collections of newspaper articles published over a period of years.

48. *Farm and the Fireside*, 14-15.

the "fanciful combinations" of Longstreet does not matter here so much as the changes he made in literary treatment. A Georgia lawyer in the tradition of the amateur humorist, Charles H. Smith began writing early enough to fall into the rough Cracker humor of cacography and vulgarity, yet he wrote late enough to react against this earlier mode.[49] For, when Bill Arp appeared between book covers, the South had developed a more delicate comic taste, lost a war, and become tender about the old times. The natural result was that Smith, while retaining some of the earlier crudeness, so prominent in Taliaferro and his mountaineer contemporary, George W. Harris, subordinated this aspect and depicted his humble friend with an affection which, at times, pointed toward the grandfatherly nostalgia of R. M. Johnston, but which also gave to his life of Bill Arp a sympathetic understanding not to be found in those of earlier Southern humorists.

In Rome, Georgia, about 1851, Charles H. Smith, then a lawyer of twenty-five, fresh from a three-months legal course, had hung out his shingle and decided to grow up with "the West" of Georgia. One day in the spring of 1861, he was reading to some fellow-townsmen in his office his first letter to Abe Linkhorn. Lolling against the door-facing stood Bill Arp, a small, trashy-looking Cracker, "his mouth open and a merry glisten in his eye." The letter having been read, Bill Arp, aware of the Southern practice of anonymity, asked the author what pen-name he would use. Smith did not know. "Well, Squire," said Bill, "I wish you would put mine,

49. *Bill Arp, So-Called*, 56.
50. *Farm and the Fireside*, 18.

63

for them's my sentiments."[50] Thus "Bill Arp so-called" entered the literary world as political commentator and cracker-box philosopher, a rôle that had little connection with the Georgia poor-white of that name, in spite of the author's opinion to the contrary: "When I began writing under the signature of Bill Arp, I was honestly idealizing the language and humor of an unlettered countryman who bears that name . . . and he declares to this day that I have faithfully expressed his sentiments. Those who know him can see more of him in my letters than they can of me . . . ."[51]

Those who know the local relations of authors, especially as they concern living originals, need not take this statement too seriously; at best, it has only a slight validity for one volume: *Bill Arp, So-Called* (1866). After all, Smith was following the practice of the period, 1855 to 1885, for, as Mr. Napier Wilt has pointed out, these pseudonyms were assumed by an author "not to develop a fictional character, but merely to use the name as a mask to express his own opinions."[52]

Bill Arp was almost a runt, weighing only one hundred and thirty pounds, but his body was tough and active as a cat's. "He could outrun, out-jump, out-swim, out-wrestle, out-shoot anybody." As the "best man" in Chulio district, he became enraged when Ben McGinnis came into his beat. "I'm no phist puppy, sir," Bill complained to a friend, "that he should come out of his deestrict to bully me." He then pounded Ben to a pulp and afterwards treated him at the whiskey barrel. Nor did Ike McCoy, "the best rasler in all Cherokee," who

51. *Bill Arp, So-Called*, 6.
52. *Some American Humorists*, xii.

"put on a heap of airs, strutted around with his shirt-collar open clean down to his waist, and his hat cocked on the side of his head," fare any better. Yet Bill Arp was no one-sport man; he also starred at gander-pullings. After other riders with weaker grips had left the gander, swinging and squawking, he seized the bird's greasy neck; "the strained tendons popped like a whip as Bill's nag went on at full speed." How sweet the hurrahs of the Crackers must have sounded to his poor-white ears when he cantered back to receive the prize, "the gander head . . . held high in his hand, the warm blood trickling from the arteries." Bill Arp *was* the "best man"—for some things.

But with that peasant who sweats all day in the eye of the sun, Bill Arp could claim no kin. He was a "no 'count." His friend, Mr. Smith, thought that "a sorry farmer on a sorry farm is a sorry sight." Bill hardly attained that level of sorriness. He worked a few bottom patches and ran a river-ferry for a wealthy man, Col. Johnson—that is, he was *supposed* to do these chores, but they usually fell to the lot of his wife and children, because Mr. Arp, like Davy Crockett, did not find breadwinning to his taste. He rejoiced in the Colonel's bounty; and "Mrs. Johnson," Bill was proud to say, "throws away enough old clothes and second-hand vittels to support my children, and they are always nigh enough to pick 'em up." Perhaps, because the reluctant ferryman realized that he was enjoying the *largesse* of slavery without its bondage, he "used to say he would rather belong to Col. Johnson than to be free."

Be it said in his defence, however, that his temptations were strong; he was a favorite not only on fields of sport, but in town. About the village, Bill hovered around the knots of big men in the hope of being asked to join them. And his "reverence for his superiors and thankfulness for their notice" always brought the call to pull up a chair. For, although this trashy Cracker "never went to school but a month or two in his life, and could neither read nor write," he had "more than his share of common sense." Equally dear to him was the ancient, tacky pleasure of gawking at trial scenes; often he deserted his ferry to sit in the courtroom a day at a time soaking up the lawyer's speeches. Afterwards, he followed the court-week mob to a saloon, where late that night his wife found him and started the reviving process for the three-mile walk homeward.

No wonder that one with such a genius for society renewed his youth in the Civil War. Wit and wag of many a campfire, Private Arp became a sort of official prankster who spared no one, not even the General himself. One day, when the C. S. A. confiscated several kegs of brandy, hidden in wagon loads of apples, one of these treasures went under the General's bed. On guard duty that night, Private Arp removed the keg and returned it next day half full. The whole company, including the robbed officer, enjoyed the joke.

How Bill Arp came to the end of his rope Smith never told us; perhaps there were unpleasant memories involved. But let us hope that Col. Johnson lived long enough to provide the merry bones of his idolator with a decent box.

Besides presenting typical and individual poor-whites, Southern humor gradually created a panorama of their social life, the separate pictures of which soon

Crackers, Woolhats, and Dirt-eaters

became *genre* writing. When this happened, definiteness of scene and character faded into generalities to such an extent that the actors might be any sort below the aristocracy. However, the fun-loving trash always shook off their malarious torpidity and, like Ransy Sniffle, came alive when a fight or a frolic was to be had. Consequently, the *genre* paintings of rousing times in the "sticks" may well reflect them more than any other class.

Down to 1847, for example, gander-pulling[53] was a favorite sport of the crudest Crackers and had its aristocratic parallel in the tournaments *à la* Sir Walter Scott held by the planters.[54] Another *genre* piece, the horse-swap,[55] with its whooping and spurring about, was a tacky institution with the upper-class equivalent of the race tracks of the wealthy. At musters,[56] the first men of the countryside commanded, but their "starveling crews" turned the drills into memorable farce and topped off the occasion with an afterpiece of bullying and fighting.[57] The shooting-match,[58] an early backwoods diversion, remained the especial delight of the poor-white who was often as much hunter as farmer,

53. C. H. Smith, "The Georgia Cracker and the Gander Pulling," *Farm and the Fireside*, 9-15; A. B. Longstreet, "The Gander Pulling," *Georgia Scenes*, 118-28.
54. D. R. Hundley's sarcastic picture: "our modern Cotton Knight, who ambles daintily on the back of a docile gelding, holding a sharpened stick under his arm, and gallently and gloriously endeavoring to thrust the same through an iron ring, which is suspended by a rope of twine from an horizontal beam" (*op. cit.*, 175). At Columbus, Miss., in 1928, I saw a more violent exhibition of such sport.
55. T. C. Haliburton (ed.), *Traits of American Humor*, I, 131-144; "The Horse-Swap," *Georgia Scenes*, 20-30. For a description of such horse traders, see Hundley, *op. cit.*, 234.
56. "The Militia Company Drill," *Georgia Scenes*, 157-64; *Farm and the Fireside*, 167; J. B. Cobb, "The Bride of Lick-the-Skillet," *Mississippi Scenes*, 194 ff.
57. Fights without reference to musters: "Georgia Theatrics," *Georgia Scenes*, 5-8; "The Fight," *Ibid.*, 53-66; *Sketches and Eccentricities*, 144-45; C. H. Smith, *Farm and the Fireside*, 246-51; *Traits of American Humor*, III, 48-60.
58. "The Shooting Match," *Georgia Scenes*, 215-35; *Sketches and Eccentricities*, 119-25; *Farm and the Fireside*, 20-23, 251; *Bill Arp's Scrap Book*, 13-14; Albert Pike, "Letters from Arkansas," No. 2, *American Monthly Magazine*, New Series, I (Jan., 1836), 27.

for, with his "old Soap-Stick," he could not only win the prize, but what he otherwise never received: some small approval. And although the camp-meeting[59] was a universal Southern habit, the orgiastic style—which became the stock one—with the jerks, holy dances, foot-washings, and love-fests, belonged to the poor-whites and other backwooders who like their religion raw. Enjoyed by all rural Southerners except the most sophisticated, the play-parties and frolics were of folk origin and have been preserved longest by the isolated poor-whites. In the early forties, "an ex-governor of a cotton-growing state" described the famous game of "Sister Phoebe," always the spice of every play-party. "The girls placed a man in the chair, and sang—

How happy, how happy, how happy was we,
When we sat under the juniper tree;
Put this hat on your head to keep it warm,
And take a good kiss, it will do you no harm.

"Then they put a hat on his head, and two of them sat down on his lap, placing their faces close on each side of his, so that he could with difficulty turn his head and kiss them. And so they went through all of the trees in the forest."[60]

The "sparking" and the wedding, like the "cocka-doodledoo" of the bully, became as inevitable as death and taxes, but seldom did versions so amusing as "Billy Warwick's Courtship and Wedding"[61] appear, for Billy

59. Hooper, *op. cit.*, 83-93. Incomparable, with satiric footnotes on political significance of such revivals, *Mississippi Scenes*, 122.
60. "Life and Manners in Arkansas," *Big Bear of Arkansas*, 154-58. See also Crockett, *Autobiography*, 45, 48; "The Dance," *Georgia Scenes*, 8-20.
61. *Big Bear of Arkansas*, 90-105.

Crackers, Woolhats, and Dirt-eaters

and Barbara had an unusual chaperon. "Old Miss cum back and sat in the chimbley corner and tuck off her shoes and tuck her pipe and went to smokin'; the way she rowl'd the smoke out was astonishin'; and every now and then she struck her head and sorter gron'd like." When the old woman went to bed (behind the backs of the couple before the fireplace), the sparkers began to hug and "buss" until the old Miss Bass yelled, "My lord!—Barbry, old Troup [the dog] is in the milk-pan! —I heerd him smackin' his lips and lickin' of the milk. Git out, you old varmint! Git out!" A pet gander that slept in the cabin started up, Billy took the cue, jumped up, chased old Troup out, and slammed the door. Looking back over this display of rural delights, one will realize that, for the first time, Americans could see how the Southern poor-white "pleasured himself"; for, be it remembered, the purpose of the Northern abolitionist was not to show the brooding pariah and victim of Southern society, happy in Zion or joyously inebriate from "bust-head," flinging his thin shanks about in a double cross-hop.

Yet Southern humor advanced beyond this to the comedy of class attitudes and thought-grooves. The basis of these was the ancient distrust of townsmen by country people, whose prejudice increased the deeper they lived in the woods. Deriving from this bias the theme of the "hick-in-town," writers have perpetrated innumerable sins in the name of humor, perhaps none less funny than G. W. Bagby's "Mozzis Addums."[62] But

62. Note Bagby's humorous attempt as indicated by this: "goin' into a sitty is atendid with a cents uv fear" (*So. Lit. Mess.*, XXVI, March, 1858, 188). Other examples of this theme: "An Arkansas Original" in *Polly Peablossom's Wedding*, ed. T. A. Burke, 119-21; "Printing a Horse," *ibid.*, 159-61.

such pointless cacography and forced, "hayseed" vaudeville were surpassed by playing upon the contradictory feelings of the Cracker toward the town.

Ignorantly prideful of his one trip to Augusta, "the *Ultima Thule* of back-woods Georgians," the Reverend Jedediah Suggs, the father of Simon, scorned anyone who had not been so fortunate.[63] What a sense of inferiority such an untraveled Cracker must have suffered, T. W. Lane tells us in his rare sketch, "The Thimble Game": "A man who had *never* been there [Augusta], was a cipher in the community—nothing killed an opinion more surely, nothing stopped the mouth of 'argyment' sooner, than the sneering taunt, 'pshaw, you ha'n't been to Augusty.' "[64]

And yet, in contradiction of such awesome worship, he feared city people and with spiteful envy longed to skin them in business. Back home on a Sunday, he might brag and strut in his Augusta store clothes, but in that city to trade, he stood defiantly on the American doctrine of equality and determined to come off the better man. Thus he could avenge himself upon the town for being made a fool by its pranksters, perhaps after the fashion of the sand-hiller, who had only "Pertaters and Turnups" to sell, but *somehow* was never asked for anything except eggs, until he drove from the town square a desperate man.[65] Likewise, Peter Wilkins, who, with his son, was victimized by an Augusta cotton buyer ("gimlet-man"), let the passion for retaliation so consume and ruin him that, years

63. Hooper, *op. cit.*, 19.
64. Meine, *op. cit.*, 373-82.
65. "Pertaters and Turnups" in Meine, *op. cit.*, 99-102. Pub. in *Spirit of the Times,* Aug. 3, 1850.

later, on his death bed, he warned his boy to "bewar of them Gimlet Fellers, down to Augusty."[66] But, another day, the country trader might catch his city customers off guard and cheat them to his heart's content, as the poor-white in Sol Smith's "A Bully Boat and a Brag Captain" (1845) did in selling wood all night long to the same steamboat, while the captain played cards and the crew loafed.

The back country people's fears of medical instruments and new-fangled remedies of the town found no better expression than the tall yarns of books like *The Louisiana Swamp Doctor* (1856); their political life, however, was given a more interpretative comic record. Perhaps, no frontier heritage was more completely preserved in the backcountry than the distrust and hatred of governmental interference. In 1728, William Byrd had observed the anxiety of the tar heels lest the survey should place them in Virginia where laws and taxes would pester them.[67] And over a century later, Johnson Hooper found that their Alabama descendants resented as hotly all prying agencies of law. In his sketch, "Taking the Census," a "chicken man" (census-taker and tax-assessor combined) stopped at a widow's gate in Tallapoosa County. On discovering his mission, she shrieked for her dogs, Bull and Pomp, to tear him, and vowed that she would like to set them on old President Van Buren himself, for "sendin' out men to take down what little stuff people's got jist to tax it. . . ." Van Buren, she swore, was " a pretty fellow to be eating his vittils out'n gold spoons that poor people's taxed for . . .

66. Meine, *op. cit.*; 382; T. W. Lane, "The Thimble Game."
67. *HDL*, 104.

the oudacious, nasty, stinking old scamp." Nor would
she report anything: "Jist put down 'Judy Tompkins,
ag'eable woman and four children.' " Nor could the
"chicken man" discover the number of fowls owned by
the next poor-white widow who jabbered endlessly and
wandered from the point, replying to his questions:
"Well, now, thar agin! Love your soul," "Well, now,
the Lord have Mercy!—less see," "The Lord Almighty
love your dear heart, honey, I'm telling you as fast as
I kin."

Resenting the power and cost of government, the
poor-white, nevertheless, enjoyed the flattery of the
ballot and the free show of elections. For Southern
politics, outside of limited aristocratic areas, was before
the Civil War (and still is in the Deep South) more an
exciting sport than anything else, and the political unfit-
ness of the poor-white trash only made the game the
merrier. Certainly, the same starved desire for excitement emotionalized the elections as well as the camp-
meetings. In J. B. Cobb's "A Political Barbecue in the
Southwest," the Mississippi clodhoppers whoop up their
speakers as they would a pair of bullies: "By jing, I
hope he'll peel him as raw as a skinned ingon. . . ."
"Yes, he desarves to have his tallow melted out'n him."
And, as already noted, Davy Crockett knew how to
catch the lubber votes with drams of the "good critter,"
German yarns, and impromptu hits. "Skitt" tells of an
Alabama Democrat, "a tall, stoop-shouldered, sallow-
faced, meek, quiet, teachable-looking man, with copperas britches . . . 'gallused' up as high as his fork
would admit" without lifting him off the ground, who
asks a Whig merchant about the presidential candi-

dates, Cass and Taylor. The Democrat, on hearing that General Taylor was "one of the people" and "in your cabin, he would . . . drink buttermilk, eat bread and butter, and yam potatoes," deserts his party's candidate: "this man Cass . . . I didn't know thar was sich a man treadin' sole leather." An equally irresponsible know-nothing was Cobe, a tenant-farmer of "Bill Arp," the Georgia humorist, who declared: "I do remember voting for a passle of fellers, and the folks told me it was against General Grant and Sherman."[68] By these glimpses, Southern humorists showed how little the "dangerous class" actually cared about its "only safeguard," the ballot, except for its entertainment value; how comical this sinister theme of the abolitionists could appear to the South.

Valuable as this balancing view was, the justifiable pride of cultivated Southerners in their statesmen definitely limited their capacity to enjoy the comedy of ignorant congressmen elected by the Rag, Tag, and Bobtail or the tomfoolery enacted in every poor-white bailiwick during every election. Nevertheless, the facts were often funnier than the humorous literature. Witness Congressman Plummer canvassing his East Mississippi, pineywoods district in company with his opponent, Judge Cage. In a tacky's cabin, the Judge scored first with the mother by kissing the smallest girl, but, on turning about, he was nonplussed to see Plummer take "a wee toddling boy, lay it on his lap, turn over its little petticoat, and go to hunting redbugs . . . [The mother] . . . never forgot that tender-

68. *Farm and the Fireside*, 208.

hearted Congressman."[69] Other aspects of this sudden democracy experienced by candidates, as well as the whole poor-white political farce, deserved a more complete recording.

As a result of this comic treatment by Southerners, the poor-white was advanced to a new literary position.[70] He was now considered a good subject for the main rôles of short sketches. His folkways had proved to be so entertaining that a humorous recreation of his sloppy world had been effected, principally, by means of short *genre* writings, which had the additional value of providing a sane antidote for the over-theoretical view of the abolitionists. In characterization the humorists had taken him through the channels of the conventional to a greater individuality. What was, perhaps, most important, these writers had steadily broken through old proprieties of language and subject matter and brought him so near to his actual vulgarity that it seemed but a step from this rough comedy to a naturalism not unlike that of the twentieth century. But the Civil War with its aftermath of nostalgia prevented any such transition for well over fifty years.

69. J. F. H. Claiborne, quoted by P. H. Buck, *American HistoricalReview*, XXXI (Oct., 1925), 52-53.
70. Hardly tenable is the claim that Southern humor "originated the American bad boy and the southern poor white" (Tandy, *op. cit.*, 95). Her use of the term *poor-white* is too loose to have much meaning (*ibid.*, 66 and *passim*). I should say that Southern humor with Northern abolitionist journalism and fiction *established* the poor-white.

CHAPTER THREE

THE SOUTH CLAIMS THE POOR-WHITE FOR WAR AND LITERATURE

To UNDERSTAND THE LITERARY RECORD OF THE poor-white after 1870, one must follow his story during the Civil War and Reconstruction, seeing him move through events that fixed his future and comprehending the motives for his actions.

According to the abolitionist's statement of the poor-white's social position, by all logic he should not have joined the C.S.A. But he did, as the most acute Northern students of the South knew he would do. Had not the South been the land of "eagle-orators"—at least since John Randolph's time? It was the easiest thing in the world for the village imitators of the master fire-eaters like Rhett, Yancey, and Toombs to harangue the clod-knocker into Confederate gray. At their hottest, spellbinders probably made the poor-whites believe that the Yankees were "miserable creatures whom they could beat five to one, and who had no other object in life but to cheat them with wooden clocks and other peddler's truck, and to make the negroes their equals."[1] Anyway, the pineywoodser was always ready for excitement.

I. THE POOR-WHITE IN THE CIVIL WAR AND RECONSTRUCTION

THE 'sandhillers,' " said Joel Chandler Harris, "were not particularly enthusiastic—they had but vague ideas of the issues at stake—but the military business

1. Editorial comment, *Galaxy*, IV (Oct., 1867), 753.

was something new to them, and therefore alluring. They volunteered readily if not cheerfully."[2] If the trashy valiant was shrewd and could find a wealthy yet pacifist Southerner who would trust him, he might have his war fun and yet get a tidy sum as a substitute.[3] But if he himself decided to let the war slide and go a-fishing, later conscription got him, that is, unless he hid deep in the woods and became a "moss-back."[4]

Once in the army, how did he fight? In some ways he was an ideal soldier. His backwoods life having preserved in him much of the Revolutionary fighter, he had a "natural adaptation to military service."[5] His squirrel rifle rarely missed anything as big as a man. Long marches like those of Jackson's "foot-cavalry" had already been made after coons and foxes. Unlike the planter's son who was used to sinking into a featherbed on a high four-poster, he had simply "loosened up" his jeans, thrown off his shoes, and slept on a floor-pallet or a shuck-bed. Sleeping on the ground? —that was nothing. Camp food was no problem: he ate anything—even dirt. A soldier who was so easily supported and who loved a "scrap" seemed perfect.

But poor-white Johnny Reb had one serious fault. He was restive under discipline:[6] he had always done things in his own way, whenever he was "a-mind to,"

2. *Balaam and His Master*, 176-77. Cf. the wild idea of S. A. Hamilton: "When the Rebellion broke out the Crackers were ripe for raping and murder. . . ." "They were on the verge of breaking out" when the war came to use "their surplus energies" (!) "A New Race Question," *Arena*, XXVII (Apr., 1902), 354.
3. Charles and Mary Beard, *The Rise of American Civilization*, II, 73.
4. W. L. Fleming, *Civil War and Reconstruction in Alabama*, 113. "Mossback": one who had hidden so long in woods from enrolling officers that moss had accumulated on his back! "Mutual men" were those who refused to join either side. See A. M. Weir, *Old Times in Georgia*, 38.
5. E. B. Seabrooke, "Poor Whites of the South," *Galaxy*, IV (Oct., 1867), 689.
6. T. N. Page, "The Two Little Confederates," *Works*, XI, 37.

not when an officer shouted. Nor did he respect military instruction. "I didn't see no use in it," drawled a Florida Cracker; "I could draw a bead and hit my mark better'n any man on 'em."[7] Thus, while Thomas Nelson Page may be forgiven the hyperbole of local pride in claiming that "the poor-white fought as valorously as the great landowner,"[8] the woolhat's hatred of routine, his limited "span of attention" to anything—even a war when nothing was happening—led to fateful consequences for Southern arms. In short, when he got a bellyful of war, he "signed off" and went home, furlough or no furlough. This act gave him his second war rôle, that of deserter. As one historian says: "Not all of the deserters were 'poor country clodhoppers,' but doubtless most of them were."[9]

Certainly, the poor-white had other reasons besides boredom for quitting the C.S.A. and most of these centered around the rich in the war. He resented the exemption of planters owning over fifteen slaves and of other "Bourbons" for a money payment;[10] while he was conscripted. If word drifted back to camp that the planters were breaking their promise to care for the pineywoods families,[11] the poor-white felt justified in deserting, especially, since he believed the exempted rich to be enjoying peace-time luxuries.[12] He complained that officers protected some of the wealthy by keeping them out of the trenches and other places

7. H. B. Stowe, "Our Florida Plantation," *Atlantic Monthly*, XLIII (May, 1879), 646.
8. *Old South*, 365.
9. A. B. Moore, *Conscription and Conflict in the Confederacy*, 332.
10. Charles and Mary Beard, *op. cit.*, II, 73.
11. J. C. Harris, *On the Plantation*, 199.
12. A. B. Moore, *op. cit.*, 332.

where the tackies and other poor men were used for gun fodder.[13] All such grievances produced the conviction summed up in the catch-phrase: "a rich man's war and a poor man's fight," and intensified by the violent resistance to conscription of the chief deserting class, the mountaineers,[14] especially those of East Tennessee. But desertion was not confined to the mountains and the upland counties near them; toward the gulf coast in Alabama, caves, swamps, canebrakes, and deep thickets called "tight-eyes" swarmed with "mossbacks" and deserters.[15]

Sometimes the sandhiller deserted to the enemy who offered both food and protection. He and his sort largely made up the great crowds of deserters that Carl Schurz, the German-American Federal officer, found every morning about his headquarters tent in Tennessee, eager to take the oath and then to eat.[16] If the tacky decided to take up home life again, he had to resist the Confederate conscription force, and this he did by patting his gun and telling the officer: "This is my furlough."[17] Such skulkers, however, led a precarious life, as Long John, a thin, loose-jointed Florida Cracker, told Harriet Beecher Stowe.

"Did you run away?" Mrs. Stowe asked.

"Wal-yes; I just tuk off and come home. . ."

"Well, and did they let you stay there?"

An ineffably droll expression passed slowly over his

13. The standard source on this is John B. Jones, *A Rebel War Clerk's Diary*, II.
14. W. L. Fleming, *op. cit.*, 111. There was talk in Northern Alabama of forming a new Union state with East Tennessee to be called Nick-a-Jack.
15. *Ibid.*, 113, 123.
16. Carl Schurz, *Reminiscences*, III, 69-70.
17. Moore, *op. cit.*, 219.

face; he spit once or twice vigorously. . . . "Wal—no—they didn't."[18]

The fact was that twice Confederate parties came after Long John, both times the skulker "getting the drop" on his pursuers. But if the Rebels couldn't catch this Cracker they *could* destroy his cabin, and crops, and drive off his stock. After that, Long John said they left him alone. A less peaceable Cracker might have joined the lawless bands of bushwhackers to gain revenge by preying upon every household, Confederate and Unionist.

Obviously, the poor-white man led a miserable life, but his "women-folks" back home also had their woes. Used to a squaw's share of the house chores and work in the swall patches, they now had to take up the hunting, trapping, and fishing of their absent "men folks"; that is, they tried. Very likely, they had poor luck, for according to Thomas Nelson Page, "they called oftener and oftener at houses of their neighbors who owned the plantations near them, and always received something."[19] Later the planter families themselves had nothing to give, and the pineywoods women had no eggs or wild honey to bring as a pitiful cover for their begging. So during the bare winter months in the far backcountry, the "weak went down and only the strong survived." If such women with their families lived within walking distance of a town, there they might escape starvation by getting a little food on the Drawing Days established by the Confederate government for the relief of the poor.

18. "Our Florida Plantation," *Atlantic Monthly*, XLIII (May, 1879), 646. See the similar story by a Georgian, J. T. Trowbridge, *A Picture of the Desolated States*, 456-78.
19. *Burial of the Guns*, 93.

The Southern Poor-White

But what of the women of Unionist families among the trash? They were soon put on the road by the Rebels with carts or wagons piled high with their "plunder." About ten thousand poor-whites poured through the Home for Refugees in Nashville, Tennessee, in seven months, and on such pilgrimages, wives did everything. When these folk arrived in Nashville: "The men . . . would sit down on their miserable furniture with stolid apathy, as if they had no interest in life or no motive for exertion. They paid no attention to anybody or anything: until their women came back and told them they had found a place to go until they could leave the city."[20]

And, of course, there was always one way to make a little money or get a snack to eat. Along the military railroads it was common talk that poor-white women were handy and willing. The superintendent of this refugee home thought these "women as dirty as their habits and their morals worse"—worse than the Negroes'.

Broadly viewed, the Civil War simply dramatized the poor-white—his social position, physical condition, and habits. The circumstance that he had undergone some reversal of feeling toward the planters and that he had done his part among the estimated one hundred thousand mossbacks, deserters, and bushwhackers who hastened the downfall of the Confederacy, threw into bold relief the facts that the Southern white population not only lacked a healthy homogeneity, but that the poor-whites' interests were inimical to those of the great landowner. His record as a soldier clearly demon-

20. James Redpath, "The New Ruling Class of the South," *Nation*, I (Aug. 17, 1865), 206.

strated that he still had enough vitality to take his place in a more democratic Southern agronomy if given the chance; but, on the other hand, his handicaps in becoming a soldier and the sufferings of his family in trying to shift for themselves revealed his frontier level of existence and also the effects of generations of living without social function.

After Appomattox, the sandhiller took up his old life, or stopped hiding if he had considered the war already over. Anyway, it required no especial labor for him to start again, for unlike the planter he had lost nothing through the war. If he had kept a grog-shop before going into the ranks, he set up a shack in the woods or swamp near the plantations—known as a "deadfall"[21] —and continued his dealing in stolen goods. An antebellum squatter back of the village continued his begging at the Freedman's Bureau as an avowed Unionist and called for the confiscation and division of the Rebels' land. One such, "a lean sallow, lank-haired inhabitant of the Spartanburg (S.C.) District suspended his chaffering with a neighboring planter for the hire of a plot of ground, and walked twenty-three miles to ask . . . [The Bureau Officer] . . . what were the 'prospects for a dividin.' "[22] Poor-white Johnny Reb was a poor-white still; in fact, after the hustling and discipline of army life, he must have outdone himself in relaxing.

A few of his tribe did try a different life. An exceptional poor-white soldier who had won the regard of a planter might rent or buy on time a small acreage from

21. Fleming, *op. cit.*, 769-70.
22. DeForest, "The Low-Down People," *Putnam's Magazine*, New Series, I (June, 1868), 707.

his land-poor friend. Usually, however, the planters considered the trash incapable of farming[23] and chose to rent to ex-slaves whom they trusted. Or after the cotton mills appeared in numbers, a lazy Cracker might move his family out of the woods to mill-hill,[24] where he could live on his children's wages. But for the whole class, both of these departures were rare. The daily life of the poor-white remained about what it was; the differences had to do with the dramatic events of the Reconstruction.

Northern writers were wrong in claiming that the trashy Cracker was unaware of the changes in Southern society and in his own social relations.[25] When he marched away to war, did not he receive the first cheers of his life? Had not songs glorified his service to the South? "Only a Common Soldier," "Private Maguire," "A Private in the Ranks,"[26]—all of them about *him!* But as already shown, he developed a reversal of feeling toward the "nigger lords," as the Alabama mountaineers called the great slave owners, only to be reunited with his planter-masters by Northern bungling of Reconstruction.

What happened in the late sixties seemed to verify for the poor-white all the scare-head orations of the secessionists about Negro equality and Yankee thievery. The plantations were so bare that the ex-slaves began

23. G. K. Holmes, "The Peons of the South," *Annals of the American Academy of Political Science*, IV (Sept., 1893), 71, 274.

24. W. W. Ball, *State That Forgot*, 265; A. M. Weir, *op. cit.*, 92-96.

25. Carl Schurz, *op. cit.*, III, 178; A. W. Tourgée, *Bricks Without Straw*, 399; Edward King, *The Great South*, 776.

26. E. P. Ellinger, *Southern War Poetry of the Civil War*, 133, 141. For another Southern literary appreciation of the poor-white's war service, see Margaret G. McCleland, "A Self-Made Man," *Lippincott's Magazine*, XXXIX (1887), 253.

to rob the hen-roosts of the tackies.[27] Loud talk about
equality in Union League meetings scared the Cracker,
for he well knew that the equalizing would start at his
own door. His women went to town and the crossroads
store in large groups for protection against rape.[28] When,
however, the blacks began to vote, hold office, and
legislate, the pineywoodser knew that his salvation did
not lie in the government, but in the power of his old
master—the planter.

Naturally, the poor-white joined the upper classes
in the Ku Klux Klan—that is, if he was allowed to do so,
because he had a greater stake in the order, more work
to do under the white hoods than anyone else. And even
if he was too trashy to get in, he probably "played Ku
Klux" for his own protection.[29] Behind the mask, he
wreaked vengeance upon "darkies" who scorned him
as "po' buckra." He burned school houses[30] built by
Northern missionaries for the Freedmen, because,
illiterate himself, he resented the Negro's rising by
education; he destroyed churches where Union League
meetings were held; and above all, "he took all sassy
niggers down a peg." Undoubtedly, by such outrages
poor-whites were in large measure responsible for the
discrediting of the Klan.[31] Nor were they in all probability incited to violence by the planters; it was not
necessary. They joined any organization to combat the

27. J. M. Beard, *K.K.K. Sketches*, 168.
28. W. L. Fleming, *Documentary History of Reconstruction*, II, 333-34.
29. J. M. Beard, *op. cit.*, 168-70. Nearly every account of the Klan records such pranks.
30. Fleming, *Civil War and Reconstruction in Alabama*, 683. Charles Nordhoff believed that the "brutal acts" of the poor-whites "in the majority of cases . . . were instigated by bad men a class above" the trashy criminals (*Cotton States. . . .*, 17-18).
31. W. M. Brewer, "Poor-Whites and Negroes in the South since the Civil War," *Journal of Negro History*, XV (Jan., 1930), 30. This article is full of misconceptions but accurate on this point.

blacks, as the warm support of the White League by the sleepy Cajuns of Louisiana clearly showed. Neither were the mass murders at Colfax and Coushatta about 1874 in the same state anything but the fear of the pine-hills folk of sinking to the Negro's social level.[32] The woolhat was merely acting on the fixed opinion that "if a feller air into the noshen that a nigger air es good es a white man, that air feller needs hell three times a day."

When the poor-buckra bestirred himself in legitimate government, he generally followed his ante-bellum grooves: he voted the ticket of the "white man's party" and swore by his old leaders.[33] And since the mountain Republicans could not stand Negroes in their ranks,[34] what could one expect of the poor-whites who lived in the black belts? Even the few renegades to the Democratic party, called scalawags, who may have got into the legislatures and constitutional conventions were an argument for "the white man's party." The woolhat, always somewhat of a hero-worshipper, hardly warmed to a party composed of carpetbaggers, Negroes, and scalawags "but little less illiterate than the blacks"— so illiterate, in fact, that about 1872 in Raleigh, North Carolina, the owner of a Republican paper, on being asked to continue the publication, stormed: "Do you think I'm a d—d fool, to print a paper for a party that can't read?"[35] To paraphrase Dryden, the scum in the South did not rise much when the nation boiled.

32. Ella Lonn, *Reconstruction in Louisiana* . . ., 16.
33. Nordhoff, *op. cit.*, 10, 11, 76, 96, 155.
34. Claude Bowers, *Tragic Era*, 419-20. A mass meeting of mountain Republicans at Knoxville, Tenn., was held in 1866 to keep Negroes out of their party in spite of Northern insistence upon the Bill of Rights.
35. Nordhoff, *op. cit.*, 97.

Civil War and Reconstruction

Often, however, when the poor-white did not return from the war or had daylight let through him for skulking or deserting, his women and children fell to new levels of misery and depravity. A Federal officer of the Freedman's Bureau at Greenville, South Carolina, understood their plight when he wrote of "The Lowdown People": "Thirteen thousand men of South Carolina dead in battle! That rebellious yet heroic fact has been a frightful one for the women of South Carolina. The State is swarming with widows and girls, who migrate after the garrisons and lead a life like that of the 'Wrens of Curragh.' Our soldiers easily provide themselves with a new set of brides or sweethearts in every village."[36] The expected result of such living was a bumper crop of bastards who were exhibited by the trashy mothers without shame.[37] Infanticide never entered such maternal heads.

The same officer recorded the visit to his Bureau of "a gaunt, crouching creature" and her barefooted daughter with an "expression as wild as that of a mustang." "Be you the man we've been a-lookin' for?" said the mother. As usual they claimed to be persecuted Unionists; their men had been killed by the Rebels, their cabin burned, and they themselves stoned from one place to another. On investigation the officer found them to be lying sluts with a long history—though their stoning was true.

And it is little wonder that so many po' buckra women wandered the country and swarmed into the Bureau to beg; their position was peculiar. One who

36. DeForest, "The Low-Down People," *loc. cit.*, 705.
37. DeForest, "Drawing Bureau Rations," *loc. cit.*, 792-93.

had charge of poor-relief and saw much of them observed that: "They will not work, and they do not know how to work, and nobody will set them to work. Such a thing as a 'poor-white' girl going into domestic service is absolutely unknown; not merely because she is as ignorant of civilized housewifery as a Comanche squaw, but also because she is untamed, quarrelsome, perhaps dishonest, perhaps immoral, and finally because she is too proud to do what she calls 'niggers' business.' "[38]

Nor would their queer pride allow them to become conspicuous public charges. "Lord's sake, don't send me to the poorhouse!" was always their reaction. They would accept beggary from door to door, wintry life in a house of pine boughs, prostitution, and thievery, rather than sleep under the roof of charity.

Aside from a little fresh blood that may have been bred into the poor-white strain by Union soldiers, the women of the "low-down people" were debased in a way unheard of before Reconstruction. Previously, some of them had undoubtedly preferred a variety of fathers for their families. The woman that Carl Schurz saw in Alabama surrounded by a lively flock of thirteen flaxen haired children told him "without the slightest embarrassment. . . that she never had any husband." Yet she was clean and her children industrious. "I left her greatly puzzled,"[39] said the Union officer—and naturally so, for he saw what might be called a happy promiscuity. Such a family was in sharp contrast to the lives of sordid garrison followers.

38. DeForest, "The Low-Down People," *loc. cit.*, 716.
39. Carl Schurz, *op. cit.*, III, 57-58.

Civil War and Reconstruction

Andrew Johnson had said that emancipation of the slaves would free more white men than Negroes, but this was bad prophecy when applied to the poor-white. For he, instead of being "emancipated," emerged from Reconstruction bound politically to his old masters and enslaved to a greater fear of the blacks. Perhaps, the greatest blessing of the sandhiller before the war had been his peace—maybe, vacancy—of mind; now, even that was disturbed.

II. POST-WAR NORTHERN REPORT ON THE POOR-WHITE: ALBION W. TOURGEE AND JOHN W. DEFOREST

FOR a number of reasons, Southerners could hardly have been expected to write of the poor-white until years after the surrender. His shabby rôle in war and Reconstruction was one that the class capable of writing wished to forget. Their glorification of him at the outset of the fighting as "Only A Common Soldier" perhaps seemed in retrospect rather ill-rewarded. But Southern authorship just after the war more than ever precluded any possibility of his being used as a literary subject: the writers were mostly war-widows and daughters of poverty-stricken families of position[1] whose twin motive was to earn a few dollars and to defend the ruling class of the Old South and the Confederate leaders. These noble but meagerly endowed women, privately educated[2] and acquainted with only a narrow range of Southern life, seized the pen—as one of them said—

1. T. N. Page, "Literature in the South Since the War," *Lippincott's Magazine*, XLVIII (Dec., 1891), 743.
2. *Ibid.*, Hence Page says he cannot criticize these women's writings. For two typical ones, see Ann Eliza Dupuy in Julia D. Freemen's *Women of the South Distinguished in Literature*, 376; Eliz. W. Bellamy in Kate A. Orgain, *Southern Authors . . .*, 141.
3. M. T. Tardy (ed.), *Living Female Writers of the South*, 504. Annie E. Barnwell, "On Southern Literature."

and became authors, writing "eagerly, hungrily."[3] In the rash of magazines that broke out all over the South to carry this second defense literature against the "defamation" by the North, one title, *The Land We Love*, perfectly exposed the roseate and lachrymose nature of most Southern writing in the sixties and early seventies. Again, as in the forties and fifties, one must turn to Northern fiction to catch sight of a Southern poor-white.

The Northerner wrote of the trash, the freedmen, and those "rascally planters," because the prostrate South was being eagerly watched as a scene of social revolution in which the poor-white was playing the rôle of violence and because, above all, there was an insatiable market for stuff about the conquered section. Whitelaw Reid, who toured the South just after the surrender, excused his book, *After the War*, by saying that "even the hastiest pencil sketch of the South emerging from the war may possess interest. . . ."[4] With his infallible nose for a vogue, John T. Trowbridge hied away on a sentimental tour of the battlefields of Dixie,[5] where, however, he found no natives loitering; they had seen enough of such places and had work to do. Only such traveling penmen and fiction-makers from the North had time for using clinical eyes on the South, and it was they who continued the abolitionists' interest in the poor-white.

No more typical abolitionist could have carried on the Northern interpretation of the trash than Albion W. Tourgée (1838-1905), a native of Ohio, who was a

4. *After the War*, 10.
5. *Picture of the Desolated States*.

judge and leader in North Carolina during the carpet-bag regime. Almost in Mrs. Stowe's words, he confessed that he "was first impelled to attempt the field of romantic fiction by the weird fascinations of Southern life."[6] A foe to realism, he threw his cap for romance and reform: "A man who paints warts and weakness, sin and shame, may tell the truth; but it is an unimportant truth, unworthy of the artist's skill, unless it bring some lesson of cause or cure."[7] And since, like his abolitionist predecessors, his obsession was the Negro, his novels were only incidentally concerned with trashy tar heels, and that mostly by way of discussion. Only once did he present a lifelike member of that class, Jordan Jackson in *Bricks Without Straw* (1880).

Without the advantage of free schools and cowed by planter scorn, Jordan came into illiterate manhood just in time to be hustled off to the battlefields. There he rose to a lieutenancy and shook off his sense of inferiority, at the same time realizing that the war was the poor man's fight and determining to get his full pay after the surrender. This he did by becoming a somewhat thriving storekeeper. So much of an exceptional poor-white is conceivable, but here Tourgée's old-style, abolitionist mind spoiled this fictional biography: Jordan Jackson had not only a "profound respect" for the United States government, but "he said that the colored man and the poor-white of the South ought to put themselves on the side of this great, busy North."[8] For such advanced thinking, Mr. Jordan was called a

6. *John Eax*, 5.
7. "An Outing With the Queen of Hearts" (1894), quoted by R. F. Dibble, *Albion W. Tourgée*, 137.
8. *Bricks Without Straw*, 344-45.

"white nigger," whipped, and urged to leave. He chose Missouri as his future home.

After all, in view of Tourgée's literary beliefs and his zeal as reformer,[9] little could be expected of him in just portraiture. He was, however, a wise literary marketer. Northern readers, he stated, had fixed Southern types in mind that were not to be disturbed;[10] hence he gave them "po' buckra" of the familiar Hildreth-Stowe-Gilmore pattern.[11]

Another interpreter of the poor-white, whose works actually preceded Tourgée's, by his attitude and method belonged definitely to the future. On the basis of two articles on the South Carolina trash, minor characters in one novel, and one short story, John W. DeForest (1826-1905) must be reckoned the most significant in literary anticipations of all the writers who depicted the "low-down people" from the late sixties to 1900.

That this man should have become interested enough in the poor-whites to write of them was as strange as Byrd's joy in lubbers. A Connecticut Yankee of good family, privately educated, and studious, author by the age of thirty of a study of the Indians of his state, a book of Oriental travel, and a novel, he served first as captain then as major of the Union army in the Shenandoah Valley and the Southwest. But it was after the war, during fifteen months as Major and Assistant Commissioner of the Freedmen's Bureau at Greenville, South Carolina, that he came to deal with and study

9. J. G. De R. Hamilton, *Reconstruction in North Carolina*, 414, and *passim*.
10. For support for Tourgée's statement, see the book by a lurid alarmist of the Chicago *Tribune*: Sidney Andrews, *South Since the War*, 335-36. He describes poor-whites in the wild abolitionist manner.
11. See the criticism of *Bricks Without Straw* for its keeping alive sectional strife: Joseph Kirkland, "Partisan Romance," *Dial*, I (Oct., 1880), 112.

"that wretched caste commonly spoken of as the 'mean whites' . . . but in my district as 'the low-down people.' "[12]

Out of this experience, DeForest published four brilliant articles that have preserved for history the daily routine of a Bureau and the lives of the people it served. Two of these: "Drawing Bureau Rations: I, The Applicants" and "The Low-Down People," contain not only the finest glimpses we have of the poor-whites in Reconstruction, but also the keenest and most complete comment upon them. How thoroughly these folk interested him may be noted from the inclusive list of section-titles in the second article: "1. Morality, 2. Drunkenness, 3. Idleness, 4. Beggary, 5. Vagrancy, 6. Social Degradation, 7. Pugnacity, 8. Ferocity, 9. History of the Family, and 10. Future Possibilities." Undoubtedly, nearly all his observations were accurate, but one should bear in mind that DeForest probably saw only the more depraved low-downers and that they harried his days!

What the Yankee Major endured from these patrons of his bounty will partly explain his later fiction about them. Since the Bureau supplied Unionists as well as Freedmen, every trashy applicant lied expansively about his sufferings for the Federal cause. A host of poor-white war-widows, genuine and spurious, swarmed through the Greenville Bureau. "Whenever my office was invaded," said DeForest, "by a woman in threadbare homespun or torn calico, grimed with mud, her down-at-the-heel shoes foxy with long wear, and perhaps tied with tow strings, on her arm a basket, and in her mouth a pipe

12. DeForest, "The Low-Down People," *loc. cit.*, 704.

with a reed stem and a claybowl, I was pretty sure to hear 'Anythin' to git?' "[13]

The first pair of such females from among the four hundred widows in the Major's District to visit the Bureau were not so well equipped.

"Mornin," they said, sat down, stared awhile, and then asked, "Anythin' for the lone wimmen?"

"Pears like I oughter git, if anyone does," added the older. "My husband was shot by the Rebs because he wouldn't jine their army."

Supposing that they might object to my pipe of tobacco, I had laid down my pipe on their entrance. Presently the eldest one inquired, "Stranger, is your pipe a-smokin'?"

"It is," I replied, wondering at such extreme sensitiveness. "But I can put it out."

"Ef it's a-smokin', I should like a smoke," was her only comment.

I may have cringed at the idea of putting my pipe between those broken teeth, but I of course made haste to do what was hospitable, and I went into the entry before I allowed myself to smile. She smoked tranquilly, and passed the luxury to her sister; then they thanked me, "Much obleeged, stranger,"—and departed.[14]

One widow wheedled a loom out of the Bureau so that she could support her children; months later she had not put it up. Sorry Crackers eyeing the plantations of ex-Confederate leaders kept asking DeForest,

13. *Ibid.*, 707.
14. "Drawing Bureau Rations," *loc. cit.*, 792-93.

"When's our folks gwine to git the land?" Men and women scuffled outside his office over what had been received. The plight of many poor-white girls during Reconstruction was impressed upon the Assistant Commissioner when a mother of fifteen appeared at the Bureau clad in a single, foul garment. "Not large enough to meet in front, it was tied with twine in loose fashion, exposing entirely one of her breasts." Held indifferently in one arm was her six-weeks-old bastard rolled in an old rug.

It was not surprising that the Major finally came to think that a poor-white's death in the war was "no great loss to him or to his country," and that when he was killed in a cabin brawl, "the respectable portion of the community, if it is interested at all, thanks God and takes courage." DeForest seemed amused that these "gems . . . of our much boasted Anglo-Saxon race" were not given to suicide and jokingly proposed that they be colonized in Abruzzi where, he hoped, "the drama of the Kilkenney cats might be re-enacted."[15] Obviously, the Union officer was repelled by the low-down people, yet their unabashed sorriness appealed strongly to the sardonic humor in his nature.

It was after the hardening experience of war and Reconstruction that DeForest, the writer, departing from his early trivial manner, came to write "with a strong, broad-nibbed pen that sometimes blots from coarseness" and to be known as "a straight . . . truthful man."[16] And since he was what William Dean Howells

15. "Kate Beaumont," *Atlantic Monthly*, XXVIII (July, 1871), 61.

16. Clarence Gordon, "Mr. DeForest's Novels," *Atlantic Monthly*, XXXII (Nov., 1873), 611.

justly called him, "distinctly a man's novelist,"[17] when he turned his satiric humor upon the poor-whites, his talent seemed to be at home.

In 1871, the "low-down people" first appeared in his most popular novel, *Kate Beaumont*, a broad satire on the *code duello* in ante-bellum South Carolina, which had so decimated the planter families of McAlister and Beaumont that old Mrs. Chester of the latter side declared that "until three years ago, our family has never been out of mourning since I can remember." Yet, excepting the portrait of that noble soul, old Colonel Kershaw, the memorable characters, as in Simms' novels, are low-lived ones.

"Redhead" Saxon, "a low-flung descendant" of a trashy strain, was the companion and guide of the dissolute planter, Randolph Armitage, in alcoholic and sexual excursions among the sandhillers. Three miles from the Armitage place, in an old field of "sand and pines and scrub-oaks" stood a cabin occupied rent-free by Nancy Gile and Sally Hugg. Nancy, "yellow-haired, white-faced, freckled, red-eyed, dirty, ragged, shiftless, idle, a beggar," had two children by undetermined fathers. Sally, an illegitimate girl of seventeen, small and square-built, had joined Nancy's household to enjoy rare liberties. Probably by the usual means, this pair "got five dollars ahead," bought a pound of candles, three gallons of raw, white whiskey, and sent word around that a "treat" was to be given. To it "Redhead" Saxon guided Randolph Armitage—well liquored. There Sam Tony, a pineywoods lad, "lean and yellow as his own fiddle" was scraping away. The dancing crowd was

17. "Some Heroines of Fiction," *Harper's Bazaar*, XXXV (Oct., 1901), 544.

"a mass of young men and girls, applauding, yelling, chattering, laughing, or staring with vacant eyes and mouth. Even the wide-open doors and windows and chinks and gaping chimney could not carry off all the mephitic steam generated by this mob of unclean people." "The forms, too, were agile, most of them tall, slender, bony, the outlines showing sharply through the calico gowns or homespun suits. . . ."[18]

"The stinted, graceless costumes increased the general ungainliness. Some of the girls were in calico, limp with dirt; others in narrow-chested, ill-fitted, scant-skirted gowns of the coarsest white cotton, such as was commonly issued to field hands; others in the cast-off finery of charity, worn . . . without remaking."[19]

But DeForest knew the taste of his time. After showing the maudlin Armitage fondling Sally, he apologized for the dance as a "nauseously interesting scene": "We only describe it because it dramatizes . . . the character of the man in his cups."[20] Nevertheless, he did not trouble himself with excusing the capital drunken scene[21] at Saxon's cabin in which sex was not involved.

There, in a drinking bout, Armitage knocked his host to the ground. Too drunk to preserve his usual abject behavior towards his friend, the "Square," Saxon demanded that they shoot it out. Aided by a companion, the Amazonian spouse of the ill-treated man gave the duellists pistols loaded with blanks and placed "each propped up in his corner . . . holding fast, their faces

18. "Kate Beaumont," *loc. cit.*, 559.
19. *Ibid.*, 61.
20. *Ibid.*, 62. DeForest's vivid and accurate description was not based on first-hand observation: "I exceedingly regret that I never attended one of these festivities" ("The Low-Down People," *loc. cit.*, 706).
21. "Kate Beaumont," *loc. cit.*, 199-200.

The Southern Poor-White

very solemn and stolid." "Square" Armitage toppled to the floor. "Set 'em up agen!" muttered Redhead calmly. With the aristocrat "once more in his corner smiling the monotonous smile of intoxication," they fired. Amazed at his failure to kill, the drunken sandhiller staggered about the room with a blazing pine-knot looking for bullet holes. "You needn't look for 'em . . ." Molly was heard to giggle, "You're too drunk to aim at anythin. You fired out o' the winder an' up the chimney an' everywhar but at him."

Excellent as is this sordid comedy of the low-downers among whom ante-bellum planters sometimes went slumming, DeForest's best study of the poor-white is that of Selnarten Bowen in the story, "An Independent Ku Klux" (1872). Not since Longstreet's famous paragraph on Ransy Sniffle had the ridiculous appearance of a trashy Cracker so delighted an author.

"Selnarten's person . . . had a made-over look. In build and features and expression he was not so much a natural human being as a sort of shabby work of art, like a totem or a fetish. . . . That grotesque and malicious sculptor and painter, Malaria, had taken him in hand from the days of his doughy infancy, and moulded and colored him in accordance with its wayward taste. He could not show a limb nor a muscle which had not been scraped down and withered and distorted by this indefatigable and pitiless carver. Malaria had hollowed his abdomen and gouged out his cheeks and sunk his eyes and pinched his temples. Then, laying aside the chisel, it had gone at him with the brush, staining him from within outwards, as if he were a meerschaum pipe; . . . taking a fresh dab at him every time it got around to a new swamp; using up on him the richness of acres of dying trees and creeks full of oozing vegetable mud . . . in short, giving him the finish of a masterpiece."[22]

"His broad-brimmed, wool hat was as ragged as though it had shaken itself to pieces in 'cold fits,'" and so much like the color of his face that it appeared "much as if his head had spread out at the top, after the fashion of a toadstool." His short-waisted, short-sleeved, buttonless coat, wizened trousers, and gaping shoes—"his entire wardrobe looked as if it needed a course of quinine."

Selnarten lived mainly on the bounty of field and stream, trusting to providence for the rest—and well he might, for he had the uncanny gift of finding wild hogs. In fact: "Selnarten was very suspicious of wildness in hogs. He hardly ever saw a porker anywhere or under any circumstances, not even when shut up in a pen, but he was ready to impute wildness to him, and wanted to shoot or otherwise slay him; and not only slay him, but tote him home, and not only tote him home, but eat him."[23] Since the war, however, so many of his kind, as well as the Negroes, had been catching "wild hogs" that the dwindling supply was being penned and carefully watched. Discovering on his "hunting" rounds that some prize "game" was in piggeries close to Negro cabins, Selnarten decided to join the Klan so that he could raid these places with impunity.

The village lawyers to whom he applied for initiation put him through a mock ceremony that only a Bowen could have taken seriously. Yet Selnarten could hardly

22. "An Independent Kuklux," *Galaxy*, XIII (April, 1872), 481.
23. *Ibid.*, 480.

be blamed. "He was simple, he was profoundly ignorant, and he was the child of simplicity and ignorance from untold generations, inheriting simplicity and ignorance as he inherited the name of Bowen. He could not read, his father before him could not read . . . there is no certainty that a Bowen of the stock ever did read— no certainty that a Bowen of this stock was ever anything but illiterate and stupid."[24]

Flushed with a sense of power, the "Klansman" went straight to the cabin of Han, a wooden-legged, Negro cobbler who had a fat shoat. Caught inside the shack chasing the pig, Selnarten fought desperately and killed the Negro. After the suppression of the Klan, Selnarten gave himself up as a murderer to the Federal authorities.

It was characteristic of DeForest to treat with ironical humor what most horrified the North: the assaults of Southern whites upon the blacks, some of which he himself had brought to light in his article, "A Report of Outrages" (1868). Here, too, was his cynical, comic version of the discrediting of the Klan, of the theory that trash like Selnarten, "this American freeman and elector," could ever become responsible citizens. For DeForest, like the planters, considered the "low-down people" socially irredeemable.[25]

In the Northern post-war interpretation, Tourgée's contribution was the repetitious continuation of the abolitionist manner; DeForest's, all of the advances toward twentieth century frankness. As social sidelights, his recreations of poor-whites around the Bureau,

24. *Ibid.*, 485.
25. "The Low-Down People," *loc. cit.*, 706-7.

their relation with planters who were going to the dogs, and their part in Ku Kluxery, have especial value. But his literary advances were equally significant. His disillusionment concerning earlier Northern hopes for reclaiming the low-downers produced a new viewpoint of humorous contempt, which, no doubt, was partly responsible for his frankness in describing sex, drunkenness, and odors; he seems to have been the first writer of fiction to suggest that the trash might be smelled! And finally his expertness of description and dialogue—both very good, even in the Bureau scenes—equals that of any author preceding him; this, in view of the date of his work, had the value of keeping the idiom and manner of the poor-white before the public until Southern writers began to use him.[26]

A number of causes operated to prevent DeForest from making his best possible contribution to the literature about poor-whites. His distaste for them and the current demand for the North-and-South romance made him waste his "vigorous art" on silly stories of spirited Southern belles won by masterful Yankees. (One would almost suspect DeForest of propaganda for breeding a superior American strain!) Having a limited yet intensive experience with these people, he was led to exaggerate their viciousness and pugnacity; by contrast, James R. Gilmore, as a result of many Southern journeys, possessed a broader acquaintance with the daily life among the tackies, but he had only a modicum of DeForest's talent. Nevertheless, without the re-

26. For an example of the contemptuous attitude towards poor-whites, see the novel by Francis H. Underwood, who before becoming assistant editor of the *Atlantic Monthly* lived in Bowling Green, Kentucky, for six years, 1844-50 (*Lord of Himself*, chap. vi, 80-81.) This chapter is entirely unredeemed by DeForest's ironic humor.

straints of the time upon language and detail, De-
Forest might well have anticipated much of the work
done by the Faulkner-Caldwell method over the half-
century mark.

III. YANKEE INTEREST IN THE NEW SOUTH AND THE
POOR-WHITE

B Y the mid-seventies in the South, men—notably
Cable, Page, and Harris—began to emerge in the
"female literary world" of Dixie; and about a decade
later, they turned to writing of the poor-white. To understand how and why this came about, one must give
this type its proper perspective as a subject of popular
and literary interest in the so-called Southern Revival
of the eighties and after.

First of all, the avid curiosity at the North about
things Southern, capitalized after Appomattox with such
alacrity by Reid and Trowbridge, steadily mounted in
the seventies. In 1875, appeared two of the best books
on this section ever written by Northern traveling
observers: Edward King's *The Great South*, valuable
pictorially but somewhat careless with facts, and
Charles Nordhoff's *The Cotton States in the Spring and
Summer of 1875*, sober, just, and thoughtful.

By the eighties this interest had reached flood stage.
Between 1882 and 1887, the annual average of articles
published on the South was about ten times that during
the preceding period of eighty years. "There is," commented a very able writer in the *Atlantic Monthly* for
1882, "a desire throughout the North for a fuller knowledge of Southern affairs. This desire is certain to in-

crease." And he was correct, for the South from the time of Washington Irving to the time of the later Howells was *terra incognita*. "You have depicted scenes, characters, and manners . . . in many respects new to me," Irving wrote to a novelist. "We do not know sufficiently of the South, which appears to me to abound with materials for a rich, original, and varied literature."[1] But from 1870 to 1890, there were especial reasons for Northern interest in things below the Line.

After the withdrawal of Union troops from the South in 1877, and after the "Age of Hate" with its gory reports of outrages had rather exhausted its venom, interest, Yankee and Southern, centered about a conception expressed in the phrase, "The New South." This phrase, by the time Henry W. Grady used it as the title of his famous address before the New England Club of New York in 1886, had already become a public fixation. About a half dozen years earlier, both Sidney Lanier and Walter Hines Page had written articles under this caption.[2]

To the North, the phrase generally meant, among other things, that the region had been newly opened to commercial adventure, if not exploitation. Certainly, the rushing of Yankees to Florida was, as Mrs. Stowe piously reflected, "mere worldly emigration with the hope of making money."[3] As a consequence of such interest, articles heavily weighted with statistics or splashed with land-office lying filled the periodicals. Nor was the South behindhand: state handbooks of

1. Letter of Irving to Capt. Gregory Seaworthy, Sept. 17, 1850, reprinted in "Introductory Word to the Reader," *Bertie, or, Life in the Old Field*, vii-viii.
2. Lanier, "The New South," *Scribner's Monthly*, XX (Oct., 1880), 840-51; W. H. Page "The New South," *Boston Post*, Sept. 28, 1881. The term was soon worn threadbare.
3. Annie Fields, *Life and Letters of Harriet Beecher Stowe*, 302.

natural resources appeared to lure the tide of capital. In 1883, Col. Henry Watterson arose before the American Bankers' Association in Louisville to unburden himself on "The New South." No Southerner ever wooed Northern cash with such rare humor in the old grand manner. "You have the money to loan," cried "Marse Henry." "We have a great country to develop . . . Whether you tickle her fertile plains with a straw or apply a more violent titillation to her fat mountain sides, she is ready to laugh a harvest of untold riches."[4]

The Colonel's speech together with the efforts of many fellow promoters was a success. Four years after its delivery, the party of journalists and artists sponsored by *Harper's Magazine* toured the late Confederacy and reported it to be "wide awake to business." And this resultant industrial awakening was especially evident in cotton mills. Everywhere cotton mills were the talk; and they concerned poor-whites. Ever since William Cullen Bryant had pictured the Georgia tackies in these mills[5] and William Gregg, "factory master of the Old South," had proclaimed that such textile plants as his splendid one erected at Graniteville, S. C., in 1847, were the panacea for the South's rural poor, the North had been aware of the tackies (also the mountaineers) as a potential supply of lint-heads. In 1875, Charles Nordhoff recommended work among the spindles as "perhaps the only means of redeeming this large population."[6] And six years later, Grady held out as bait to Yankee investors the low living costs and

4. Henry Watterson, *Compromises of Life*, 291-92.
5. *Letters of a Traveller*, 345-50.
6. *Op. cit.*, 108.

consequent low wages of available factory hands—
meaning, of course, poor-whites and mountaineers.

These overtures were especially alluring to outsiders,
for the revolution in Southern society after the war
had produced changes clearly favorable to a business
civilization. Perhaps none of these was more keenly
watched by the North than the fading of class lines.
The exodus of ruined planters to the cities created many
democratic countrysides in which "humble 'Mr.' and
plain 'Sir' " predominated. Even the great families that
clung to their lands were often leveled by poverty to
poor-white squalor like that in Miss Woolson's story,
"In the Cotton Country." Or, at least, the wasteful
board and the finery of old times gave way to corn pone
and patched clothing—a fact hit off brightly by George
W. Bagby in his jingle, "Fill Joanses":

> Oh times is sadly changed since then;
>   The Yanks have got us for thar oanses;
> Thar's not a man, not one in ten,
>   Lives like they lived at Fillip Joanses.[7]

People so poor had to labor with their hands—or
starve. And, thus, pride began to confer upon toil some
of the dignity which the abolitionists had demanded for
their theoretical poor-whites whose supposed desire to
work had been so long denied. But this came slowly,
even grudgingly, in some quarters. In 1882, a traveler
in Texas found many young aristocrats from the Old
Dominion, working hard to get a start, because "it was
not yet the fashion for young Virginians of good family

7. *Old Virginia Gentlemen and Other Sketches*, 310.

to engage in hard, rough work near their homes. . . ."[8]
In sections of less elegant tradition, such as the hemp
country of Kentucky, where "men young and old,"
according to James Lane Allen, "who had never known
what work was, were replacing slaves," "hands" had
come to mean not so much "hired men" as what everyone had to use.[9]

Such signs of growing democracy and industry en-
couraged immigration to the South, both for business
and for pleasure. Union officers with commercial eyes
set up as cotton planters; many Yankee soldiers had
settled in Arkansas by 1894, according to Alice French,
"to enjoy or hope for pensions from a grateful country";[10] Northern city-dwellers who had never seen a
sheep, took up herding in Tennessee; and Mrs. Stowe
and her son came to grief as cotton growers in Florida.
Most, if not all, of these newcomers encountered those
queer people, the poor-whites; and at least one of them,
the author of *Uncle Tom's Cabin*, gave to the home-
folk in the North a fine sketch of the Florida Cracker.[11]

But it was the Northerners sojourning in the South
for health and pleasure who had the curiosity, talent,
and time for writing about the Crackers. And Florida
was their destination. In 1882, George M. Barbour in
his book, *Florida for Tourists, Invalids, and Settlers*,
observed that the state "is rapidly becoming a Northern
colony." A number of winter residents, like Mrs.
Margaret Deland, in their tramps and boat trips discovered what to their eyes seemed almost a new racial

8. Anon., "Studies in the South, III," *Atlantic Monthly*, XLIX (May, 1882), 683.
9. *Reign of Law*, 53.
10. "The Farmer in the South," *Scribner's Magazine*, XL (Apr., 1894), 402.
11. Stowe, "Our Florida Plantation," *loc. cit.*, 641-49.

type: the Florida Cracker. As an indirect result of the resort boom, he received more complete portraiture in articles during the eighties than any other poor-white.

Toward the mid-eighties, this general interest in the "New South" was brought to fashion by the public awareness that a brilliant group of Southern writers had emerged and thereby shifted the literary locale from the West to their section. The suddenness with which this realization came to North and South alike lent to the Southern Revival an exciting and dramatic quality. Back in 1874, the year after Cable's first published story, Paul Hamilton Hayne, inveighing against the "Fungous School" of writing females in Dixie, had thought that "the literary future of our unfortunate South would appear to be as dark as her political."[12] Yet during the next fourteen years, the continuous series of notable literary debuts by Cable, R. M. Johnston, Harris, Page, Murfree, King, and others attracted so much attention that by 1887, the apex of the vogue, a writer on the Revival claimed "the establishment of a characteristic Southern literature."[13] So wildly uncritical was the reception of these authors that attacks were soon leveled at the "outburst of eulogy," "this malady of undue panegyric." "The Southern writer," said one critic, ". . . is but getting his wings, and the North, having long regarded him indifferently as a tobacco-worm, is suddenly anxious to admire his flights and colors as a butterfly. Southern literature is a sort of craze."[14] The tables had been turned just before and

12. "Literature at the South," *Southern Magazine*, XIV (June, 1874), 653.
13. C. W. Coleman, "The Recent Movement in Southern Literature," *Harper's Magazine*, LXXIV (May, 1887), 855.
14. Anon., "Literature in the South," *Critic*, X (June 25, 1887), 323.

after the Civil War the South had been forced to blow her own literary horn; now the North was blowing it for her—only louder.

With so much encouragement and such a variety of geographical backgrounds, Southern writers might have been expected to depict for sale "up North" every local type—even the tacky. But several intentions back of the writing in the Revival caused a relative neglect of the trash.

Perhaps the most notable of these was the glorifying of the Old South. Southern writers before the War had already done this, but with bitterness and defiance; those of the Revival strove to create for the nation a new picture of their region, one that would be both admirable and lovable. A natural consequence of this was that the aristocracy, as the highest development of Southern culture, received the earliest and perhaps the major literary attention from native authors. Indeed, the reception of stories like Frances Courtney Baylor's "In the Old Dominion" (1882), Thomas Nelson Page's "Marse Chan" (1884), and Mrs. W. B. Harrison's "Crow's Nest" (1885) proved that a general American audience was ready to love—even to weep over—what E. C. Stedman termed "the unspeakable charm that lived and died with the Old South." Thus, although the motives were different, Southern literature was again— as before the War—putting her best foot forward; it was not, of course, the bare, itchy one of the trash.[15]

The persistent, underlying thought of such literary

15. A checking of the articles on the South in *Poole's Index* and *Reader's Guide* indicates that the nation from 1802 to 1901 has been interested most in (1) the aristocracy of the Old South and in (2) the commercial and resort aspects of Florida. The states of most interest are, in order, Virginia, Louisiana, South Carolina, and Kentucky.

endearment was the reconciliation of the North and the South; and thus it still further operated against the poor-white as a literary subject. Southern writers hardly cared to win public sympathy for a class whose rôle in the late war and Reconstruction was so sorry.[16] To depict new Ham Rachels and Ransy Sniffles would have been poor strategy in allaying the prejudices of the two sections. Had not Northern novelists from Hildreth to Tourgée and "outrage mongers" during Reconstruction used the poor-whites as living indictments of the very class now being made lovable by Southern authors? After the war "outrage mongers" had continued to repeat riots and murders of 1865-69 as examples of Southern conditions in the seventies; and these same "hireling incendiaries" after Reconstruction had become bug-eyed "foreign correspondents" with what Joel Chandler Harris called "the habit of making yearly raids" upon the South. Thus it was well-nigh impossible for Southerners to regard the low-down people with concern; a typical reaction was to ignore or deny the existence of these reverted Southerners. It is not surprising, therefore, to discover that all of the articles about the trash in the 1880's were written by Northerners.

Besides glorification and reconciliation, there was an equally unfavorable barrier to the literary use of Ham Rachels: the cult of the picturesque which so obsessed the local color of the Revival period. Ever since Bret Harte had popularized his formula of picturesque characters against backdrops of striking scenery, writers

16. R. C. Beale finds no stories of the Civil War in Southern periodicals until after 1870 (*op. cit.*, 48-49).

had been busy placing it like a stencil on every quaint locality in America. Such a ready and easy way to authorship brought into being a species of peripatetic color hunters.

Of these, Constance Fenimore Woolson, grandniece of James Fenimore Cooper, staked more literary claims on the Southern scene than any outsider. She was a tourist-writer "in search of the picturesque"—within convenient distance from the resort porch. "I always walked abroad at sunset . . . "she said. "No doubt there was plenty of busy, prosaic reality . . . in the mornings, but I never saw it."[17] No wonder that she wrote a poem, "The Pine Barrens," and located two stories in the Florida pinelands but failed to note the Crackers who lived there. In the ten stories of *Rodman the Keeper*, there are no poor-whites; the sole allusion to them, however, explains their absence. Writing in "King David" of the loneliness experienced by a Yankee teacher, ostracized for serving in a Southern Freedmen's settlement, she remarked that "There were no 'poor-whites' there; he was spared the sight of their long, clay-colored faces, lank yellow hair, and half-open mouths; he was not brought into contact with the ignorance and dense self-conceit of this singular class."[18]

Clearly, Miss Woolson was repelled by these folk whose placid faces were so inscrutable to a sundown stalker of the picturesque. This eagerly sought quality she did find in decayed aristocrats, with what F. L. Pattee calls "the pathos of forever vanished glory"[19] about them, Minorcan fishermen in Florida, consump-

---

17. *Rodman the Keeper, Southern Sketches*, 179.
18. *Ibid.*, 261.
19. *Development of the American Short Story*, 253.

tive city artists among the healing Southern pines, Negroes, and mountaineers. In her neglect of the poor-white, in her quest after the picturesque, Miss Woolson was a typical, if somewhat exaggerated, example of the local colorists everywhere, even those native to the South.

To such writers, the drab, uncommunicative poor-white obviously had small appeal, for their slogan might have been that of William Combe's Dr. Syntax:

> *I'll prose it here and verse it there,*
> *And picturesque it everywhere.*

The Cracker was not a character for sweetness and quaint sentiment; his home rarely had a pretty setting; he did not appear to have much "serio-comic oddity" like that of the mountaineer and the funny "darky"; and, most disappointing of all, his dialect exhibited only a small part of the Negro's outlandish jargon or the poetic quaintness of the "Southern highlander," who— as everyone had been repeatedly told—still spoke the language of Shakespeare! In view of such deficiencies, writers whose method was to "scratch away on the surface" and "strike 'color'" would strike at types of more obvious promise.

Glorification, reconciliation, and the picturesque— these caused the poor-white to be overshadowed in the Revival by all of the distinctive Southern characters. A Boston critic in 1887 complained that only the Negro, the Creole, and the mountaineer had been given to American readers; "aside from these . . .," he said, "no other figure identified with the South has been clearly and definitely depicted."[20] Inaccurate as this is, it may serve as a fair index of public impression; even as late as 1900, a reviewer could say that "the 'poor-white' has been neglected almost as much in fiction as in our philanthropy and our politics."[21]

IV. SENTIMENTAL AND HEROIC POOR-WHITE: JOEL CHANDLER HARRIS AND THOMAS NELSON PAGE

SOMEWHAT paradoxically, however, the Southern writings about the poor buckra were, largely, the incidental result of the same three emphases in the Revival together with the natural continuation of Southern humor, particularly in Georgia by R. M. Johnston.

As the work of glorification and reconciliation progressed, literary interest was extended to the lower levels of Southern life, so that, after 1880, Joel Chandler Harris and Thomas Nelson Page came to write a few stories giving the trash a more appealing, that is, sentimental, portraiture, without the bitterness or contempt hitherto found in Northern works or the clownishness in earlier Southern humor. And there was another cause for the appearance of the poor-whites. The local color method of the Revival with its ideal of the picturesque was soon repeating monotonously its types—decayed Colonels, great ladies, faithful black Uncles and Aunties. By 1891, four years after the vogue's height, Thomas Nelson Page noticed among Southern writers "an apparent tendency to copy old work."[1] The resultant

20. Anon., "Southern Literature," *Boston Literary World*, XVIII (June 25, 1887), 200.
21. B. W. Wells, "Southern Literature of the Year," *Forum*, XXIX (June, 1900), 512.
1. "Literature in the South Since the Civil War," *loc. cit.*, 756.

search for newer types brought some poor-whites into fiction; and they were a welcome departure. "In the 'poor-whites' of Georgia," commented a writer in 1882, "Harris has found material as fresh and picturesque as anything in the delightful experience of Uncle Remus."[2]

That Joel Chandler Harris in democratic Georgia should have been the first in the Revival to write a story of the poor-white was very appropriate in that his own humble origin and experience gave to him a deep sympathy for the lowly. His father—whose name cannot be found in print—was an itinerant Irish laborer who deserted Mary Harris soon after Joel's birth. When forty-eight and famous, Harris recalled with understandable and affectionate exaggeration the Georgia countryside that was so generous and kind to "Miss Mary" and her red-headed boy. In "Georgia . . . the most Democratic part of the country," he said, "the poorer whites had no reason to hold their heads down because they had to work for their living. . . . The humblest held their heads as high as the richest."[3] This love of plain people remained an abiding passion throughout his life. As editorialist on the Atlanta *Constitution* from 1878 to 1890, no less than Grady, he lent his pen to what he called "the poor-man's chance."

Inevitably this sympathetic interest was reflected in his literary ideas, of which he had a good many, in spite of his usual over-modest denial that he had "no literary training and know nothing at all of what is literary." Full of gratitude to the kindly Georgians of Putnam County where his boyhood was spent, he felt that "no

2. Quoted by Julia C. Harris, *op. cit.*, 200.
3. *Stories of Georgia*, 241.

novel or story can be genuinely American unless it deals with the *common people*, that is, the *country people*."[4] Advising a young writer, he declared that "what is really great in literature is the *Commonplace*."[5] But not only should the best literature deal with people on the soil, it should be "absolutely impartial and invariably just."[6] And besides being "dreadfully sentimental" as well as romantic and hedged about by taboos in subject matter, Southern authors, like all the rest in America, had been blind to half of rural life. Writing in 1884, Harris declared: "It is a fatal weakness of American literature that our novelists . . . can perceive only the *comic* side of what they are pleased to term 'provincial life' . . . It is a remarkable fact that the most characteristic American story that has thus far been written should approach rural life on the tragic side. This is *The Story of a Country Town* by E. W. Howe."[7]

All of this brave pronouncement was right and tonic both for the South and the time. But no man escapes his age and in practice Harris was the victim of all the influences he condemned. The heroines of this Georgia democrat "went skipping into the parlor" exactly like the hoopskirts of Mrs. Hentz and Mrs. Stowe. Nor could a story be more sentimental than "Balaam and His Master." And, as for tragedy, he bogged down in the pathetic.

But there was yet another influence on Harris' portraiture of the Georgia tackies. In addition to his

4. Julia C. Harris, *op. cit.*, 204.

5. Quoted by Julia C. Harris in "Joel Chandler Harris, Constructive Realist," *Southern Pioneers in Social Interpretation*, ed. H. W. Odum, 150.

6. Quoted by Julia C. Harris (ed.), *Joel Chandler Harris, Editor and Essayist*, 46.

7. Quoted by Julia C. Harris, *Life and Letters*, 208.

Joel Chandler Harris and Thomas Nelson Page

humble origin and Southern emotional heritage, Harris'
tendency toward sentimentality was accentuated by
his zeal as a conciliator of the North and South. In editorials and literature, he was the perfect counterpart of
his oratorical fellow worker on the *Constitution*, Henry
W. Grady, in the "healing of the nations." By nature
Harris was what the Anglo-Saxons called a peace-
weaver. When a mere boy of fifteen, working on a newspaper at Turnwold plantation, he wrote an essay, placing "the ambition to be a peace-maker on earth" above
all others. About twenty years later, this belief had
become a conviction, sustained by such missionary
courage that he attacked Jefferson Davis for "his restless petulance and ridiculous rhetoric"[8] by which the
idol of the South was keeping alive sectional bitterness.

So intent was this "cornfield writer" (so Harris called
himself) on making Yankees and ex-Rebels good neighbors in the old-fashioned Georgia sense that he began
to minimize—even deny—the differences between the
two sections. There were, he maintained, "remarkable
points of resemblance between the typical down-easter
and the typical Georgia Cracker. . . . Major Jones is
Brother Jonathan thinly disguised in a suit of Georgia
linsey-wolsey. . . . Stand them up alongside Hosea
Biglow . . . and the parallel is complete. Bring Hosea
Biglow to Georgia, turn him loose in a pine thicket,
show him a bunch of dogwood blossoms . . . give him
a suit of jeans . . . then, you have your Major Joseph
Jones of Pineville, who is 'yours till death.'" Typical
regional types, he went on to say, were mostly popular

8. Atlanta *Constitution*, Jan. 24, 1882. As quoted by Julia C. Harris, *Joel Chandler Harris, Editor and Essayist*, 67.

illusion. Witness "sectional contradictions" like Hosea Biglow, the Yankee supposed to be ever tending pennies, but actually jabbering over politics; and Major Jones, the Southern Cracker thought to be politically mad, but really concerned most in telling of his love affair.[9]

In 1883, four years after these remarks, Harris traveled in New England, where he saw *through train windows* that he had been correct: New England had poor-white trash, and they were exactly like those in Georgia:

"Here, too, was Bud Stucky, the Georgia Tacky, though what he was doing hanging barefooted around the little station of Bethel on the Vermont Central the Lord only knows. . . . Bud Stucky's New England name . . . is Webb Brown; but what is in a name? He wore here the same striped shirt and red jeans trousers he used to wear in Georgia, and he had the same pale, watery eyes, the same straggling sandy beard, and the same habit of fingering his weak chin and mouth. And, then, when the train boy, with true Southern accent called out 'Northhampton,' why should a group of E. W. Kemble's Georgia Crackers be standing near the station? All this is more than I can make out, unless the leagues that stretch between Vermont and Georgia are a dream and sectionalism a myth . . . wherever I have gone in New England I have found . . . this 'poor white trash' . . . the Sandhillers, the Dirt-eaters, the Crablanders, the Tackies—as large as life and quite as natural . . . forlornest of all is the poverty that is acquiesced in—that has become a habit. It is found here in New England, and it is not . . . cut off

9. Editorials, Atlanta *Constitution*, Sept. 28, and Oct. 5, 1879.

into communities as in the South, but it hovers on the edge of prosperity. . . . The wonder is, not that New England should have its Tackies and its 'poor-white trash,' but that the restless Northern correspondents should not have found it out. Or did they think their discovery would give offence?"[10]

The evangelist of good will had seen what he went forth to see. Indeed, he was so carried away with his message that he deceived himself. What he really believed about things Southern came out thirteen years later when writing on Georgia wit and humor. Like Georgia watermelons, they were unique; "they have no counterpart in any other section of the country."[11]

All errors of zeal aside, the creator of Uncle Remus probably wrought better as a conciliator than any literary man of his time.[12] At Atlanta in 1905, President Theodore Roosevelt was speaking for the nation when he said of Harris: "He has written what exalts the South in the mind of every man who reads it, and yet what has not a flavor of bitterness toward any other part of the union."[13] But however noble it may have been to inspire readers toward "solving American problems aright," definitely bad was the effect of such propagandizing on Harris' work, as may be seen from his treatment of the poor-white.

Because of his rôle as conciliator, his great sympathy for the poor, and his weakness for sentiment, Harris claimed the trashy Crackers for pity. He was out to

10. "Observations from New England," one of the three articles which Harris wrote on his trip for the *Constitution* in 1883.
11. *Stories of Georgia*, 240.
12. Typical stories of reconciliation by Harris: "Little Compton," "Aunt Fountain's Prisoner," "Azalia," in *Free Joe and Other Sketches*.
13. Julia C. Harris, *Life and Letters of Joel Chandler Harris*, 141.

defend and win sympathy for them. To him, the
Georgia pineywoodsers were not the malicious villains
of Simms, or the moral perverts of Gilmore; they were
the unfortunates of his state, not a class to be ridiculed,
but human beings to be pitied. This view he presented
during the decade 1882 to 1892 in four stories and a
part of *On the Plantation*. In these, Harris did four
notable things: (1) he added to the gallery of Southern
poor-whites three memorable characters; (2) in Emma
Jane and her half-witted son, Bud, he introduced the
pathetic or sentimental poor-white; (3) he came nearer
the tragic conception of the tacky in Mrs. Feratia
Bivins than any other writer of the nineteenth century;
and (4) incidentally he made comments which constitute a sort of chronicle of the type as well as a redefini-
tion of his lot.

By 1887, Harris was so absorbed by section-welding
that he spoiled his story, "Azalia," which contains his
most extensive picture of Georgia tackies. It is merely
another North-South love affair with baldly pointed
social morals. Helen Eustice, anemic Bostonian, went
to the Georgia pinelands, where she found not only
health but a lover, General Garwood. The marriage
in Massachusetts, according to Harris, was "practical
Reconstruction." But, in this tale, as in Simms' novels,
the poor-white characters are by far the most real;
nevertheless, Emma Jane and Bud Stucky serve only
as an obligato of compassion to the aristocratic love
theme. Certainly, Bud's childlike devotion to the
Boston girl, as well as General Garwood's wooing,
reconstructs her. And Emma Jane's fierce mother love
for Bud is as touching as Harris could make it.

Joel Chandler Harris and Thomas Nelson Page

Of course, Simms had employed an idiot girl as a device of pity in *Richard Hurdis;* but Harris, by virtue of his superior knowledge of and sympathy for the lowest Crackers, achieved an actuality denied the Charleston author because of his condescension. The Stuckys are important sentimental poor-whites in the Revival.

Having walked into the village of Azalia from the pinelands, Emma Jane arrived at Mrs. Haley's tavern. There, silent and staring, she awaited her usual hand-out:

"Her dirty sunbonnet had fallen back from her head, and hung on her shoulders. Her hair was of a reddish gray color. Its frazzled and tangled condition suggested that the woman had recently passed through a period of extreme excitement; but this suggestion was promptly corrected by the wonderful serenity of her face—a pale, unhealthy-looking face, with sunken eyes, high cheekbones, and thin lips that seemed never to have troubled themselves to smile: a burnt-out face that had apparently surrendered to the past, and had no hope for the future.

"You must be tired, Emma Jane, not to say howdy," said Mrs. Haley. . . .

"Ti-ud! Lordy, Lady! how kin a pore creeter like me be ti-yd? Hain't I thes natally made out'n i'on?"[14]

After Emma Jane had gone with her victuals, the Boston newcomer was deeply touched. "Her eyes will haunt me as long as I live," she said. But Mrs. Haley made quick rejoinder:

"You nee'nter be sorry for Emma Jane Stucky

14. *Free Joe* . . ., 177-78.

117

neither. Jest as you see her now, jesso she's been a-goin' on fer twenty years . . . [she] . . . is like one of them there dead pines out there in the clearin' . . . Bless your soul and body, child! . . . if you're going to let that poor creetur's looks pester you, you'll be worried to death, as certain as the world. There's a hundred in this settlement jest like her, . . . I reckon maybe you ain't used to seein' pineywoods tackies. Well, ma'm, you wait till you come to know 'em, and if you are in the habit of bein' ha'nted by looks, you'll be the wuss ha'nted mortal in the land. . . ."[15]

Nor was Harris behindhand in building up sympathy for Bud, who, in his queer twisted mind, had a love of beauty. He had been chore-boy and hound-like follower of several pretty women of the country-side. And he loved nothing more than music. While Bud was listening to organ music played by the Boston girl at the tacky mission, his face was symbolic of the age-long misery of his class: "It suggested loneliness, despair, that was the more tragic because of its isolation. It seemed to embody the mute, pent-up distress of whole generations."[16] He would slink around the Garwood plantation house to hear piano-playing, even though the Negro servants threatened to set the dogs on "the nasty stinkin' ondacious villyun."

And all the while, Emma Jane humored him trying to keep his addled wits at ease. Anxiously she guarded Bud's feelings toward the Boston girl, especially after he had seen her walking home from church with General Garwood.

15. *Ibid.*, 181. This an excellent impression of the middle-class Southerner's taking the poor-white for granted.
16. *Ibid.*, 201.

A. B. FROST IN "HARPER'S MAGAZINE," 1894

Pineywoods Folk of North Carolina

Joel Chandler Harris and Thomas Nelson Page

"I seed 'er," said Bud. "He sent some yuther gals home in the carriage, an' him an' the Yankee gal went a-walkin' down the road. He humped up his arm this away, an' the gal tuck it, an' off they put. . . . Yes, siree! she tuck it an' off they put."

Mrs. Stucky looked at this her grown man, her son, for a long time without saying a thing, and finally remarked with something very like a sigh—

"Well, honey, you neenter begrudge 'em the 'er walk. Hit's a long ways through the san'."

"Lordy, yes'n!" exclaimed Bud with something like a smile; "It's a mighty long ways, but the giner'l had the gal wi' 'im. He jess humped up his arm, an' she tuck it, an' off they put."[17]

Later when the Boston girl went to the Stucky cabin to see Bud die and let her tears flow freely, Emma Jane scorned her. "Watter you cryin' fer now?" she asked with unmistakable bitterness. "You wouldn't a-wiped your feet on 'im. . . ."

But the finest single poor-white created during the Southern Revival appeared in Harris' first story of the trash, "Mingo" (1882). Mrs. Feratia Bivins is even more than that: she is the nearest approach before the twentieth century to the tragic poor-white.

Just before the Civil War, her son—apparently an exceptional Bivins—had made a runaway marriage with Cordelia, the daughter of aristocratic Judge Wornum. The girl was disowned by her parents; her husband was killed in the war; and she herself died in childbirth. Now her little girl, Pud, was being reared

17. *Ibid.*, 202-3. Bud's repetitive speech suggests later dialogue by Sherwood Anderson and others.

by Mrs. Feratia and Mingo, an old Wornum Negro, who had followed Cordelia. Year by year, this great, bony woman with Mingo's help had slaved on her little piece of ground to save toward giving Pud a chance. And year by year her hatred of the aristocratic Wornums increased.

Thus, when Mrs. Wornum relented and came to the Bivins' cabin to see her granddaughter, Pud, Mrs. Feratia's loathing knew no bounds.

"Mizzers Bivins is come to that time of 'er life when she's mighty proud to git calls from the big-bugs."

"Things is come to a mighty pretty pass when quality folks has to go from house to house a-huntin' up pore white trash, an' a-astin' airter the'er kin."[18]

Suddenly all the wrongs she had suffered at the hands of Mrs. Wornum flooded her mind: "how she'd 'a' bin a-houndin' after me an' my son, an' a-treatin' us like as we'd 'a' bin the off-scourin's er creation. . . ." Then the cruel pride of the aristocrat now in her house—pride which had let a daughter die in want and grief released all of the personal and class hatred in Mrs. Bivins. Thinking of Cordelia's death, she turned on her visitor: . . . "an' ef hit hadn't but 'a' bin for *her*, Emily Wornum, . . . I'd 'a' strangled the life out'n you, time your shadder darkened my door. An' what's more . . . ef you er come to bother airter Pud, thes make the trial of it. Thes so much as lay the weight er your little finger on 'er . . . an' I'll grab you by the goozle an' t'ar your haslet out."[19] The great lady, fearing the rage of Mrs. Feratia, departed hastily.

18. *Mingo and Other Sketches in Black and White*, 21.
19. *Ibid.*, 24.

Joel Chandler Harris and Thomas Nelson Page

This story, told by Mrs. Feratia herself at a picnic, was tragedy and, as Harris said, "seemed to represent the real or fancied wrongs of a class and to spring from the pent-up rage of a century." But Uncle Remus knew not the ways of tragedy. He apologized for not being able to give an "imitation of the remarkable dramatic fervor and earnestness" of the story. He apologized for his poor-white heroine as a tragic figure: "It was not merely Mrs. Feratia Bivins who had been speaking, but the voice of Tragedy." Such pointing and bolstering seem to indicate that Harris was afraid of making Mrs. Bivins pathetic rather than tragic. All of "Mingo" excepting the fine scene of anger is pure sentiment.

And besides winning sympathy for the Georgia poor-white in these three characters, Harris also re-defined for Southern literature the history of "that indescribable class of people known ... as the pineywoods 'Tackies.'" Of these folk in the "squalid settlement," mentioned in his story "Azalia," he wrote: "They had settled there before the Revolution, and had remained there ever since, unchanged and unchangeable, steeped in poverty of the most desolate description, and living the narrowest lives possible in this great Republic."

Certainly, Harris represented these pitiful Crackers in the period before and during the Civil War as kind, harmless, mistreated creatures. In "Free Joe," old Micajah Staley and his sister, Becky, are the only friends that the free Negro had. "When he was a slave," Harris observed, "Free Joe would have scorned these representatives of a class known as poor-white trash, but now he found them sympathetic and helpful. . . ."

But when Harris wrote of the tackies in the Civil

The Southern Poor-White

War, he was more than sympathetic; he was resentful. In 1891, he set down in "Mom Bi" what must be reckoned the finest fictional representation of the aristocratic pre-war attitude toward the trash. In this story, it is expressed in the contempt of a Charleston-bred slave woman. The unidentified poor-whites are used to illustrate Mom Bi's resentment of her young master's going to war.

At the summer resort for Charlestonians in the pinelands, "the sandhillers . . . marketed their poor little crops" and received the tongue lashing of Mom Bi: "De Lord knows," she would shout, "I glad I nigger. . . . I mought bin born lak dese white folks what eat dirt un set in chimley-corner tell dee look lak dee bin smoke-dried. . . ."

With her master's children, she watched the tackies drilling in the village—poor devils, "hollow-chested. . . round-shouldered, and exceedingly awkward . . ." who had been harangued into the C.S.A. by local spread-eagles. "Look at um!" she cried, "I done git skeered myse'f, dee look so vigrous. Ki! dee smell dem vittle what dem Yankee got, 'tis goodby, Yankee! Look at um, honey! Dee gwine fight fer rich folks' nigger."[20]

This to her was as it should be. But when young Master Gabriel joined the cavalry of the C.S.A., Mom Bi's dander rose. The quality should have things done for them—even to fighting a war. On being told that Gabriel must defend his country, Mom Bi became the mouthpiece through which the Georgia writer delivered a little history lesson. "Wey dem san-hillers bin gone at?" she asked, *"Wey de country what dee fight fer?"*

20. *Balaam and His Master*, 177.

Joel Chandler Harris and Thomas Nelson Page

Nor was Mom Bi convinced by her master's answer that the South was also the tacky's country. "Whut dem po' white trash gwine fight fer? Nuthin' 'tall ain't bin tell me dat. Dee ain't bin had no nigger; dee ain't bin had no money; dee ain't bin had no lan'; dee ain't bin had nuthin' 't all."[21]

More than anything, she resented "her boy's" serving in the same army "longside dem trash . . . *dem whut de Lord done fersooken dis long time.*" But the old "darkie's" cup ran over when Gabriel was killed. Then she rocked and moaned: "Whoffer dee no lef dem no 'count san'hillers fer do all de fightin'? Who gwine fer cry wan de git kilt?"

The last words of Mom Bi are the "cornfield writer's" bitterly ironic comment on the callous indifference of the great planter families towards the tackies, for the old Negro acquired her attitude from South Carolina "quality." Not that Harris made the specific charges of the abolitionists against the aristocracy; he merely implied some blame. And was he not at one with De-Forest, who, years earlier, had said that the decent people of the South thanked God and took heart when one poor-white killed another?

How ironic the story, "Mom Bi," really is and how much Harris pitied the wretched sandhillers in the Civil War, may be learned from the self-defence of Pruitt, the deserter, in the work, *On the Plantation* (1892): "What do you call the fellers what jines inter the army arter they 'er been told that their families 'll be took keer of . . . by the rich folks at home; an' then arter they've been in a right smart whet, they gits word that their

21. *Ibid.*, 180.

wives an' children is a-lookin' starvation in the face. . . .
Bimely they breaks loose an' comes home . . . what sort
of fellers do you call 'em?"

With "Mingo" and "Azalia" Harris brought his
incidental chronicle of the poor-white to a close by
showing the wrongs of pre-war days poisoning the life
of Mrs. Bivins and the persistence of the pineywoodsers, outside of Azalia, unchanged by war and peace.

Emma Jane and Bud Stucky, Mrs. Bivins, Micajah
and Becky Staley—all are pitiable, if not lovable; they
represent Harris' main contribution—the pathetic poor-
white. That he did not achieve tragedy instead of
pathos may be accounted for on many scores. Besides
the influences of great sympathy for the lowly, current
sentimentality, and reconciliation, there were other
causes. Harris shied at sex and the sordid details
inherent in the poor-white as tragedy. "He disliked
Zola and the French realists intensely . . . because of
the mass of sordid details"; and wrote to a publisher,
"In all my writings you will find nothing that cannot
be read and explained to a young girl."[22] And, above
all, his love of the lovable was the preference of a genius
suited to happy "darkies" of childlike fancy, not to the
degraded tacky.

A co-worker of Harris in the cause of reconciliation
was Thomas Nelson Page, who declared that he had
"never wittingly written a line which did not . . . tend
to bring about a better understanding between the
North and the South. . . ."[23] And he added to the
pathetic poor-white the qualities of heroism and

22. Julia C. Harris, *Life and Letters* . . ., 574, 497.
23. Introduction to *Works*, I, xi.

Joel Chandler Harris and Thomas Nelson Page

romance. His great successes in making the nation love
the Old Dominion of Marse Chans and Meh Ladys
finally led him to record for sympathy and admiration
those forgotten Virginians in the swamps and thickets.
One story, "The Two Little Confederates" (1888)
concerns these folk incidentally, but "Little Darby"
(1894) is all poor-white. In both of them, Page views the
tackies from the plantation porch and in that respect
continues the ante-bellum Southern tradition.

Yet in these stories—contradictory as they are as
pictures of the trash—he recorded two possible and
vivid rôles of this group in wartime. The one, "The Two
Little Confederates," presents the Holetown[24] settlement as the hide-out of deserters; the other, "Little
Darby," the poor-white as hero.

Hidden in "virgin forest and old-field pines," Holetown, said Page, had a reputation of an unsavory
nature, though its "harmless people" had vices no
worse than "intemperance and evasion of the tax laws."
"Usually so thin and sallow that one had to look at
them twice to see them," they "eeked it out" like all
poor-whites by hunting, fishing, and patch-farming.

Nearly all of the Holetown men joined the C.S.A.,
"thinking war was more like play than work." Soon
Holetown had many of its soldiers back home to stay.
Tim Mills told his Colonel: "I'm gwine back . . . an'
I'm gwine to fight, ef Yankees gits in my way; but ef
I gits tired, I's comin' home; and 'taint no use to tell
you I ain't, 'cause I *is*. . . ." Consequently, the Con-
script Guard often descended upon Holetown, only to

24. Holetown was to Page almost a foreign country. Even if he had known it well, his dainty conception of novel content would have prevented intimate depiction (Roswell Page, *Thomas Nelson Page*, 198).

125

see "a rush of tow-headed children through the woods" or hear a horn tooting the number of the raiding party. On being questioned by a guard, one old woman bugler replied sullenly: "Jes' blowin' fur Mallindy to come to dinner."

But the poor-whites in "Little Darby" are something else. Sentiment, heroism, romance—all the qualities of Page's best "Ole Virginny" manner he applied to Little Darby and the Mills family.

Strangely enough, these poor-whites, living in pine barrens or swampy bottoms much like Holetown, were not sallow like their cousin, Tim Mills, in "Two Little Confederates"; "A clean-limbed, blond, blue-eyed people," they became weather-beaten and hard-visaged only in middle age. But, in accounting for his valiant hero and heroine, Page carried this romancing even further. "There were often among them," he said, "straight supple young fellows with clean-cut features, and lithe, willowy looking girls, with pink faces and blue, or brown, or hazel eyes, and a mien which one might have expected to find in a hall rather than in a cabin."[25] Certainly this is more than enough to explain Little Darby. A sort of latter-day Crockett, he "was but a poor hand with the hoe." Even his neighbors "dilated on his worthlessness." Yet with a rifle he was a dead shot, and his hawk-like eye could find "a squirrel flat on top of the grayest limb of the tallest hickory in the woods . . ."

But in the Civil War, Little Darby found himself. Davy Crockett was hardly so valiant a soldier. Thrice the Virginia poor-white became the hero before losing his life for Dixie: once, when he cut down a post in the

25. *Burial of the Guns*, 51.

direct fire of the enemy so that Confederate artillery could advance; again, when he crawled out between the lines to silence a sharp-shooter; and finally as a spy, when he led Union cavalry to a bridge which his sweetheart, Vashti Mills, was burning.

How utterly ignorant Page was of the poor-white mind may be observed in his rhapsodies over Little Darby leading the Federals: "What he thought of, who might know?—plain, poor, ignorant, unknown, marching every step voluntarily nearer to certain and ignominious death for the sake of his cause." Certainly, Page could not know; and, as a result, except for the description of Little Darby's early life and home, one might mistake the poor-white hero for any high-souled Randolph or Lee in gray.

Nor is Vashti Mills much less than a Virginia Joan of Arc. While the men are away, she hunts, traps, fishes, and chops wood, and so keeps less able war-widows from starving. But her daring hike to the bridge which she was to burn for her lover, wading in water up to her neck with matches in her teeth and carrying rails to speed the fire while Federal cavalry shot at her—that was a deed for no Emma Jane Stucky. But, according to Page, Vashti came of heroic stuff: her father, after his two boys had joined the army, took down his squirrel rifle and left for the front.

In "The Two Little Confederates," Page told the truth about Virginia pineywoodsers; in "Little Darby," he forgot the facts and gave the poor-white to glory.

The Southern Poor-White

B ESIDES this pathetic and sentimental poor-white of
Harris and Page, there appeared another in the
Southern Revival which was largely inherited from ante-
bellum humor. But no more Ransy Sniffles and Ham
Rachels appeared: the new humor had been cleansed
and sweetened. This, William Dean Howells unwittingly pointed out in 1894 while accounting for the
shift from romance to "realism" in Southern fiction.
"This development," he stated, "was on the lines of
those early humorists . . . who were often in their
humor, so rank, so wild, so savage, so cruel, but the
modern realism has refined both upon their matter and
their manner."[1] And Howells was right: his type of
realism with now and then a vestige of the old Southern
humor was being applied to the poor-white.

Of the writers using this mode (which amounted to
Dickens plus Longstreet) none suited the taste of the
eighties better than Richard Malcolm Johnston. Publishing his first book, *Georgia Sketches*, in 1864, he
bridged two periods of Southern writing. Like Longstreet, he insisted upon a large factual basis for his stories
and wrote to preserve "the memories of the old times:
the grim and rude but hearty old times in Georgia."
Many of Johnston's stories reflect the attitude of his
pair of old Georgians who sat under a tree with their
mint juleps and cried over the "blessed old times" of
family visits *en masse* and chicken pies.[2] In praising

1. *Southern Lights and Shadows*, vi.
2. *Dukesborough Tales*, 180.

Old-South Humor

Johnston, E. C. Stedman stated accurately the nature of this newer Southern humor: the "expression of both the pathetic and the comic sides of life move us often to weep, and yet always to smile through our tears."[3]

The best known story of Johnston, "The Goosepond School" (1864), points back to Longstreet's sketch, "The Turn Out," and forward to sentimental stories of mother love like Harris' "Azalia." To the Goosepond School went Brinkly Glisson, a raw-boned, freckled lad, with "beautiful eyes, very blue, and habitually sad." Before he could read well enough, he was put into geography by the schoolmaster who thereafter flogged him unmercifully for poor lessons. Unable to prepare his work and to endure the whippings, even for his mother's sake, Brinkly beat the master into a bloody pulp before the whole school. The widow Glisson on hearing her son's story became both joyous and tearful. Later her ambitions for Brinkly were realized under a kind teacher.

But stories like "The Goosepond School," except for its horseplay, do not represent the lingering strength of the Old South humor—especially in Georgia. In 1872, an elegant Southerner declared that Bret Harte and the humorists had reduced Americans to literary ignorance and vulgarity; no one recognized any more a reference to Homer or Plato, but "describe how—'Sut Lovingood's daddy played hoss' and see if you do not touch a familiar chord."[4] And to the turn of the century, Johnston and Harris extolled Georgia wit and humor.

3. "Literary Estimate . . . of Richard Malcolm Johnston," *Publications of the Southern History Association*, II (Oct., 1898), 315.
4. M. F. Taylor, "The Turning Point in American Literature," *Southern Magazine*, XI (Sept., 1872), 325.

The Southern Poor-White

For to both of them, as Harris said: "Middle Georgia was and is the center of the most unique [sic]—the most individual civilization the Republic has produced. *Georgia Scenes*, *Major Jones's Courtship*, and all that is racy in *Simon Suggs*, and Colonel Johnston's characters, all came out of Middle Georgia."[5] Nor was Johnston behindhand in continuing this partly justifiable boast in his fine article, "Middle Georgia Rural Life."

Thus, while Georgians did not devote themselves mainly to the poor-white, it was natural that they should have noticed him in the old humorous way. In Harris' rare chapter, "Georgia Wit and Humor," written for *Stories of Georgia* (1896), he recounted the life of a sallow lad from the Dark Corner of Lincoln County, the scene of Longstreet's "Georgia Theatrics." Born among the "tackies, the clay-eaters, and no-accounts that . . . had given themselves over to thriftlessness for good and all," this boy became Judge Dooly, the most noted practical joker of his time. On one occasion he shamed a wooden-legged challenger out of a duel by refusing to fight unless allowed to shoot with one leg in a bee-gum made of a hollow log.

It was Johnston, however, who in one story, "The Various Languages of Billy Moon" (1881), carried over the old humor about the poor-white into the post-war period. For this yarn tells of a fight at a muster, one of the most popular genre subjects in the pre-war era. Placed beside "The Fight," by Longstreet, this story of Johnston reveals perfectly what had happened to American taste and Southern writing in a half century. At the outset Colonel Johnston informed the reader

5. Quoted by Julia C. Harris in *Life and Letters of Joel Chandler Harris*, 316-17.

that fights at Georgia musters were not bloody, fist-and-skull onslaughts—such as Ransy Sniffle loved—but merely trials of strengths which lasted until one valiant cried "enough," that is, "gave the word."

After the muster, Oglethorpe Josh Green, self-styled O.J.G., who was the undefeated, visiting bully, cried his challenge. The crowd made up the bet and brought their champion—a tall, stringy, yellow-headed Cracker, Billy Moon, who began to make signs. "Deaf and dumb!" said Oglethorpe. "Ain't he a egiot?" O.J.G. refused to fight "it," for the mute could not "give the word," nor could "it" hear him if *he* yelled the word. Bewildered by the mute's wild gestures and squeakings, O.J.G. agreed to one friendly fall and was promptly slammed on his back. Dusting himself off, the bully, in a daze from the fall and the gibbering of Billy Moon, offered to buy his conqueror a drink. But Billy began squeaking and pointing; "it" wanted to treat the crowd. O.J.G. was now so thoroughly confused that his tongue grew heavy. "My gawnamighty . . ." he drawled, "what kind o' wordth wath them?"

Never did O.J.G. bully again. In after years, when others told of strange things, he would point his thumb down South and say: "Gentlemen, it were a kind of egiot; and it were grippy as a wise, and it were supple as a black snake, and it were strong as a mule and a bull both putten together. And, gentlemen," he would add, "egiot as it were, it were smarter'n any man ever I see; and as for its langwidges—well, gentlemen, they wa'nt no eend to its warious landwidges."[6]

6. "The Various Languages of Billy Moon," *Harper's New Monthly Magazine* LXII (Aug., 1881), 399.

The Southern Poor-White

The old-time fight of gouging and ear-chewing had become clean and picturesque. Not only did the gentle Colonel omit all swearing and blood, he apologized for the callousness of "country people of the humbler and less cultivated sort" who in those times called idiots and mutes, "it." Nevertheless, despite all such sanitizing, the muster fight of ante-bellum humor still had enough life in it to be excellent fun.

In the Southern Revival no other piece of writing about the poor-white had so much of the old humor as "The Various Languages of Billy Moon." Whenever a theme used by the Longstreet era re-appeared, it was warmed and sweetened by sentiment. In "The Thimble Game" (1847), T. W. Lane told, as a joke, the story of a Georgia Cracker fleeced in town; in "An Elephant's Track" (1897),[7] Mary E. M. Davis repeated the tale as a tragi-comedy of West Texas poor-whites. Newt Pinson lost all the money saved for months to a card sharper at the circus; so that the family was forced to return home, having seen none of the wonders except an elephant's track in the road. But like Col. Johnston, Mrs. Davis added the soft note. Before starting home Newt's wife told her disappointed brats that she would cowhide them till they could not sit down "if any one o' you says a word to yer paw 'bout this here misfortin' o' his'n, or 'bout hankerin' a'ter the show. . . ." Not so good, yet in the same convention of the sentimentalized joke is "A Born Inventor" (1889)[8] by Harry Stillwell Edwards; yet this story of a Cracker boy whose inventions, such as a peg-leg for a mule, always bring

7. M. E. M. Davis, *An Elephant's Track and Other Stories*, 1-20.
8. H. S. Edwards, *Two Runaways and Other Stories*, 209-25.

disaster contains an interesting social note: the poor-whites' taking over of "ghost plantations." The easy-going family of the "inventor" lives in a log cabin and lean-to on "the site of one of the great ante-bellum houses that disappeared when Sherman marched through Georgia."

However, in 1889, there appeared a comic poor-white woman that was not derived from ante-bellum Southern humor. Mrs. Sophrony Mathis, who provides comic relief in Louis Pendleton's novel, *In the Wiregrass*, is in the tradition of Gilmore's Mrs. Mulock and the bedraggled females that visited DeForest at the Freedmen's Bureau in South Carolina. Although not degenerate like these literary ancestors, she is nevertheless "taller-face, po' buckra" and talks and acts in much the same manner.

Sophrony, a laconic, pipe-smoking angel-of-mercy, was a concocter of vile medicines. Whenever she heard of illness, to the neighbor's backdoor she went with her elixirs. "Jes'a strong cup drawd from red pepper—with a lettle grain er sassafras root an' sage leaves throwd in," she knew was good. But better, perhaps, was "water from biled hops an' poke root, an' sweetened wi' lasses and spiked wi' good strong whiskey." In Sophrony's opinion, apparently, a dose to raise the dying must taste like death and smell like the dead. "Nothin' 't all in the world but water," she said after smelling arsenic.

No richer piece of comic writing about the poor-white was done in the later nineteenth century than a scene in which Pendleton recorded one of her mercy visits. Left in a room alone to smoke and drink brandy, Sophrony puffed and guzzled, rocking happily and, after each

wheezy cough, hoisting her skirt to wipe her mouth.
Needless to say, when the plantation mistress returned,
she was no less amused than Major DeForest had been
in lending his pipe to his sloppy callers at the Bureau.

In general, the Southern humor of pre-war style that
lingered was weak stuff. Victorian prudery and sentimentality had washed all of the tang out of it. And, for
the poor-white in literature, this was unfortunate, because he had received major attention in the uncurried
age of comic writing in the South.

VI. PICTURESQUE BACKGROUNDS AND LOUISIANA CAJUNS: GEORGE W. CABLE AND KATE CHOPIN

IN addition to this latter-day humor and the other
writings about the poor-whites motivated partly by
the twin desires of local glorification and sectional
reconciliation, there was the contribution of "the picturesque."

The weaknesses of this cult notwithstanding, it both
sharpened and broadened the outline of poor-white
life. It continued the work of journalists like J. R. Gilmore in keeping these sorry Southerners before the
nation in some sixteen articles and several books of
travel as well as fiction. It substituted the picturesque
for earlier Northern propaganda, and it helped to make
available for the public a fuller and more varied view
of Cracker life than it had ever enjoyed. In doing so, the
picturesque made two specific additions to the story of
the "forgotten men" of the South: the creation of a
literary geography for the poor-white and the depiction
of the Cajun of Louisiana unnoticed since Longfellow's
Evangeline had appeared in 1847.

Picturesque Backgrounds and the Cajuns

Before 1865, the habitat of the Crackers was a stereo-typed stage set. Without first-hand observation, most of the Northern authors had placed their Southern pariahs in vague pine barrens and swamps, or any place sufficiently drab and Godforsaken. These standardized haunts were not only to be sharpened by details from actual experience, but three new ones were introduced. Furthermore, noters of the picturesque made an effort to understand the relations of place and people. Thus, from Virginia to Florida and west to Texas, the panorama of the poor-whites spread, usually from one strip of sterile land to another—always outside the stream of Southern living.

Until after the Civil War, no writer of much imagina-tion had told America the nature of the Southern pine-lands, which had for well over a century hidden the tackies. But in the seventies and eighties these woods in Florida appalled more than one sojourner. In his poem, "From the Flats" (1877), Sidney Lanier longed for his Georgia hills, because on the peninsula "the drear sand-levels drain my spirit low." The aspect peculiar to the Florida pine country was its tropical coloring, which one Northern hiker found "oppressive to the last degree." No outsider, however, conveyed so fine a sense of its atmosphere as Margaret Deland in her charming book, *Florida Days*, the record of this Pennsylvanian's boat trip into the backcountry. The multitude of long-leafed pines with their bare trunks, tall as cocoa-nut trees, made a strange impression upon her; she thought of them not in the mass, but as individuals, countable only if one had an eternity. And the soughing of their needle-tops called to her mind the Latin hymn

The Southern Poor-White

beginning: "Infinitas! Infinitas." But there was nothing exalting about this hideaway of the Florida Crackers.

"The solitude," Mrs. Deland lamented, "is overpowering; the still air brings the strong balsamic fragrance in burning gusts, but there is no wind; at noon, on the barrens, even the dance of gorgeous butterflies and the clumsy booming of bumblebees, cease; the stillness is appalling and never restful. It is a relief to see motion anywhere—lizards slipping over a wrinkled root that buries itself in the sand like a veined and withered finger, or two buzzards sweeping upon rigid wings through the shadowless blue, in vast curves and circles.

"It is a relief here in the barrens when night suddenly falls . . .; darkness shuts out these appalling distances and lifts the weight of consciousness from a man's soul."[1]

Such country, even in less semi-tropical east Mississippi seemed a nightmare to the vitriolic Yankee traveler, Stephen Powers, who recorded his disgust in an article, "With the Yam Eaters."

"The sallow, ashen or yellowish soil," he explained, "is full of ague seeds and unmeasured potentiality of yams and ugly spiders. There are the wide flats beneath the pines, with the straggling wisps of brown-grass, where the sullen hiss or rattle of reptiles makes a sudden fluttering in the blood, and black swamps among the cypresses, full of miasmas and fevers and all biliousness . . . the pines move with an uneasy stir, as a fever patient sighs . . . and rustles the covers . . . as he tosses in his burning."[2]

1. *Florida Days*, 126-27.
2. "With the Yam Eaters," *Lippincott's Magazine*, IV (Dec., 1869), 264-65.

Picturesque Backgrounds and the Cajuns

Viewing these frightful places mostly from train or boat, travelers like Mrs. Deland and Stephen Powers naturally included the folk that would live in such country. The poor-whites thus became the inevitable still-life figures in this survey of Southern landscapes.

"These silent people of the swamps and woods," said Mrs. Deland, . . . "can only be thought of as upon the very spot where one chances to find them, and as this feeling of their permanence increases, the less human they seem to be . . . less human, not at all in the sense of brutishness, but only as they become more and more a part of physical nature, less and less spiritual expressions of God."[3]

The same identity of land and people, James Redpath noted in Alabama when, with the Union army, he had "scoured the bottomlands between Huntsville and Stevenson, which are exclusively occupied by poor-whites." "The people," he said, "are like the country— as dull-eyed and stupid as the lowlands, as gaunt, angular, and vacant as the bluffs."[4]

During the period, however, three new locales of the tackies appeared in fiction. They were different from the usual pineywoods settings in being picturesque and, sometimes, beautiful. Such places made colorful backgrounds for natives that had been considered rather drab.

Before the discovery of commercial fertilizer in the late nineteenth century, the wiregrass region of south-central and southeast Georgia was a country of pines, sand, wiregrass, and swamps. Into it the poor Crackers

3. *Op. cit.*, 176.
4. "The New Ruling Class of the South," *loc. cit.*, 207.

had been pushed by the great planters of the Black Belt
to the north and those of the coast to the east. Toward
the Florida line, Spanish moss, magnolias, and live oaks
began to appear. Here Louis Pendleton located his novel,
In the Wiregrass (1889), which contains one of the really
excellent backgrounds achieved by the local color
school. In this country of upturned hurricane roots and
white old logs, fallen before the storms of fargone years
and lying in the dry wiregrass, lived Mrs. Sophrony
Mathis with her Cracker household.

After Alice French ("Octave Thanet"), a Middle-
Westerner, had moved to Clover Bend, Arkansas, in the
Black River country, she brought into fiction a second
unfamiliar and picturesque locale of planters and poor-
white "renters." It was all ridges, cypress swamps, river-
bottoms, and cane brakes. During the Civil War, escaped
prisoners and, afterwards, runaway convicts had
"crouched among the sodden grasses," dreading the
time when the "cane would be crushed by the leaps of
the panting hounds." But Miss French employed
scenery with no more functionality than Miss Woolson.
Her best poor-white story, "The Mortgage of Jeffy,"
she told against a scenic sampler of autumnal color in
the Black River bottoms; whereas the chill-giving
miasmas of the lowlands which cause the heroine's
death were the sole descriptive need. To Alice French
as to Miss Woolson gorgeous swamp scenery was its
own excuse for being in fiction.

But it was in Louisiana, after the mid-eighties that
lovers of the picturesque were provided with a poor-
white locale to their liking: the Bayou Teche country,
the home of the Acadians or latter-day Cajuns. There,

Picturesque Backgrounds and the Cajuns

George W. Cable located his prose idyll, *Bonaventure* (1888). Before that book, America, fed upon Cable's fiction of New Orleans Creoles, had lost sight of the French Canadians since what M. Ditchy proclaims as "la description lamentable, lugubre de ce drame odieux, qu'en fait Longfellow dans *Evangeline*."[5] But once Cable had enchanted the public with his color re-creations of the Old French Quarter of New Orleans and the pastoral beauty of the Cajun country, Louisiana joined Virginia and Georgia as a literary center of the Southern Revival. By 1891, Alcée Fortier, a distinguished Creole scholar, observed that "everything concerning French Louisiana . . . seems to possess an interest for the public."[6] To satisfy this curiosity, Northern travelers, native commentators, and among writers, Cable and Kate Chopin, set before the United States a complete Cajun world, one that was at the same time a new sort of poor-white life in setting, nationality, language, and folkways.

Unlike other poor-whites, most of the Cajuns had settled in "the loveliest part of Louisiana," the Bayou Teche and the Attakapas prairie to the west.[7] In the early seventies, Edward King in *The Great South*, had written ecstatically of this region. But after Cable had delighted the nation with his stories, many sentimental journeys were made into the land of Evangeline by boat up the bayous and by carriage over the Attakapas and the Opelousas. In 1886, Major Burke, editor of the New Orleans *Times-Democrat*, took Charles A. Dana's party

5. J. K. Ditchy, *Les Acadiens Louisianais et leur parler*, 223.
6. "The Acadians of Louisiana and their Dialect," *Publications of the Modern Language Association* (1891), 64.
7. See Cable's description of part of it in *Bonaventure*.

of Northern visitors up the bayous to the Cajun country. On approaching a bankside settlement, a cannon (especially mounted on the launch for the occasion) was banged away to wake up "the sleepy *habitans* [sic] who rushed down to the landing to see what was the matter."[8] On deck the journalists danced with the supposed descendants of Evangeline and later at New Iberia halted to have sentimental thoughts on the bridge over the Bayou Teche. About the same year, both Charles Dudley Warner and Mrs. Rebecca Harding Davis hied thither. On the Teche, Warner found no "lack of the picturesque," and "the vast prairie,"[9] "dotted with small round ponds like hand-mirrors," reminded him of a green ocean whose long swells had begun to settle into a calm. Though perhaps even more tremulous than Warner in the midst of such beauty, Mrs. Davis excelled him in transferring the lush landscape to her pages; only Cable, indeed, has done better. She saw the Attakapas as "interminable plains of tall grass . . . webbed by a labyrinth of bayous and rigolets glittering like lanes of silver, and dotted here and there like blots of shadow with forests of hoary old trees . . . shrouded . . . with funeral moss."[10] The wind brought "gusts of the odor of magnolia or roses or jasmine," and "bent the grass in long furrows . . . but made no sound." Overhead buzzards wheeled and Gulf clouds shifted about letting through bright sunshine or casting quick shadows on the grass, in and out of which darted colored lizards.

In this green and pleasant land, the Acadian exiles

8. H. M. Field, *Blood is Thicker than Water*, 87.
9. "The Acadian Land," *Harper's Magazine*, LXXIV (Feb., 1887), 337-38.
10. Rebecca H. Davis, "Here and There in the South," *Harper's Magazine*, LXXV (Nov., 1887), 915.

had settled in 1766. Yet instead of persisting in the rather industrious ways of Nova Scotia, they had rested under their fig trees and lived a poor-white existence on whatever prodigal nature let fall into their laps. Perhaps, the loss of their Canadian homes had discouraged them in accumulating worldly goods. However that may have been, Cable stated most of the causes of their sluggardly life in *Bonaventure:* "In France their race had been peasants; in Acadia, forsaken colonists; in Massachusetts, Pennsylvania, Maryland, Virginia, exiles alien to the land, the language, and the times; in St. Domingo, penniless, sick, unwelcome refugees; and for just a century in Louisiana, the jest of the proud Creole, held down by the triple fetter of illiteracy, poverty, and competition of unpaid, half-clad, swarming slaves."[11]

And so, like the pineywoodsmen, the Cajuns lived apart in a little world of their own. After suffering exile for resisting the British in Nova Scotia, they had done with meddling in outside affairs. To be at ease, to have peace and contentment—that was best. So they became lazy and, eventually, decadent.

There can be no doubt, however, that before the Civil War, Cajun life was picturesque. Therefore, it had what the local colorists generally failed to see in poorwhites of English blood. These French-Americans had a charming *patois;* their peasant origin had provided them with quaint folkways and crafts; and their Latin natures were demonstrative and sentimental. On the bayous, at seasons filled with water-flowers, they fished in *pirogues,* made of logs, scooped out shallow and as

11. P. 101.

gracefully modeled as a half pea pod. They climbed high trees to cut away and throw down the moss which, when weather-rotted, they sold to mattress makers. Little patches of cane, sweet potatoes, corn, and cotton required little work; the ponies and cattle, none at all, since they grazed at large on the unfenced prairie. Naturally, the Cajuns had time to play, and they did so in frontier style, for the early Attakapas was a pastoral land of horsemen who were much like Texas cowboys or Argentine *gauchos* in garb. These "men in broad hats and dull homespun, with thin soft, untrimmed brown beards" loved the pony race, the cock fight, and the shooting match. But best of all, perhaps, was a stout bottle, poker, and a Saturday night dance—one that lasted until five in the morning, when the fiddlers went outside, fired a pistol, and shouted, "Le bal est fini!"[12]

This old life in the unpainted huts or *cabanas* was disrupted by the Civil War. General Richard Taylor, Louisiana planter and son of President Zachary Taylor, in whose command served many Cajuns, said that "upon this simple race . . . the war came like the tree of knowledge to our earthly parents." "Many an Acadian volunteer and many a poor conscript," declared Cable, "fought and fell for a cause that was really none of theirs, simple, non-slaveholding peasants." And again the author of *Old Creole Days* was correct in recording the effect on them of the war as well as the following commercial development of the South: The Cajuns were pulled into the circle of American life. In *Bona-*

12. *Bonaventure*, 6, 68; Fortier, *op. cit.*, 77-79; Kate Chopin, "At the Cadian Ball," *Bayou Folk.*

142

venture, the widow Zoséphine knew what had happened: "Yass, 'tis so," she said, "Dawn't see nobody seem satisfied—since de army—since de railroad." The open Cajun country was eventually fenced into farms; the pastoral age had passed. Then the English language and the public school, sewing machines, and Horsford's Acid Phosphate brought in the discontent of progress. And thus, as the Cajuns came into a new life of outside trade and education, the results of a century's isolation and decadence in Louisiana were first completely realized by keen observors; the "descendants of Evangeline" were poor-whites.[13]

Nor can there be any doubt that they were so regarded by Creoles, other whites, and Negroes. They had been, as Cable said, "the jest of the proud Creole" —the French aristocracy, who often had a word for the poorer Cajuns: "Canaille!"—that was their way of saying poor-white trash. Even a low white man like Bud Aiken in Kate Chopin's story, "In Sabine," would abuse his wife as one of "them Cajuns." In 1896, James Ralph, a Northern journalist, noted in his book, *Dixie*, that the Louisiana Negroes scorned the Cajuns "as the darkies elsewhere look down upon the 'poor whites.'" Indeed, this attitude was apparently so fixed that its expression became automatic. Aunt Mint in "A Rude Awakening," by Mrs. Chopin, shouted at a little Cajun girl: "Dah you is, settin' down, lookin' jis like w'ite folk!"

And as the tackies resented being called poor-whites,

13. Generally true of them; yet, as among the Georgia Crackers, occasional men of mark, like Alcibiade Le Blanc, who led the war on carpetbaggers, and Alexandre Mouton, Governor and Senator, came from the Cajuns. However, there were more poor-white Cajuns than any other sort.

so the Acadians raged at the word, *Cajun*. To James Ralph, "it was strange . . . to hear that we must not call them Cajun to their faces lest they be offended, that the term is taken as one of reproach." Kate Chopin used this feeling in her delightful story, "A Gentleman of the Bayou Teche." Evariste, a ragged, sorry Cajun, whom a painter had thought picturesque, agreed to sit for a portrait. But when a Negress, Aunt Dicey, said that the artist would write on the picture: "Dis heah is one dem low-down Cajuns o' Bayou Teche," he rebelled. Nor would he start posing until his own title was accepted by the painter. It ran: "Dis is one picture of Mista Evariste Anatole Bonamour, a gentleman of de Bayou Teche." As cruel as such class contempt always is, it indicated definitely that a great many of the Cajuns were what a traveler called them in 1866: "good representatives of the white trash."[14]

Yet long before that, the Acadians had a good start toward becoming "low down Cajuns"; even in Canada they were so ignorant that nearly all of them made their mark in signing the oath of allegiance.[15] And in 1803, a report to Thomas Jefferson on Louisiana stated that not more than half of the people could read and write.

More than that: besides the usual causes of such poor-white illiteracy in the old South, two others operated in Cajun-land: the barrier of the French language and the opposition of Roman Catholic priests to education. "Isolated up to the time of the war," wrote General Richard Taylor, "they spoke no language but their own

14. A. R. Waud, "Acadians of Louisiana," *Harper's Weekly*, X (Oct., 20, 1866), 670.
15. J. R. Ficklin, "Historical Sketch of the Acadians," *In Acadia*, ed. Margaret H. A. Johnson, 19.

patois; and, reading and writing not having come to them by nature, they were dependent for news on their curés and occasional peddlers, who tempted the women with chiffons and trinkets."[16] After the Louisiana purchase, the neglect of the Creoles gave way to the American task of making the Cajuns bilingual. In doing this, the schoolmen, Yankee or native, ran into hostility from the priesthood. One of the fathers told Mrs. Rebecca Davis in 1887 that the Cajuns were sweet, simple peasants: "Would you teach them 'progress,' politics, newspaper gossip, American ideas?" So long as these people remained ignorant and spoke only French the power of the church over them was safe. This fact Cable placed bluntly and courageously in *Bonaventure.* Therein, the priest who preached at a Cajun mission once a quarter attacked the new school taught in English: "Why do you Grande Pointe folk allow it?" he shouted. "Do you want your children stuffed full of American ideas? . . . to learn English is to learn free-thinking . . . You silly 'Cadians think your children are getting education. . . . Do you know what comes of it? Discontent. . . . It will soon be . . . goodbye to the faith of your fathers."

And with the advantage of these peasants' heritage of ignorance, the priest had temporary success when a crowd of Cajun fathers attempted futilely to close the school. "I t'ink dass all humbbug, dat titchin' English," said old Catou. Others agreed with St. Pierre in his words to Bonaventure, the schoolmaster: "You say ed'cation—priest say religion—me, I dawn't see neider one make no diff'ence."

16. Richard Taylor, *Destruction and Reconstruction,* 135.

The Southern Poor-White

Nor was Cable misrepresenting the pitiful illiteracy of this priest-ridden folk. In 1894, six years after *Bonaventure* had appeared, a Frenchman writing of the Cajuns "dans l'ignorance absolue" recorded as fact the attitude which Cable had illustrated: "L'éducation, disaient-ils, c'est beau, mais ça rend trop souvent l'homme canaille. J'ai pu gagner ma vie sans éducation, mes enfants en feront autant."[17] In Louisiana, their ignorance had long been a byword. Charles D. Warner's driver, an ex-Confederate soldier, expressed the popular opinion when he said "[they] don't known no more'n a dead alligator; only language they ever have is 'no' and 'what?'"

Along with ignorance and isolation, existed the usual shiftlessness and, oddly enough, poverty in the midst of plenty. When Dan'l Dennett, "a resident of the Gulf States more than thirty-four years," wrote his book, *Louisiana As It Is . . .*, in 1876, he referred to the Cajuns as "not a thrifty people."

"Many of them," he said, "are mere squatters. . . . Their houses often half framed and half built of mud . . . are . . . often without even a garden enclosed. . . . With thousands of cows roaming on the prairies, you seldom see butter and milk in their house. With the means around them of living well, they fare no better than the people who live on the poor lands."

In *Bonaventure*, Cable made the same charge and also presented Cajun Chaouache's family as discovered by the Confederate conscript officer: a barefooted lot, the wife and girls in dingy homespun dresses like pillow-

17. L. F. Peytavin in *L'Athenee Louisianais* (1894) as quoted by J. K. Ditchy, *op. cit.*, 247.

slips. But it was Kate Chopin, a St. Louis woman, long a resident of Louisiana, who best etched the shiftless Cajun, especially in two stories. In "A Rude Awakening," Sylvestre Bordoin, whom his daughter, Lolotte, called "de lazies' man in Natchitoches pa'ish," always went fishing when any work was mentioned. More worthless still was Arsène Pauché in "Azélie." Ordinarily living with "that triflin' Li'le river gang," he at times deceived some planter into taking him as a tenant, for Arsène now and then hankered after sugar, *café noir*, and *perique* tobacco from the commissary. He merely went through the motions of making a crop in order to keep his credit at the store. When there was no more coffee and tobacco for Arsène, he bundled his family off to the river, crop or no crop.

Still, it was not only this prevalent shiftlessness among the Cajuns that led to decadence; their isolation proved to be disastrous. In 1875, Edward King declared that they were very likely victimized by political sharpers in the way that the Creole scholar, Charles Gayarré, had demonstrated in his novel, *The School for Politics* (1854). The most serious consequence, however, of their isolation was inbreeding. Clannish by nature and held together by persecution and outside contempt, the Cajuns allowed kin to marry kin until the state of Louisiana had to pass the "first cousin" law forbidding such unions. A. R. Waud, an artist traveling in Louisiana in 1866, noted that "by dint of intermarriage" of blood relations the Cajuns were "down in the social scale." Thirty years later, James Ralph, puzzled at the heaviness and uncouthness of Cajun faces, guessed that these were the result of marriages with Indians. But although Cable records one such marriage, the paramount fact in the decay of this French-American peasantry was inbreeding. However, the literature of the nineteenth century said nothing about it; that was reserved for the twentieth.

What did primarily interest writers like Cable and Mrs. Chopin in the Cajuns was their picturesque community life and their Latin natures. Yet both authors in dealing with them were more than local colorists.

In Cable, the itch to propagandize, that eventually ruined him as an artist, asserted itself as early as 1888 in *Bonaventure*. This, of course, was partly sentimental special pleading. He condemned those who viewed "these illiterate and lowly ones" as "dull and insensible" of ordinary emotions and thereby made "these people extremely offensive." Yet Cable's plea was not all sentiment; he stated boldly the causes of Cajun poverty and ignorance, placing the blame exactly where it belonged. All of this, he mixed with the love story of Bonaventure, a Creole orphan, reared among the Cajuns, who became a schoolmaster, laboring for the uplift of his adopted people.

By credo, though less by practice, Kate Chopin was no local colorist; certainly, she eschewed propaganda. In reviewing *Crumbling Idols*, by Hamlin Garland, in 1894, she delivered herself of the opinion that "social problems ... by their very nature are mutable ... social environment, local color, and all the rest of it are not of themselves sufficient motives to insure the survival of the writer who employs them." And Zola's work she considered a "mass of prosaic data, offensive and

nauseous description and rampant sentimentality."[18]
Like the later James Lane Allen, Mrs. Chopin joined
the movement away from local color and propaganda
toward a purer art.

And, for the interpretation of the Cajun, this was
fortunate; inasmuch as ten stories in her volumes,
Bayou Folk (1894) and *A Night in Acadie* (1897), concern poor-whites and constitute an even wider view of
them than that in Cable's novel. Besides, her fictional
emphasis was different. She concentrated upon the
emotions called forth, both by the French natures and
by the daily grooves and conditions of the Cajuns. The
description of the locale of her Cajun stories around and
west of Natchitoches—a pine and cotton country to
the north of Cable's Bayou Teche—was to her unimportant in comparison with the making of an artistic
record of Cajun sentiments. And, be it said to her
credit, that, more often than any other writer in the
Southern Revival, she kept sentiment from melting
into sentimentality. As a result, her Cajuns, though
displayed on their quaint and sweeter sides, are not
merely picturesque types in a pastoral such as *Bonaventure*, but humble human beings, feeling and thinking
according to long-set patterns. Consequently, at the
end of nearly every story, Mrs. Chopin crystallized the
feeling which she had already built up beforehand.
Emotional reality—that was her primary concern.

And this she might have achieved in tragedy had
public taste been different. But Kate Chopin, a widow
with a family to support, knew that the market de-

18. *St. Louis Life*, Oct. 6, 1894, as quoted by Daniel S. Rankin, *Kate Chopin and her
Creole Stories*, 143-45.

manded sentiment, comedy, and at least a few dashes
of local color. As a result, she used tragic elements
merely to give a glow to sentiment. In *"A Visit to
Avoyelle,"* Doudouce went to see his old love, Mentine,
now the misshapen, shrill-voiced mother of six, living
desperately on a worn-out farm. Yet when the old
lover started home, he realized that Mentine was
watching not him, but her sorry husband going back
to the plough-tail. Lalie, the heroine of "Love on the
Bon Dieu," "slender with a frailness that indicated a
lack of wholesome and plentiful nourishment," had "a
pathetic uneasy look—in her gray eyes." When she
crossed the churchyard after mass, the Cajuns who were
better off whispered: "She's real canaille, her," because
Lalie lived near the swamp with a half-crazy grand-
mother in a cabin which even the darkies had refused
to rent. Nevertheless, Azenor, a young carpenter, found
that love could level ranks and therefore married her.
Such typical narratives show that Mrs. Chopin evaded
the tragic implications of her material.

Nevertheless, within the province of comedy and
sentiment, she penned three short stories of poor-white
life that were unsurpassed until the advent of Erskine
Caldwell. And even today, they stand apart as faultless
art records of poor-whites who happened to be French.
In the two and a half pages of "Boulôt and Boulotte,"
Kate Chopin left a comic miniature of Cajun childhood.
The twelve-year-old-twins, Boulôt and Boulotte, having
saved money enough for a first pair of shoes, started for
Natchitoches and were watched out of sight by the
whole troop of younger children. Toward sundown, the
watchers, having again assembled to see the new shoes

E. W. Kemble in "Century Magazine," 1887

Cajun Fathers at the Schoolhouse

Cajun Fathers at the Schoolhouse

coming down the road, were sorely disappointed: they saw the twins carrying the shoes in their hands. All go into the cabin crestfallen—that is, all except haughty Boulotte and the "littlest" Cajun in arms who did not care.

Even better were the portraits of two girls. Azélie was neither exceptional nor pretty. Only her dark, wide eyes redeemed her face, colorless except for her lips. Her hair, "plastered back," was usually covered by a pink sunbonnet. Listless and indifferent, most of the time she let silence serve to say "no." She was a true daughter of Arsène Pauché, a trifling tenant when he was not a river rat. Like her tribe, she had no sense of property rights. Naturally enough, when Polyte, the overseer in love with her, but ashamed of the fact, caught her one night in the plantation store filching goods, she was not sorry, but resentful. "I was'n steal-in," she cried, "I was jus' takin' a few lil' things you all was too mean to gi' me." No matter how much her father overlooked the fact that he was supposed to farm, she resented the cutting off of his store credit. Like all low white tenants, she became furious when the planter rewarded one of his hard-working Negroes with a new buckboard. She would gladly steal to get her mistreated "poppa" his dram and *perique* tobacco. Naturally enough, when Arsène decided to rejoin the shanty trash on the river, Azélie refused to stay on the plantation and marry the overseer. If Polyte wanted her, he would have to quit his job and take up a river life. After many restless nights, he did so.

"In Sabine" is Mrs. Chopin's story of 'Tite Reine, a gay, illiterate girl of Natchitoches parish, who had eloped with the roving, drunken Texan, Bud Aiken. After this, 'Tite's life had been one backwoods clearing after another in three parishes; now Bud swore that "Sabine's a damn sight worse than any of 'em. . . . I'm fixin to sell out an' try Vernon." And so, when an old acquaintance, Gregoire Sentien, chanced upon the Aiken cabin, 'Tite poured out her woes to him. Bud had treated her like a dog, forced her to pick cotton while he lay around drunk, and put her on his bucking mustang to laugh at her being thrown. Worse than that: "I tell you," 'Tite Reine whispered to Gregoire. "He beats me; my back and arms—you ought to see—it's all blue." Among Bud's other joys was telling her that a drummer had married them as a joke and that when he got to Vernon Parish he intended to "turn her loose." Besides all of this, the lonesomeness of the piney-woods was driving 'Tite distracted: "It's no pos' office, it's no relroad,—nothin' in Sabine." Yet mail service really meant nothing; for being unable to write, she had no way of sending her parents word to come for her. No wonder, 'Tite Reine, lost in the pinelands, crawled in the dark to Gregoire's pallet on the porch and convinced him that he should take her away. One morning, Bud discovered that he had no wife, no mustang, and no guest.

Azélie and 'Tite Reine, along with Lalie in "Love on the Bon-Dieu," stand out as the only memorable poor-white girls created during the Southern Revival. Also, in so far as their lives are mixtures of sentiment and fairly sordid conditions, they assume added significance as literary ancestors of the tenant women depicted by Paul Green and other sensibilists in the next century.

Alice French and Her Arkansas Rednecks

To the literature of Cajun life, Cable contributed pastoral background, folkways, and propaganda; Kate Chopin, the emotional values of these facts presented by Cable.

VII. NATURALISTIC MATERIAL AND LOCAL-COLOR METH- OD: ALICE FRENCH AND HER ARKANSAS REDNECKS

B UT of all the writers of the eighties and nineties, Alice French advanced the poor-white furthest towards naturalism. Harris created the pathetic Bud Stucky; Page, the heroic Little Darby; Johnston, the humorous "O.J.G."; and Cable and Kate Chopin, the pastoral and shiftless Cajuns. But all of these were idealizations, or at least no more than current "realism," that is, factual backgrounds and narratives of sentiment or romance. Alice French, also this sort of realist, was something else; she was a social propagandist.[1] As such, she re-introduced the poor-white in his rôle of violence and immorality. By doing so, she placed her six pieces about the Arkansas rednecks in a class by themselves in this period.

As one might expect, Alice French's fiction about the poorest Arkansans is contradictory. In local color technique she is the twin sister of Miss Woolson. Nor did she become less misty-eyed over Cracker halfwits than Harris and Johnston. Indeed, "a little child shall lead them" served her as the theme of three stories about the rednecks. But this sentimentality was largely the natural result of her experience and consequent view-point.

1. In the early 1880's she wrote politico-economic articles; others about the working classes in 1896; a volume of labor stories, *Heart of Toil* (1898).

The Southern Poor-White

Spending her winters in the Black River country of Arkansas, Miss French, a Middlewesterner, looked upon the renters and croppers about her plantation house both like a hunter of the picturesque and like a neighborly social worker. She liked to imagine that the ragged croppers near her place were descendants of noble French families and that French blood, with perhaps a dash of Spanish, had given to them physiques resembling those of the Canadian *habitants*. For readers of the *Atlantic Monthly* in July, 1891, she hymned "Plantation Life in Arkansas." "A poor man in this country," she said, "whatever he lacks has air, space, and beauty." Furthermore, he "misses the cankerfret of envy, the suffocation of merciless crowds." She joyed in being friends with the croppers, whom she regarded "as individuals, not as 'the poor.' " And finally, she lamented the coming time when "the country will be so well drained that it cannot even summon an old-time chill."

But occasionally Miss French had to believe her eyes. The renter of "grave imperturbability" and "stoical soul" had, she thought, as "the keynote of his existence . . . a patient endurance of avoidable evils." She saw also that the renter's living was "often a bare and gaunt one" and that he usually buried from three to five wives.[2]

Yet sentimental great lady and neighbor though she was, Miss French managed to indicate much of poor-white violence and thereby made a notable advance toward naturalism. Not since DeForest's ironic story of Selnarten Bowen had a writer dwelt upon this always

2. "The Farmer in the South," *Scribner's Magazine*, XV (Apr., 1894), 402.

present aspect of the low-downers. Their depravity, which always produced acts of knuckle, knife, and gun, had been reported by Harris and Page, but they dramatized no such deeds. This omission was corrected somewhat by Alice French in two volumes of short stories: *Knitters in the Sun* (1887) and *Otto the Knight*. . . . . (1891), and one novel, *Expiation* (1891). Of course, the author did this after the fashion of sweetened local-color manner, yet in contrast with other works of the Southern Revival the result was striking.

Instead of presenting the poor-whites in the Civil War as pathetic or comic deserters and heroic Little Darbys, in *Expiation* she displayed them as pillaging guerillas or graybacks. In "The Farmer in the South" she described the activities of the guerilla bands and their cruelties: "The outlaws tormented men by fire, pouring hot coals down their backs or slowly roasting them; twice they pulled out a man's nails . . . .The result was that they were hunted down and exterminated like wolves." Such atrocities she attributed to the poor white weaklings and degenerates who largely made up the outlaw bands in her novel. However, the only member sketched separately is Lige, a hireling murderer, who repented his crimes on his death bed.

In formula, this novel follows the Simms border romance: a love story of planter folk imperiled by fierce outlaws. Lige is merely Ben Pickett of *Richard Hurdis* sentimentalized. Nevertheless, in the late nineteenth century, *Expiation* remains significant in the literary story of the poor-white, first, as the re-creation of the historical fact that poor-whites in wartime

scoured the South in guerilla bands, and second, as a
record of their bestial cruelty. But, according to the
stories of Miss French, these Arkansans of the Black
River canebrakes did not lay aside violence after the
war. In "Whitsun Harp, Regulator,"[3] the hero was
"called" at a camp-meeting to regulate the morals of
his neighborhood. This he carried out by "licking"
wrongdoers, until one of them shot him from ambush.
But these people would pull a trigger over lesser matters.
Dock Haskett fired at Luther Morrow's dog as it dragged
a ham from Dock's smokehouse. Somehow, part of the
buckshot went into Luther's leg. Later, in a swamp,
Dock and Luther were preparing to shoot it out when
the sweet sight of their little girls, Mizzie and Doshy,
playing house caused them to forgive and forget. Thus,
in "The Loaf of Peace,"[4] Miss French had an initial
situation for comedy that would serve Erskine Caldwell;
instead she used it for a heart-throb.

The author's work points most clearly, however, to
the naturalistic material of the twentieth century in
"Trusty, No. 49," a story of homicide and penal abuses.
Definitely belonging to the literature of social reform,
the narrative was aimed at convict-leasing in Arkansas,
the inhumane practices on the chain-gangs, and the
perversion of justice. As an indictment of the Southern
penal system, her story may be considered the forerunner of such later books as *I Am a Fugitive From a
Georgia Chain-Gang* (1932).

How much Miss French differed from her predecessors
and contemporaries may be noted in this story. The

3. From *Knitters in the Sun.*
4. *Otto the Knight,* 160-80.

156

initial situation is that used for a joke by T. W. Lane in the "Thimble Game" (1847) and by Molly E. M. Davis for sentimental humor in "The Elephant's Track" (1897): the poor-white "rube" cheated out of his money by a town sharper. In "Trusty, No. 49,"[5] the Arkansas tenant shot the gambler. At his trial, one of the jurymen, hitherto unknown to his neighbors as an ex-convict, declared that "in the present state of convicts in Arkansas, if you don't find this man not guilty, you had better find him guilty enough to be hanged." Then he told of his life as a convict on the chain-gang, describing the swamp stockade, sixteen by twenty, in which thirty-three men lay chained on water-soaked mattresses. The "awful steam rising up from the swamp" soon had all the convicts "chilling," yet the leasers demanded that the guards drive the sick men to work. One of them having become insane was killed by the guard, supposedly in self-defense. A note smuggled to the outside by the narrator, then Trusty No. 49, brought about an investigation and temporary reform. But the juror continued: the gambler killed by the poor-white tenant on trial was the murderous guard. Of course, the prompt verdict was "not guilty."

A tract for the times, "Trusty No. 49," stands alone in its attack upon the vicious circle set up by the bestiality of the chain-gang. Rarely have any but the poorest Southern whites been so disgraced as to serve in this penal group with Negroes. To work on the roads in stripes and with blacks has been and is the poor-white's ultimate shame. And because of the average Southern juror's horror of thus destroying the

5. *Ibid.*, 216-61.

last bit of self-respect, even of a poor-white, he perverts justice and encourages violence. Alice French wrote the sad truth.

No less important than these glimpses of violent rednecks in the Black River country was the author's introduction of a new group: the roving bands of cotton pickers. And she did not blink at the loose ways of these "movers." Sabrina Matthews, known as "Headlights" because of her bright eyes, is the promiscuous heroine of "The Mortgage of Jeffy" (1891).[6] She is also the first immoral poor-white woman to appear in fiction since Mrs. Bony Mulock.

No trashier trash existed than these cotton pickers. Even the croppers and tenants thought them "mighty onery folks." After the pickers swarmed into a community, every theft and misdemeanor was laid upon them. That the shacks and sheds furnished them were no longer fit even for Negroes showed what Arkansas farmers thought of them. And, with a little money ahead, on Christmas Day, the pickers became a "howling mob" of cavorting drunks. Living desperately on seasonal wages, they usually had poor health. "Cotton pickers," said one old woman, "never had no ruggedness."

In shuttling about the cotton country in these gangs, "Headlights" had given birth to a bastard that she packed around with her. When the story opens, she had "taken up with" another picker who did not want any "boot." To please him, she hid the baby under the counter of the plantation store and "lit a shuck" for other parts. After her man had plied her with a hickory stick and she had cowed him with a knife,

6. *Ibid.*

158

she returned for her child, only to find that a recently bereaved mother had taken it. How under pressure "Headlights" "mortgaged" little Jeffy to the woman for twenty-seven dollars, worked and starved to save that amount, and finally died from the exposure of bringing the money to reclaim the boy brings the story to a tearful close of self-renunciation.

With a perfect factual background for naturalism, Miss French, like Page, told a story of sentiment. Nor is she less romantic than the Virginian in presenting "Headlights," a loose-living picker from a group—by the author's own statements—characterized by anemia, drunkenness, and free sex-life. "Headlights" was "a tall woman, whose wild beauty could not be obscured by her wretched dress . . . Her battered hat shaded a bold profile, cut cleanly, like the head on a Roman coin. . . . She was as graceful and unconscious as a panther."

From this woman to the cotton-patch strumpet of Erskine Caldwell is a far cry; yet the living original of both is the same. Neither Miss French nor the time was prepared to be frank about roving pickers.

In retrospect, the contribution of the period from the late sixties to 1900 reveals some of the literature about poor-whites following pre-war channels. Tourgée extended the life of the older Northern interpretation; Thomas Nelson Page perpetuated the plantation view of Kennedy; the old humor of Longstreet lingered in a story of R. M. Johnston; and the border romance of Simms found late expression in *Expiation* by Alice French.

There were, however, important divergences. A central fact in the literature about poor-whites during the Southern Revival was that the tackies were sentimentalized in a new way. Before the Civil War, abolitionist novelists had specialized in pathetic po' buckra as a means of causing readers to hate the planters. But Hildreth's Jimmie Gordon and Trowbridge's Dan Pepperill, pitiful as they are, do not elicit affection, but repulsion. On the other hand, Southern authors in the Revival, when occasionally they left off parading colonels and old "darkies," set their hands to making their poor-whites not only pitiable, but likable.[7]

Such a literary intention precluded the more sordid and tragic aspects of Cracker life. These, thought Southern authors, had been emphasized enough by abolitionists; it was, therefore, entirely legitimate to balance the picture by representing the more normal side of these drab people: the emotions and affections common to all men, but colored by their status. Harris, Page, Cable, and others insisted upon viewing their unfortunate fellow Southerners as human beings, not as mere symbols of economic wrong. Nor did they care to see them as comic dirt-eaters or lecherous Mrs. Mulocks.

The results of this attitude, however, were not irredeemably bad. Discount, as one must, the lachrymose themes of reconciliation, the decorative picturesqueness, and the current prudery in detail, still from this fiction there emerge characters of such uncommon reality as to force the conclusion that Southerners

7. Henry S. Canby's statement that, aside from the artistic shortcomings of the local-color story, its "service to curiosity and the broadening of human sympathies, has been immense," may be fittingly applied to the poor-white (*Short Story in English*, 321). For similar earlier opinions, see Gertrude Atherton, "Geographical Fiction," *Lippincott's Magazine*, I (July, 1892), 112-14; T. W. Higginson, "The Local Short Story," *Independent*, XLIV (Nov. 3, 1892), 1544-45.

wrote better than they knew; their immersion in the native achieved for them a partial, unstudied success. Otherwise, there is no accounting for Harris' Mrs. Feratia Bivins and the Stuckys, or Johnston's O.J.G. or Kate Chopin's Azélie and 'Tite Reine.

Besides this, during the eighties and nineties, the poor-white in literature made several gains. The period had filled out his backgrounds, added the Florida Cracker and the Louisiana Cajun to his company, devoted to him many short stories and the first novel, Cable's *Bonaventure*, whereas earlier he had in the main been used incidentally or in short sketches.

However, no marked change in the literary conception of him occurred until far past the turn of the century; the pathetic Cracker introduced by Harris remained the dominant type throughout the period. In *Northern Georgia Sketches* (1900), Will Harben, the last significant Georgian of the local-color era, included four stories which "speak the idiom of the soil" with more flavor than any written about the poor-whites in the later nineteenth century.[8] Yet the blight of sentimentality is upon them, as one titled, "The Tender Link," abundantly proves. Indeed, Harben may stand for all of the later writers in localism.[9]

Little wonder, then, that the Southern Revival was "a backward glance over traveled roads" and consequently failed to deal with the contemporary plight of farmers and poor-whites in Dixie. No fiction writer of any importance told what had happened to the poor-

8. See W. D. Howell's praise of this fact: "Harben's Georgia fiction," *North American Review*, CXCI (March, 1910), 356-63.

9. Typical examples: Matt Crim, "An 'Onfortunist' Creeter," *Century Magazine*, XXXI (Feb., 1886), 582-88; Ruth M. Stuart, "Bud Zant's Mail," *Harper's Magazine*, LXXXVIII (Dec., 1893), 58-70; Opie Read, *An Arkansas Planter*.

whites since Reconstruction or hinted that unrest and populism were among them or chronicled the rise of demagogues like Ben Tillman of South Carolina on the bony shoulders of the "woolhat boys." Only Sidney Lanier spoke out in literature. In a few dialect poems[10] and "Corn" (1875), an effective adaptation of eighteenth century landscape verse to the purposes of economic parable and propaganda, he warned his fellow-Georgians on the land of the evils that have since made poor-whites of so many of them. Sidney Lanier saw there were Jeeter Lesters to come.

But neither the Georgia poet nor any other writer of the century could have been expected to deal tragically with the sordid aspects of lower Crackerdom as displayed, for example, by J. R. Gilmore in "The Sum of the Whole" (1866). Page, Harris, and Alice French—all tried varieties of tragic approach. The age denied them achievement, the age asked only for pathos. The timid use of naturalistic material by Alice French in "The Mortgage of Jeffy" and "Trusty, No. 49" represented the limit of license. The sordid tragedy of the poor-white had to wait until public taste could stand it; that came about over a decade after the World War. Not until two hundred years after Byrd's lubbers and over sixty after Gilmore's Mrs. Bony Mulock did fiction achieve the frankness allowed in magazine articles.

10. "Thar's More in the Man Than in the Land," "Jones's Private Argymint," "Nine from Eight."

CHAPTER FOUR

AMERICA MAKES THE POOR-WHITE A CAUSE AND A LITERARY VOGUE

THE STORY OF THE POOR-WHITE SINCE RECONSTRUC-
tion may be told briefly: overtaken by settlement
and forced into the Southern agronomy, he became a
tenant or, worse, a sharecropper.[1] Yet it is necessary to
recount some particulars of how this new status proved
to be a *cul de sac*, more tragic than anything in his
earlier history; and out of it, he has failed to escape
despite two definite efforts. Otherwise, most of the
literature about the contemporary poor-white, especially that of critical realism and naturalism, the result,
in part, of economic pressure, cannot be fully appre-
ciated.

I. TENANT AND SHARECROPPER: THE CONTEMPORARY POOR-WHITE

THE ever-encroaching development of natural resources and settlement finally caught up with the
descendant of William Byrd's lubber, Little Darby, and
the squatter or hunter-fisher-farmer like Davy Crockett.
Even his favorite haunt was invaded when sanitoria for
"lungers" arose in the pinelands; rich men fenced in or
land-posted the country as game preserves; and the
lumber companies reduced the woods to wastelands,

---

1. Tenant: one who rents a farm paying cash or cotton and furnishing his own stock
and machinery; sharecropper (sometimes called "cropper"): one who supplies only his labor
and that of his family for a share of the crops.

The Southern Poor-White

which seemed to William Faulkner in *Light in August*
"a stump-pocked scene of profound and peaceful deso-
lation . . . gutting slowly into red and choked ravines
beneath the long quiet rains of autumn." And here were
the rotting shacks of deserted sawmill villages "not even
remembered by the hookwormridden-heirs-at-large who
pulled the buildings down and burned them in their
cookstoves and winter grates." The dead end of this
natural and human tragedy John Peale Bishop chanted
in his poem, "Southern Pines":

> *Cut pine, burnt pine,*
> *The fourth man's eyes burned in starvation,*
> *Bone-back cattle, razor-back hogs*
> *Achieve the seedling, end the pinewoods.*

This typical American rape of the land spelled the end
of freedom for many poor-whites. Only in the most
remote swamps or places like the Florida scrub could
the squatter make his "deadnin" as of old. And even
there the arm of the law reached him at will. Trapped
by society, this "white Indian" could no longer "sign
off," as Henry Thoreau would say, from the outside
world of work. He had to "join up," and he did so by
moving from his backwoods cabin to a sharecropper's
hut.

Yet the poor-white (as well as many small farmers)
who owned a few acres or perhaps at the breaking up of
the plantations had added to them, more often than not,
came to the same end. This Henry Grady explained in
his prophetic article, "Cotton and Its Kingdom,"[2]

2. *Harper's Magazine*, LXIII (Oct., 1881), 719 ff.

Tenant and Sharecropper

belaboring the new agricultural system that "threatened re-absorption of the small farmer." Its greatest evil, he rightly saw, was credit. After the failure of planters following the immediate post-war boom and slump in cotton prices and the consequent withdrawal of many from planting, the banks cut down their agricultural loans, considering the new farmers too small to justify credit. In this exigency, the vicious system of farm finance arose: commission merchants borrowed money from banks and loaned to storekeepers who made loans to farmers usually in the form of supplies on which a rate of over fifty per cent interest was originally charged. To protect himself, the storekeeper demanded a large cash crop of cotton. Consequently, what with enforced one-crop farming, the introduction of improved machinery,[3] the expense of commercial fertilizer, and the low prices of cotton— the poor-white (as well as other farmers) soon mortgaged himself into sharecropper estate. Sidney Lanier not only told this story in his poem, "Corn," but in 1880 warned the small farmers of the South that, after escaping the planter monopoly, they were headed for another form of "control": corporation farming[4]— a prophecy to some extent fulfilled in the Southern Delta. Because of various influences the tenant and the cropper have had little chance of escape from this economic trap. Aside from the credit system and the world conditions of the "poverty crop," most of these influences have to do with the Negro.

Even the wretched health of the tenant, which has

3. Herbert Agar, *The People's Choice*, 231.
4. "The New South," *Scribner's Monthly*, XX (Oct., 1880), 840-51.

made him "no 'count" and unambitious, is to be traced, in part, directly to African slaves who planted in Southern soil the scourge of the poor-white: hookworm. For perhaps a century, hookwormed descendants of Ransy Sniffle have been eating dirt and subsisting on sowbelly, sorghum, and corn pone, compounding their listlessness with each generation until by the twentieth century, thirty-nine per cent of the Southern rural white children examined by the Rockefeller Commission for the Extermination of the Hookworm Disease proved to be victims of the "big lazy."[5] Add to this malady, undernourishment and the other curse of the poor-white, malaria; then one need not wonder why so many Southern croppers have been too trifling to become landowners.

Equally tragic is the presence of the color line, splitting the tenant class and rendering it incapable of group action. Once the poor-white's relation to his Freedman competitor had been fixed during the Reconstruction, he was lost economically. "On many a lonely highway," wrote William G. Brown in 1902, "they pass each other. . . . They stare at each other in helpless antagonism. . . ."[6] This feeling has been intensified, for many planters prefer the hardier and more resourceful Negro tenants because they will work for less and are easier to manage; that is, few blacks will dare to question the accounting of the landlord. Thus, while California farmers have been protected somewhat from the ruinous competition of the Japanese, the Southern cropper for over a half century has been debased economically and socially by the presence of his Negro

5. R. B. Vance, *op. cit.*, 282, 384.
6. W. G. Brown, *Lower South in American History*, 251.

rival. Living on the level of the blacks, doing the same work, being treated in much the same way by the landlord, the poor-white tenant has felt even more degraded than he did during slavery times; for then he could stay in the backlands away from humiliation.

Worse still: the race prejudice underlying the economic rivalry between the white and black tenants, which, of course, redounds to the planter's advantage, has been kept at high temperature by Negro-baiting demagogues.[7] By scaring the "one-gallus" tenants with what Walter Hines Page called the ghost of Negro domination, the Vardamans, Hoke Smiths, and Bilbos have preserved the absolute power of the "white man's party"[8] and thereby prevented any concerted political action by the croppers, tenants, and poor farm owners.

Yet despite such fanning of race prejudice with its inevitable flattery in the doctrine of "white supremacy," the tenant has been without political recourse, for even his political "leaders" have betrayed him. Ever since Andrew Jackson's era, every Southern office seeker has had to pose as "the plain man's friend" and "the farmer's friend." But in the nineties, when Populism became a political force in the South, the poor-whites, thinking that at last they had a party, flocked to its standard-bearers. And no state in Dixie had so promising a farmer's champion as South Carolina. "Ben Tillman," wrote Ludwig Lewisohn, "led the revolt of the agrarians, the 'poor-white trash,' the 'wool hats' of the 'upper country' against the old Charlestonian aristoc-

7. A. B. Hart, *The Southern South*, 160.

8. For an excellent account of Vardaman, the "most brutal negrophobe," and others of his stripe, see Virginius Dabney, *Liberalism in the South*, chap. xiv.

racy. He won. The time-spirit was with him."[9] But, as
W. W. Ball in his spirited defence of the Charleston and
Wade Hampton regime claimed, Tillman won by setting
"ablaze the worse passions in plain men's hearts."
From his "brass throat" poured such harangues of class
hatred that his woolhat followers howled down opposing
speakers and hurled clods at them. In the end, the poor-
white—as usual—got nothing and "plowed on"; Gov.
Tillman was glorifying himself by building two state
colleges which few if any children of his tenant sup-
porters could attend. And Tillmanism has been the
story of the "woolhat boys" in politics ever since.

Yet once more they attempted to relax the economic
pressure in order to obtain a livable existence. This time
they did not try politics. Instead they adopted the
method of industrial labor. In Arkansas the weight of
poverty became so great that, for the first time in
Southern history, croppers, white and black, realizing
their common plight, formed a local organization which
in 1934 became the Southern Tenant Farmers' Union.[10]

This seemed to presage great things. But the poor-
white never has any luck: his saviors, both at home and
above the Line, have usually brought him to grief. As
if the struggling Union did not have enough opposition
locally, socialist and communist deliverers swarmed into
Arkansas and injected the issues of race and com-
munism into the situation, thereby tainting the Union
in Southern eyes and destroying much of its usefulness
for years to come. For the zeal of visiting "comrades"

9. "South Carolina, A Lingering Fragrance," in *These United States*, ed. by Ernest
Gruening, I, 84.
10. A first-hand account: C. T. Carpenter, "King Cotton's Slaves," *Scribner's Magazine*,
XCVIII (Oct., 1935), 193-99.

Tenant and Sharecropper

gave to enemies of the Union the perfect excuses of "nigger-love" and "Red Russianism" by which might be justified acts of intimidation and violence—acts which enabled our contemporary outrage-mongers to equal their Reconstruction forebears. Naturally the planting class resented this new-abolitionist portrait; Joel Chandler Harris' South, "the galled jade," balked once more. And the tenant union was the loser.

It was natural, therefore, that, as the poor-white entered the 1930's, completely pocketed economically, the increasing awareness[11] of his tragedy in the preceding decade culminated in a frank, critical, and sometimes pessimistic literature.

II. POOR-WHITE AND THE SECOND LITERARY REVIVAL IN THE SOUTH

TOWARD the middle 1920's the literary region of productivity shifted from the Middle West to the South as it had done in the 1880's from the West.[1] During the decade following the World War some three hundred volumes of various kinds by Southern authors were issued by national publishers. By 1927, Herschell Brickell felt safe in prophesying "that the Renaissance is only beginning." Indeed, a section that could produce novels like James Branch Cabell's *Jurgen* (1919), Ellen Glasgow's *Barren Ground* (1925), and Elizabeth

11. A typical Southern reaction fifty years ago was to deny to outsiders the existence of "any poor-whites" ("Studies in the South," *Atlantic Monthly*, XLIX, Jan., 1882, 80); in 1910, the South was "little awakened" to the poor-white problem (A. B. Hart, *op. cit.*, 244-45); by 1929, the discussion of the farmer in congress and in the press "catapulted [him] into the public consciousness" (Anon. *Sat. Rev. of Lit.*, VI, July 27, 1929, 1, 4); after 1933, the flood of articles about sharecroppers began.

1. Herschell Brickell, "The Literary Awakening of the South," *Bookman*, LXVI (Oct., 1927), 138.

The Southern Poor-White

Madox Robert's *The Time of Man* (1926); a play like
DuBose Heyward's *Porgy* (1927); and poetry like that
of John Crowe Ransom and others of the *Fugitive* group,
might well be said to be in revival.

True to past literary history, in this "outpouring of
books by Southern writers," the Negro characters out-
numbered all other local ones, as was the case in the
eighties. Literature in the South as well as trouble seems
to start with the "darky." T. S. Stribling's *Birthright*
(1921), DuBose Heyward's *Porgy* (1925) in novel form,
Julia Peterkin's *Black April* (1927), and Paul Green's
In Abraham's Bosom (1927) are merely examples of the
flood of Negro books in the twenties. But Negro life of
the folk sort being a shallow literary vein soon worked
out, writers like Heyward and Green either deserted
the field or devoted less time to it.

And so, once more in literature the poor-white got
his inning after the John Henrys, Porgys, and Scarlet
Sister Marys. But to explain how this came about, it is
essential to follow the converging of popular and literary
interest upon him.

Various matters, some of them annual, have served
to keep the poor-white in the public eye almost since
the turn of the century. Of these, perhaps the most
dramatic was the announcement by Dr. C. W. Stiles in
1902 that he had discovered the cause of a great menace
to health among the rural poor of the South—hookworm
or *Necator Americanus* (American murderer) as he
called it before its African origin was known. This "poor
man's malady," Dr. Stiles showed, was most pronounced
in the sandy poor-white areas and caused dirt-eating
and bloated stomachs; in fact, all of the abnormalities

of Longstreet's Ransy Sniffle were at last explained. Newspapers and journals played up the sensational discovery[2] as "the germ of laziness" and the "vampire of the South." Nor could the hookworm surveys of the Rockefeller Commission have had an abler promoter and more thoughtful advertiser than Walter Hines Page.[3]

Three other events in quick succession have exposed the wretchedness of the croppers. From reports of the press and of the Red Cross, America learned in picture and story what the Mississippi floods of 1927 and 1930 in the Southern cotton country meant to tenants, especially when closely followed by the drought of 1931.[4] Their plight, both physical and economic, was thrown into bold relief by utter destitution.

But some reminders of our contemporary poor-whites have become regular and uniform enough to be called traditional. On the appearance of each illiteracy report always with the eleven Southern states showing the highest percentages and one of them with a large tenant class, such as South Carolina or Mississippi, leading the nation, the Negroes and then the poor-whites are hauled out by apologists to excuse Southern illiteracy. Nor is illiteracy an isolated matter of note. Not a year has passed since Emancipation that the press with its horror stories of Southern lynchings did not remind the public of the section's illiterates. For tenancy, illiteracy, and lynchings are a social trinity;[5] the areas of rope and

2. See Mark Sullivan, *Our Times* (New York, 1930), III chap. ix, for excitement and amusement over Dr. Stiles' report: cartoons, verse, jokes, and skits.
3. B. J. Hendrick, *The Training of an American*, 370-71.
4. See especially *Mississippi Flood Disaster of 1927*, and *Relief Work in the Drought of 1930-'31* (Washington, D. C., 1930).
5. Frank Tannenbaum, *Darker Phases of the South*, 141.

faggot and the circumstance that the assaulted white woman is usually a poor-white are obvious illustrations of the fact.

Yet news from the South has for over a half century been filled with another sort of violence—queer, because it is both comic and tragic. Never since the days in South Carolina when the "clodhoppers" shouted for Ben Tillman: "Bring out the one-eyed plowboy!" has the South been without headline-making demagogues like "Tom Tom" Heflin and "The Man" Bilbo, every one of them a loud "friend" of the poor farmer and a past-master at garnering the votes of the trash.

To this constant popular attention to retarded Southerners has been added the increasing interest of social scientists and historians in them. This concern, however, lagged behind literature: when Ellen Glasgow's *Voice of the People* appeared in 1900, not one Southern college or university had a department of sociology and only seventeen offered courses in the subject.[6] But the pioneer work of the Institute for Research in the Social Sciences at the University of North Carolina with such an excellent monograph as *How Tenant Farmers Live* (1922) by J. A. Dickey and E. C. Branson first made scholars and social-minded laymen acutely aware of "Southern peons." And this stimulus led to standard scholarship like the historical article, "The Poor-Whites of the Ante-bellum South" (1925) by P. H. Buck and the Dutch sociological treatise, *De Landelijke Arme Blanken. . . .*(1933) by A. N. J. Den Hollander.

The growth of social sciences in the South and the

6. Odum, *American Epoch*, 312.

consequent concern over the section's degraded folk abetted the change toward more realistic fiction with social implications—a change which began in Southern writing around 1900. Before 1912, Ellen Glasgow had considered the lot of the Virginia poor-white after the war in four novels. But at the University of North Carolina, as a result of the general interest in the tenant farmer, the new social interpretation first got under way. The Carolina Playmakers, founded in 1918, applied themselves to writing about and portraying our contemporary poor-whites as well as the mountaineers, the Negroes, and the other Southern folk types. It was, therefore, no coincidence that both Harold Williamson's one-act play, *Peggy*, and *How the Tenant Farmer Lives*, by Professors Dickey and Branson, were published in 1922. After this date, the new literature about the poor-white began springing up in all parts of the South. Still, at Chapel Hill, Paul Green, the most important product of the Playmakers, starting with "Fixins" in 1924 has continued to write plays, stories, and novels that have bulked largely in the mounting literary vogue of the poor-white.

Nevertheless, his work was only a part of the rising stream of such writings in the 1920's. In that decade over a score of publications, fiction and drama, presaged the outburst of the 1930's, in the first three years of which as many titles appeared as during the entire preceding ten years. By 1933, every Southern state except Tennessee had produced a literary treatment of the poor-white. The day of the Southern poor-white in literature arrived a half dozen years earlier than Albion W. Tourgée had prophesied in 1888.

The significant fact about this vogue of the thirties
is that it marks the introduction of the naturalistic
conception of the poor-white. Yet, like all literary
departures, it was not unanticipated. For example, in
frankness of description, the Old South humor, the
Abolitionist fiction, and the stories of Alice French in
the late nineteenth century pointed toward the complete license of William Faulkner and Erskine Caldwell.
Indeed, from the early beginnings of Ellen Glasgow in
1900, there was a growing frankness and social preoccupation that culminated in the naturalistic thirties
with Faulkner's *As I Lay Dying* and Caldwell's *Tobacco
Road*. This progress may be viewed in three sorts of
interpretation for convenience styled local color, criticism and propaganda, and sensibility and realism.

III. LOCAL COLOR ONCE MORE: MARJORIE RAWLINGS' RE-DISCOVERY OF THE FLORIDA CRACKER

THE old methods of local coloring, practiced by literary carpetbaggers and natives in the South from
Woolson to Harben, have proved to be equally popular
in the twentieth century. In searching for the market-
able picturesque, these writers found that the poor-
white could be used for a variety of things: color
sketches, for example. About 1904 Clifton Johnson discovered some pitiable Georgia backlanders whom he put
into his sketch, "Among the Georgia Crackers."[1] In
Sandhills Sketches (1916), William Haynes declared that
"the Tar Heel is as fascinating and romantic as his
cousin up in the Cumberland Mountains." Yet despite

1. *Highways and Byways of the South*, 96-120.

174

Haynes' tourist-eye for oddity and his mindfulness of literary parallels, he wrote one valuable sketch: "Them Huggins Boys." It is not only amusing and pictorial as fiction but wise as social comment.

The Huggins boys lived in "poor old Moore County," North Carolina, where the sandhills section was so sterile that one could hear the cotton grunting in an effort to grow. The rewards from tending their sandy farm seemed so meager that the Huggins boys did not bother, but now and then hired out as laborers or burned tar. Meaner than a mad mule, these work-hating brawlers and petty thieves were a nuisance to the countryside. Having become their neighbor for the quail-shooting season, Haynes decided that they were "not vicious or mean; they are frightened and suspicious." When Northern capital developed dairying, vineyards, tobacco, and Pinehurst, the Hugginses learned nothing; they still rode about in their broken down phaeton, pulled by a moth-eaten mule, trying to discover, like DeForest's Selnarten Bowen, something "wild" or free for the taking. "They are helpless and hopeless," said Haynes. "They are the tattered remnants of an outworn age." Such sketches contain nothing new except later economic developments; they are a continuation of previous work always being done from Byrd to the present. But the poor-white had other literary values than mere oddity for sketch-work. In view of the technical expertness of the modern short story, one would expect the local-colorists to find new uses for the Cracker and his typical surroundings. Three of their stories showing high mechanical perfection illustrate the manipulation of poor-white elements for incidental ends.

The Southern Poor-White

For the purposes of the terror story, the pinelanders and swamps of Alabama were strikingly employed by F. S. Greene in "The Cat in the Canebrake" (1916). Sally Gantt met her death by means of a rattlesnake head dropped by a cat near her pallet on the morning she was to run away with a surveyor. A pineywoods tacky, living near swamps for all of her twenty-two years, Sally has a "clear skin and white teeth" and hates the "bare grassless country, its flat miles of monotonous pine forests, its flatter miles of rank canebrake" as if she had been brought up in a green and pleasant land. The author's enumeration of the external facts of pineywoods life is correct; his use of them, spurious.

It was inevitable that sooner or later scribblers would use the poor-whites in a murder story. In 1922, Irvin S. Cobb won the first O. Henry Memorial prize for his story, "Snake Doctor," based on the theme of "The Man and the Snake" by Ambrose Bierce. The point of it is the double ironic twist: Japhet Morner, "just plain white trash," jealous of his wife's kindness to an old "snake-doctor" who collects reptiles for trade, kills his spouse by mistake, and apparently, after trying to rob the old man's cabin, dies of snake-bite. The queer thing was that the snake which "bit" Japhet was a stuffed one! Here again, as in Greene's story, are all of the outside facts of the poor-white swamper's life in the Deep South, where "biliousness was the lot of every man." Yet they have little validity; they are simply parts to be knocked into place by one of our most expert literary cobblers. That Miss Blanche C. Williams should have felt it necessary to point out that "the villainous nature of Japhet Morner is not typical of the poor-white . . .

[but] that in the main he runs true to type," is surprising. For, on the score of character or motivation, the story has no standing whatever.

The third story illustrating the use of poor-whites for special effects is unique among the fiction herein considered: some degenerate Florida pinelanders are viewed through the eyes of a small Northern girl, who with her mother goes South to join her father. "Innocence" (1922) by Rose Wilder Lane unfolds through the child, Mary Alice, a story of disillusionment and tragedy. Uncle Charley has fallen to the pineywoods level and married Molly, who, barefooted and clothed in red, reminds Mary Alice of "Grandfather's big brown horse that lived behind bars and had once killed a man." Molly despises her husband's "uppety" brother and his family, tries to poison Mary Alice with a ball of sweet gum, and hamstrings her brother-in-law's cow. Fearing arson or the pollution of their well, Mary Alice's parents return North, leaving Uncle Charley forever. This story of the degeneracy and viciousness of Florida poor-whites is made terrible by means of the limited viewpoint of the little girl's innocence.

More significant than these stories were two one-act plays. John W. Rogers' "Bumblepuppy, A Comedy of Climate" (1926) takes its title from a game in which two men with palm-leaf fans sit equidistant from two lumps of wet sugar and try to keep the flies from alighting upon their sticky chunks. Gnats, bees, and tassel flies do not count. Andrew Bugg, an Arkansas woolhat, extols the points of this pastime while playing: "There ain't no game that suits this climate like bumblepuppy," he drawls . . . "Sugar ain't hard to get and

The Southern Poor-White

I ain't never seen flies no rarity. Shoo! A man can't afford to wear hisself out in this climate. He'll get all pulled down by the hot weather if he do."[2] Never has the laziness and stupor of the poor-white in the Southern heat been so perfectly represented.

The other play is the one interesting portrayal in the twentieth century of the Cajuns, who, because of Cable and Chopin, were of literary importance in the eighties and nineties. Ada Jack Carver takes for her theme in "The Cajun" (1926) one which is pat for hard, sordid handling: the inbreeding among the Cajuns which brought about the enactment of the so-called "first cousin" law in Louisiana.[3] When this new statute stops the wedding of Pierre and Julie, a Mississippi elopement becomes imperative: the girl is pregnant. This is a subject for a writer like Faulkner; Ada J. Carver gives it the heart-break of the local-colorist. But that she should have used an aspect of Cajun life ignored by both Cable and Chopin indicates the drift away from the sweetness of earlier local-color depiction of the poor-whites.

Such sketches, plays and stories, except for a few economic and regional notes or technical tricks, had nothing new to offer about the poor-white. The contemporary local-color novel, however, has added two unfamiliar groups and settings to American fiction: the shanty-boaters on the Mississippi and the Crackers of the Florida backlands. By 1918, R. S. Spears had used the first group, sometimes called "river rats," in his novel, *River Prophet*, as background for an absurd romance between a newspaper reporter and a runaway

2. In *American Scene*, Clark and Nicholson (eds.).
3. *Ibid.*

Re-Discovery of the Florida Cracker

wife. Spears obviously had little knowledge of or interest in these river folk. As a local-color field they lay fallow until cultivated in theatrical manner by Ben Lucien Burman in "Minstrels of the Mist" (1927) and *Mississippi* (1929). Here for the first time are to be seen convincingly in fiction, the dregs and driftwood of society that settled down on or by the river bank. Like the tackies in the inlands, they have been the objects of contempt in the river world, no man knows how long. They live in shanties or shanty-boats patched together out of wrecked box cars, junked automobiles, piano cases, discarded stove pipe, or anything lying about or floating down the river. They exist by fishing, muscle-shucking, working little bankside patches, bootlegging, and petty thievery. Nor has their filthy existence any more stability than their shanties: one day a landowner may find his cow milked dry or his chicken roost forlorn and order his riverside guests to shove off. Or, civic pride may cause a town to decide that two miles is not sufficient clearance between its wharf and the shanty-boat colony. They are poor-white trash afloat.

During the great days of steamboating, the shanty people were always stealing from the big ships or their cargoes at landings. In retaliation the boat captains cursed them for river rats and swamped their shanties with high waves from their paddle wheels. Often a gun fight ensued. Against this feud, Burman in *Mississippi* placed his improbable story of Capt. Lilly, who stole a shanty-boy and reared him to hate his people. Having learned his origin, the boy deserts the captain, marries a shanty girl, and, by a well-timed accident, the couple are reunited to the captain and his cleaner world. Four years after *Mississippi*, Mr. Burman wrote *Steamboat Round the Bend*, no less well received and no better in notebook local-color or story than the first novel. What the author did for the Southern poor-white was to photograph an unfamiliar group and suggest its peculiar ways and attitudes.

By far the most talented of the local-colorists recently dealing with the poor-whites is Marjorie K. Rawlings, a Northern journalist, who after a few years in Florida re-discovered the Cracker. He had, of course, been there all the time. Fifty years earlier Miss Woolson's grand eye had overlooked him, and somewhat later Margaret Deland sketched his strange placidity, but no one before Mrs. Rawlings realized the fictional possibilities of his life or the fascination of his haunts.

As a result of a series of her writings, which began in 1931 with "Cracker Chidlings," the Florida Cracker has at last become the literary rival of his long-famous Georgia cousin. For not only do we know from Mrs. Rawlings' fiction to some extent what his history has been but what he is like.

First of all, the origin of this Florida type explains his hatred of the Georgia Cracker. The wilds of Florida were the last refuge on the Atlantic coast of the migratory poor-white. There the murderer, the thief, the shiftless hunter-fisher-farmer could relax amid forests full of game and streams stocked with fish. And just as the lubbers and tar heels of North Carolina hated Virginians, so the Florida Cracker hated the people of his old home. In "Cracker Chidlings," Marjorie Rawlings tells of a host at a Florida country feast, who, after bragging that the stew or "purloo" had been made by

Re-Discovery of the Florida Cracker

his wife, a native of Brunswick, Georgia, was assailed by one of his Cracker guests: "The food ain't fitten to eat, dogged Georgia rations. . . . And he's done cooked the squirrels' heads in the pur-loo, and that suits a damned Georgia Cracker, but it don't suit me. . . . I don't want no squirrel eyes lookin' at me out o' my rations."[4] This is the old story of a crude people hating their somewhat more civilized neighbors. As we have seen in the foregoing period, the Florida Cracker was held to be the most trifling in Crackerdom; naturally, he fought back against such contempt.

But in another sense, this Cracker, enjoying the anachronistic life of a Davy Crockett in the fastnesses of a semi-tropical country, actually considered himself superior to the land-grubbing poor-whites of a well-settled state like Georgia. It is to this incongruous sort of frontier existence that Mrs. Rawlings has devoted her talent. Mart in "Jacob's Ladder" (1931) and Old Lant and Young Lant in *South Moon Under* (1933) are decadent, latter-day Crocketts, whose careers reveal what would have happened to Davy had he lived to see civilization closing tightly about him.

In "Jacob's Ladder," Mart meets Florry at a Cracker dance in the northern Florida pinelands and takes her away to a trapper's hut in the marshy "prairie." Here begins the heart-breaking fight against outside forces that are making the old backwoods life almost impossible—forces given meaning by the title song:

> *Jacob's ladder's steep an' tall—*
> *When I lay my burden down!*

4. *Scribner's Magazine*, LXXXIX (April, 1931), 128.

The Southern Poor-White

If you try to climb, you boun' to fall—
When I lay my burden down!

Scarcity of trapping forces Mart into poaching, then into illegal fishing. But these are soon stopped, and outlaw ways lose to the encroaching influence of society: to avoid starvation, the Cracker becomes the hired man of a Yankee orange-grower—a degradation Mart never dreamed of! Impatient of Mart's slovenly, inept ways and ignorant of the poor-white's resentment of being treated as a Negro servant, the Northerner goads the Cracker beyond endurance. But no sooner has Mart established himself as a sea fisherman about the Gulf islands than his livelihood disappears; the great commercial boats have ruined his fishing ground. There is one last resort: moonshining in the scrub, a desolate place of saw palmettoes, scrub oaks and pines, sand, and terrific heat. But here again society thwarts the Cracker, for revenue officers smash his still, and the law sends him to the chain gang. Ill from brutal treatment while serving his sentence, he and Florry wander back to their first home, the prairie, where he secures food on credit at a store and unearths his hidden traps. But Mart had not reckoned with the Florida equivalent of the cotton country storekeeper. By the sheriff's orders, his traps are taken from him for the merchant's security. Completely destitute, Mart and Florry decide that Jacob's ladder cannot be climbed and return to her father's cabin in the pinelands. And so their wanderings come full circle in a parable of fading independence in the Florida backlands.

In method and background, *South Moon Under* is

merely a repetition and amplification of "Jacob's Ladder." Old Lant, a fugitive from justice, lives out his Indian-like existence in the Florida scrub, but Young Lant feels the pinch of the converging outside. He can no longer wrest a living from the scrub as his father had done. Failing to secure a mill job, he takes to moonshining only to be betrayed by a spiteful neighbor to the revenue forces.

What many Florida Crackers are at present reduced to may be inferred from the life of Grampa Hicks in "Cracker Chidlings." Since nearly everything in Florida is imported—tourists, vacationers, booms, and writers —it was perhaps inevitable that some of the oldest citizens of the state, the Crackers, in whom no one was interested, should have become the parasites and leeches of wealthy sojourners and sportsmen. At least, Grampa Hicks found them to be fat pickings. Living in a ten-by-twelve palmetto-log shack, he subsisted by illegal trapping of fish, renting other Crackers' boats without permission to city fishermen, and supplying sportsmen with moonshine. But to Grampa, "Man's law is one thing, God's another. . . . I don't fish on Sundays," he said. . . . . "I wan't raised up that-a-way."

Informative as Mrs. Rawlings' work undoubtedly is, when considered as a contribution to literature about the poor-white, its claim is small and amounts to this: the introduction into fiction of a Cracker type, hitherto used only in travel sketches, his strange semi-tropical home, and some interesting notes on his story. Mrs. Rawlings' method is exactly that used a half century ago by her predecessor in Florida, Miss Woolson: types against panels of scenery. The differences are those of taste. Miss Woolson would hardly have spoken of a girl in the scrub, "who would always mate here and there like any rabbit," but neither would she have used any prettier words than Mrs. Rawlings does when she says: "The Cracker speech was soft as velvet, low as the rush of running branch water." Romantic local-color remains much the same. Mart and the rest have only typical reality; the moonshiner-the-law-and-the-girl plots were threadbare fifty years ago. Mrs. Rawlings has expanded the range of poor-white literature: she has added little to its quality.

All in all, local color in the twentieth century has followed the formula of the eighties. The use of shanty-boaters and Florida Crackers has been its contribution.

IV. CRITICISM AND PROPAGANDA: ELLEN GLASGOW TO T. S. STRIBLING

IN the present century, the critical and sometimes propagandist treatment of the poor-white in fiction has been a continuation of the work of Caruthers, the abolitionists, Tourgée, Harris, and French. But this interpretation, while motivated by much the same intention as preceding examples, differs in that current formulae and modes lend some originality to it. And, again, the present dilemma of the poor-white as share-cropper and tenant gives new point to old indictments.

In this sort of contemporary fiction, Ellen Glasgow, because of her earlier venturing, must be recognized as the pioneer. Indeed, it is suprising that a Virginia woman, closely identified with aristocracy and tradition, should have chosen an illegitimate poor-white for the hero of her first novel, *The Descendant*, which appeared in 1897 when its author was only twenty-three. Moreover, she has since used the poor-whites in four other novels, two of which contain heroes from that class.

There are several probable explanations for this. First of all, Ellen Glasgow is endowed with fine, hard sense, a "vein of iron," which made her revolt against Southern sentimentality of the traditional sort and condemn the "evasive idealism," "sham optimism," "sugary philosophy utterly without basis in logic or human experience"[1] which she found in the American novel of the "sugary years" around 1916. Educating herself by a directed course of reading, she emphasized science and such full-bodied writers as Fielding and the nineteenth-century Russians. But this austerity of mind was tempered with the benign charity of the genteel—"help from the greater to the least," as she expressed it in her poem, "A Creed" (1902). Such a person would naturally question and criticize the social order about her, and in doing so, she recognized that the poor-white was the obvious contrast for the ruling class of Virginia as well as an effective means of protest against caste. From this, one may infer that Miss Glasgow has never been interested in the Virginia poor-white for himself; like James Lane Allen, she is concerned incidentally with the lower or primitive levels of folk only as they represent a relation to or progress toward the goal of all society: a culture of social justice and gentle living.

Bearing this in mind, one can understand why the

1. Grant Overton, *Women Who Make Our Novels*, 22.

three poor-white heroes of Miss Glasgow are all self-made men: by rising to public regard or great place they can by their solid worth rebuke those who have scorned them.

Witness the first hero, Michael Akershem in the *Descendant* (1897), the bastard poor-white, produced by "an awkward woman of the fields" and an unknown father. Reared in a yeoman farmer's home, Michael is persecuted almost daily by the snobbery of the country-side, until he accepts his ostracism and with a Lincoln-like avidity for learning devours the whole library of the local minister, refuting theological sophistry as he goes like any born iconoclast. As a consequence of this double stigma of birth and class and also of his voracious study, Michael becomes a bitter Poe-esque editor and radical in New York, only to have his ideals defeated and his life ruined by his morbid impulsiveness: the direct result of Virginia class cruelty.

This is Miss Glasgow's first venturing with the "lost people" in literature. Poor-white life is not described; Michael, by rearing, is no poor-white. The novelist was interested in working out the after-effects of social scorn visited upon Virginia's lowest class.

Three years later, using again the formula of the self-made man, Miss Glasgow created, in *The Voice of the People*, a believable hero, Nick Burr, and described his youth against the background of poor-white family life. Nick's story is again one of fighting against odds for an education, but he has his reward when the people of Virginia elect him to the governorship. And this distinction was achieved in spite not only of the contemptuous aristocrats, but of Nick's father.

Criticism and Propaganda

Amos Burr, a sorry overseer before the War and a sorrier farmer after the surrender, never planted or did anything on time in any way except an ignorant one. Content with his own illiteracy, he hated Nick's zeal to learn. "I never saw nothin' come of larnin' yet," he said, "cep'n worthlessness." In his later days, when the Farmer's Alliance and Populism began to flourish, Amos discovered the cause of his own life-long failure: the government had helped everyone except the farmer.[2] So Amos mouthed about his rights and let the weeds grow.

But the opposition of the aristocracy was more serious. The ambition of Nick to get an education and enter the gentleman's profession, the law, caused a hot flurry in post-Reconstruction Virginia. For, just then, the aristocracy, forced by poverty into the leveling intercourse of trade with all classes, was intent upon preserving class lines. It seemed to them, as to the old "darkie," Uncle Ish, that the Negroes were going out of their heads and the poor-white trash out of their places. No wonder that Judge Bassett's admission of Nick to the private school taught in his house apparently threatened to undermine Virginia society. The pupils called the freckled boy "common as dirt"; the tutor abused him for not staying in his social class; an elegant and icy mother demanded of the Judge that Nick be dismissed from the school. Only little Eugenie Battle, with the democracy of childhood and the unconscious snobbery of her training, walked home with Nick,

2. As far as I have been able to discover this is the only literary allusion to the agricultural unrest of the eighties and nineties in the South. There was no Hamlin Garland to record it.

offering him on the way the queer consolation: "I don't mind about your being poor-white trash."

Scorned by Negroes and planter-folk alike, Nick achieved the bar and the friendship of Judge Bassett, only to strike another class barrier. Both he and Eugenie Battle agreed that they could not marry until he should win distinction and property. And so Nick went upward, breaking down all prejudices against him, until he arrived at the Governor's mansion.

Obviously Miss Glasgow stacked the cards too completely against Nick; yet by doing so she has provided a comprehensive exhibit of Virginia scorn of the poor-white; and by allowing Nick to win the respect of his state, Miss Glasgow has added a much-needed footnote to the Northern view of the trash: the Old South never refused—after definite proof—to recognize ability and character, regardless of class.

In 1904 appeared *The Deliverance*, subtitled "A Romance of the Virginia Tobacco Fields." The only poor-whites in this story, Sol Peterkin and his hussy daughter, Molly, are unimportant. Sol is a humorous character inserted for expository purposes. Having arranged for his fourth wife, he reflected that each spouse had worked less, lived fewer years, and cost more; "as the price goes up the quality gets poorer." Molly, "that yaller-headed limb of Satan," being unable to hide longer the evidence of her promiscuity, demanded that Sol do something. Her weak-kneed father proposed to three suspected louts that they draw straws for the honor of becoming Molly's husband.[3]

3. The incident is without the drollery of Mrs. Mulock's bargaining in Gilmore's *My Southern Friends*.

Criticism and Propaganda

The Peterkins are of significance only by contrast with the poor-whites of similar level created by Erskine Caldwell; Miss Glasgow states the facts about poor-whites as the source of rural whoredom; Caldwell dramatizes the facts.

Miss Glasgow presented her third poor-white hero in *The Miller of Old Church* (1911). Abel Revercomb is placed in a more tragic and complex pattern of class relations than that which the author had constructed in the *Voice of the People*.

Like Michael Akershem and Nick Burr, Abel rose by character and ability but only to the humble estate of countryside miller. And as Nick was aided by his foster-parent, Marthy Burr, so Abel was even more indebted to his mother. Mrs. Revercomb had fought the laziness of her trashy husband, who, she said, "was born shiftless an' he died shiftless. He never did a day's work in his life that I didn't drive him to." Yet despite her influence, a younger son, Archie, became noted for his "inherited idleness." Against the debasing pull of family and kin, Abel, the capable exception among the Revercombs, had to fight, and, in the end, raised his status among the plain people so that he was no longer referred to as "slack fisted poor white trash." But to the planter class, he was still a poor-white, and so, when he fell in love with Molly Merrywether, an overseer's granddaughter and bastard of a planter, Abel's suffering from class prejudice began anew. How after marrying a fool, Abel became a widower and eventually Molly's husband constitutes his story of deserved success.

But Abel's rise and his crossed love are not the most important social considerations here. *The Miller of Old*

The Southern Poor-White

Church contains Miss Glasgow's most complete illustration and outright discussion of the poor-white. And what is equally significant: the novel in its method and indictment constitutes a remarkable latter-day adaptation of the abolitionist formula, that is, a novel of many contrasted types in a plot so managed as to illustrate specific social weaknesses. There is, however, one notable difference: Miss Glasgow omits Negro relations and studies the position of the poor-whites in the first generation after the war as it was conditioned by antebellum class lines. "To rise under the old system" says the author, "had been so impossible that Abel's ancestors had got out of the habit of trying. In that pleasant, idyllic period the one act which went unhonored and unrewarded was the act of toil. So in the odor of shiftlessness, Abel's father died."

This favorite indictment, iterated ceaselessly in every abolitionist novel from *Archie Moore* onward, Miss Glasgow elaborates in explaining the serf-like acquiescence of Reuben Merrywether in the seduction of his daughter by Jonathan Gay, his landlord. Thus "paralyzed by the burden of slavery" and inured to a docile acceptance of their lot, the "poorer whites"— yeoman and trash—were bewildered by the changed order after Reconstruction. There had occurred a sudden, not a "gradual evolution of class"; and, consequently, the lowly whites were unprepared for the political responsibility which was thrust upon them. A new generation of this lowest class, without the abject regard for the "wheel-horse Colonels," would have to come on before the new order could be realized. That is, capable men from the poor-whites like Abel Revercomb and others from the plain people would have to lead that part of the Southern citizenry so long helpless.

But the hitch in Miss Glasgow's parables of progress, as far as their propagandist inferences are concerned, is that they were based upon two assumptions: first, a certain capability in poor-whites and, next, the desire to improve themseves in the New South. This was exactly the view and prophecy of the abolitionists. Consequently, in her stories of striving successful poor-whites, Miss Glasgow has told particular, not general social truth. Between 1911, when *The Miller of Old Church* appeared, and the publication of *Barren Ground* in 1925, Miss Glasgow seems to have given the poor-whites a closer scrutiny in their new rôle of tenant farmer.

The scene of *Barren Ground* is Pedlar's Mill, a community over which, after the breaking up of the plantations, tenant farmers had swarmed "as buzzards after a carcass." By the first quarter of the twentieth century, they had truly made it barren ground, most of which was now deserted old fields, cut by gullies and covered with broomsedge and scrub pine. This gutted and forlorn land is tangible proof of the curse of the tenant system, which derives, says the novelist, from the truism that "no man will work himself to death over somebody else's land." But even more fundamentally it was the result of stupidity, laziness, and ignorance—weaknesses which are not confined to tenants. For the poor-white landowners are as trifling as the croppers, more trifling than the blacks. "The negro," says Miss Glasgow, "who owns his ten or twelve acres is a better manager than the poor-white with twice the number."

The Southern Poor-White

The significance of Ellen Glasgow's poor-white novels is not so much intrinsic as initiatory. They contain little that is new as social criticism, for she has simply adapted old indictments. Nor do the major poor-white characters have much class reality, because they always rise out of their level. Indeed, the abstraction of social contempt seems to have interested the novelist more than the unsanitary poor-white in the flesh. Nevertheless, great credit is due her, for during the days of *Mrs. Wiggs* and "The Rosary," she was applying her critical intelligence to the lot of the despised people of her state. By doing this, she, more than any other writer, initiated the vogue of the poor-white in this century—a vogue, ironically enough, which has developed along lines extremely distasteful to her.

Other writers followed Ellen Glasgow's lead. In the *Atlantic Monthly* for 1906, Walter Hines Page published anonymously his "Nicholas Worth," later issued as *The Southerner*. This novel of Reconstruction and the New South is closer to the abolitionist formula than any of Miss Glasgow's works. In it, Page inveighed against the cult of the Colonels or Confederate die-hards as obstacles to progress and charged the old aristocracy with victimizing the poor-whites not only by slavery but after the war by waving the flag of white supremacy. For these, "forgotten men," as he called them, Page demanded the free popular education so long denied them. And although there are no trashy tar-heel characters in the novel, their need of education is the main concern and propaganda of the book.

A timid follower of Ellen Glasgow was Mary Johnston. After the appearance of *The Descendant* and the

Criticism and Propaganda

Voice of the People, Miss Johnston put aside her cape-and-sword romancing long enough to write *Lewis Rand* (1908), the hero of which rose from humble estate to the governorship of the Old Dominion. Thus Lewis Rand's career, in Mr. Jefferson's time, like the later one of Nick Burr, became a living criticism of aristocratic prejudices. But the hero is only the grandson of a poor-white; the effect of his somewhat removed poor-white origin was Miss Johnston's utmost concession to the work of Ellen Glasgow.

During the twenty-five years after Page's "Nicholas Worth," novels of criticism and propaganda showed an increase of economic emphasis rather than any change in method of interpretation. The later trends of such fiction are of prime importance here. How this type of novel has become a sort of economic illustration, or at best, documentary realism, may be observed in the work of four authors: *In the Land of Cotton* (1925) and *Can't Get a Red Bird* (1929) by Dorothy Scarborough; *Cotton* (1928) by Jack Bethea; *The Cabin in the Cotton* (1931) by Harry H. Kroll; and *The Store* (1932) by T. S. Stribling. All of them deal primarily or in part with the popular version of the twentieth-century poor-white, the tenant farmer, but *In the Land of Cotton* is by far the most satisfactory; in fact, no more thorough study of the present lot of the tenant has appeared in American fiction. And since it and Kroll's novel represent the ultimate development, or perhaps deterioration of critical and propagandist fiction about the po' buckra, they will be discussed last.

In *Cotton*, Jack Bethea followed old ruts. Len Maynard, son of a poor-white tenant, at last completes an agricultural course and returns to Alabama as the evangel of progressive farming—of course, he proved invincible. Propaganda could scarcely become more naïve.

Beyond a doubt, the most perfect survival of the abolitionist method of depicting poor-whites appeared in T. S. Stribling's *The Store* (1932), a novel of Florence, Alabama, and the surrounding country during the eighties. The parallels between the tenants in this book and the poor-white trash in *Dred*, for example, are almost exact. The Alabama woolhats as minor characters are mere illustrations of class hatred, victims of planter-merchants, and foils to noble Negroes.

Alex Cady, an evil wretch and trifling tenant, is the very reincarnation of a Negro-hating poor-white of an abolitionist writer. He resents the Negro school, and after discovering that the colored teacher is coaching his illiterate daughter, he burns the schoolhouse. He baits the noble octoroon, Touissaint, so that he may murder him. But failing thus to break down the Negro's dignified control, he tries to agitate a mob into hanging this "white nigger" for bringing suit in court against his landlord. The fiendish persistence of Alex is rewarded at last. When a mob breaks into the jail to lynch a pair of jewel thieves, Alex has the pleasure of slipping the noose around the neck of Touissaint, who, although he had merely accepted the protection of the prison after his suit, is strung up to clean out the cell block.

At least since *Birthright* (1921), Stribling has apparently been more interested in the Negro than in the poor-white; and this, again, was true of the abolitionists. But Stribling is also a humanitarian and a careful documentor of his works. Consequently, he put into *The Store* an illustration of the poor-white victimized by the supply merchant. Gibeon Dalrymple made four bales of cotton one year and eight the next, yet both times he broke even—according to J. Handback's store account. How this came about Stribling explains with proper indignation. The rascally storekeeper befuddled the tenants with complicated ledgers and the victims acquiesced, for they well knew that the landlords preferred Negro renters who could be cheated even more outrageously.

Of course, Negro-baiting, schoolhouse burning, lynching, and the like are a matter of record, but Stribling does not use them for interpretation. His method is the exaggerated contrast of the abolitionist novel. In fact, Stribling writes like an old-fashioned scalawag.

With Dorothy Scarborough's *In the Land of Cotton* (1923), the type of fiction initiated by Ellen Glasgow was given a somewhat new direction and pushed to its ultimate limit. Miss Scarborough, instead of devoting herself to class contempt, explored and defined the economic plight of the tenant in the cotton country of Texas. But, at the same time, her novel runs in several old grooves. It has definite alliance with the local color and sweetness of books like *The Deliverance* (1904) and "Jacob's Ladder" (1931); its story is the rise of a common man, who, like Nick Burr, dies a martyred leader. For Ben Wilson, the son of a tenant farmer, driven by "a strange eagerness" within him, graduates from Baylor University; and afterwards when the planter who loaned him money on which to begin his education needs his services, he returns to oppose some

195

night-riding tenants and at their hands meets his death. But as in the proletarian novels, Ben does not die in vain; the plans which he formulated to aid the cotton tenants are to be carried on.

As an economic study, *In the Land of Cotton* must be placed above all other twentieth-century novels about the poor-whites by virtue of its three-fold distinction: it exhibits a superior grasp of the entire problem of cotton farming and tenancy not only in its local but world setting; its view-point is characterized by fairness and tolerance; its propaganda constitutes a remarkable economic prophecy.

Miss Scarborough is not out to make anyone or any class the goat for the plight of the tenant. She takes a somewhat deterministic view, seeing in the cotton system a vicious cycle of relations produced both by immediate and far-removed causes—flood, drought, insects, stupid farming, European war, shifts in manufacture, inadequate financial machinery, and others. No wonder that an ignorant tenant like Jeff Wilson, unable to comprehend many of the forces which were defeating him, became a fatalist. "If I was to start to hell with a load of ice," he swore, "there'd be a freeze before I got there." Cotton tenants, stupid and hopeless as Jeff, could scarcely be expected to help themselves; yet they must be saved. Just how this is to be done Miss Scarborough tells us in detail.

All artistic considerations aside, the propaganda in this novel, both by its wisdom and its completeness, amazes one. No better tract for the times could be prescribed as required reading for Southern cotton growers. In a chapter entitled "Reality," the whole problem of the tenant is rehearsed in the conversation of a planter, a tenant, and a lawyer. But Miss Scarborough is a daring propagandist; she does not stop with analysis and criticism; she offers a solution. Mr. Bob, the lawyer who is to devote his life to carrying on the reforms of the martyred tenant boy, Ben Wilson, outlines in the last chapter a program that prophesies the Agricultural Adjustment Act and other farm measures of Franklin D. Roosevelt's administration. "We've simply got to have laws," says Mr. Bob, "that make it possible for farmers to borrow money at reasonable rates, not only to carry them through the year and raise and market their crops, but to buy land as well." More than that, national and state governments must come to the farmer's aid—by instituting crop limitation, providing warehouses and other means of co-operation, and encouraging diversification.

Obviously, Miss Scarborough does not at times distinguish between pamphleteering and novel writing. Nor did she learn to do so in her next novel of the Texas cotton country, *Can't Get a Red Bird* (1929), which is equally overloaded with discussions of farm problems and repeats the elements considered here in her earlier work. Certainly, in dealing with the tenant, economic illustration in fiction can not go beyond Miss Scarborough's work—and it need not.

It can, however, be more dramatic, as Harry H. Kroll's *The Cabin in the Cotton* (1931) definitely proves. The unfair system of bookkeeping in plantation stores, which Stribling merely explained, Kroll translates into human terms of considerable power. And he does this by placing Dan Morgan, a poor-white tenant or Mississippi peckerwood, educated by his landlord, in the plantation store as bookkeeper. Thus from the lad's viewpoint of divided loyalties we see the injustices of the Delta cotton system—injustices which lead to thievery, arson, and lynching. In the end, Dan casts his lot with his own people, the peckerwoods, and forces some of the great planters to adopt a more honest and humane form of tenant contract.

As a lively social document, *The Cabin in the Cotton* has considerable value. Like Miss Scarborough, Kroll tries to balance the scales fairly between planters and peckerwoods, but his sympathies so pull him to the underdogs that his book becomes by far the most effective indictment we have of the traditional planting system of the Deep South.

What, then, did the novelists of special purpose, from Ellen Glasgow to Stribling, add to the literature of the poor-white? They established as a convention: the poor-white hero in a Lincoln-like story of the rise of a common-man—the theme illustrated by R. M. Johnston's Brinkly Glisson in "The Goosepond School" and Cable's Claude St. Pierre in *Bonaventure*. Miss Glasgow made a valuable analysis of the aristocratic attitude toward the poor-white. Equally important was the introduction of the economic study of the poor-white as tenant by Dorothy Scarborough and Kroll.

The historical significance of these novels is their position in the drift toward the naturalistic manner of William Faulkner and Erskine Caldwell. From Miss Glasgow to Miss Scarborough, the trend is toward a documentary and factual method, which leads logically to outright, if not brutal, frankness. And yet all of these novelists evaded this development. Miss Scarborough, for example, says that her tenant farmers are "little better than animals." But one would never suspect it from reading *In the Land of Cotton;* the poor-whites in its pages are certainly not brutish. The author and all of the others, except Kroll, in the propagandist group, shied away from human nature, made beast-like by toil or other causes, mainly because they are all basically romantic and refused to follow through to the logical conclusions of their method.

V. SENSIBILITY AND REALISM: EDITH S. KELLEY, ELIZABETH MADOX ROBERTS, AND PAUL GREEN

SINCE the early 1920's, there has been appearing a treatment of the poor-white, which, compounded of sensibility[1] and idealism[2] in character and of rather hard realism[3] in situation and background, has added a notable body of writings to this history: *Weeds* (1923) by Edith S. Kelley, *The Time of Man* (1926) by Elizabeth Madox Roberts, and a number of plays and pieces of fiction from "Fixins" (1924) to *The Laughing Pioneer* (1932) by Paul Green.

And while this method marks an original departure from preceding ones in depicting the poor-whites, yet it has definite connections with both the local-color and the critico-propagandist groups already considered. This can be more easily explained if it be shown that the major attention of these three writers in their works

---

1. Herein the usage of this term is the ordinary one: mental receptivity and capacity of feeling.
2. By this term, nothing more formulated than a vague desire is meant.
3. The term here indicates the accurate representation of the facts.

about the trash has been given to the tenant woman.

Earlier, in local-color, there had been presented a sizable group of pineywoods girls who longed to escape to something better, for example, Kate Chopin's 'Tite Reine and Caline, Addie M. Lee's Nervy Dixon, and Frederick Greene's Addie Gantt. The poor-white heroines of Miss Kelley, Miss Roberts, and Mr. Green are of different stuff: they are not merely animated figures against scenic backdrops; their tenant world is part of the flow of their lives;they are regional characters, following the daily grooves of their kind.

This metamorphosis, while, in one light, a natural development from the local-colorist to the regionalist conception of character, was very likely hastened by the popularity of "soil novels," such as Willa Cather's *O Pioneers* (1913), with its conquering, poetic heroine, Alexandra Bergson. Nor was, in all probability, the acclaim in 1914 of Robert Frost's *North of Boston*, with its poems of sensitive, tortured, and sometimes insane farm women like those in "Home Burial" and "A Servant to Servants," lost upon these three Southern authors.

The relation of this new poor-white woman to the works of the Glasgow-Scarborough group is definite, but less important. Judy Pippinger in *Weeds*, Ellen Chesser in *The Time of Man*, Patsy Tate in Green's *The House of Connelly*—all of them struggle against their lot to achieve a more decent existence. From similarity of theme, they would seem to be Miss Glasgow's self-made heroes with a change of sex, if it were not for the fact that the women, with the exception of Patsy Tate, do not win. Nor do they move in a morass of economic illustration like that in Miss Scarborough's *In the Land of Cotton*. Miss Roberts ignores economic factors completely; Miss Kelley works them into the lives of her people with funtionality; and Paul Green, except in the preface to his novel, *The Laughing Pioneer*, avoids them.

With these connections established, the exact nature and originality of the new tenant heroine of sensibility can be understood best by presenting sketches of the five most important ones.

The advent in 1923 of Judy Pippinger as the heroine of Edith S. Kelley's novel *Weeds* opens a new literary province in this history. For the first time a poor-white woman became the leading character in a novel; for the first time, her mind was fully studied against the rounds of her daily life. Hitherto, she had nearly always been depicted from the outside as was the case with Kate Chopin's Azélie, the riverbank Cajun, and Alice French's "Headlights," the itinerant cotton picker. Before the twentieth century, the nearest approach to the inner reality achieved by Miss Kelley was the self-revelation of Mrs. Feratia Bivins in Joel Chandler Harris' "Mingo," which, however, is merely a short story, only in part devoted to the poor-white virago. But in *Weeds*, we can follow the alteration of Judy's mind through the years.

Among the dull, bony girls of the Kentucky tobacco tenants, Judy was like a flower among weeds. She was a bright, tomboyish girl who liked to draw malicious cartoons of the schoolmaster, ride her father's nags, and do the outside chores about the farm. And partly because of her fine zest in living, she possessed an unreasoned faith that somehow she would not repeat the brutalizing existence of the tenant wives who, bent and angular before their forties, sat against the wall at dances, staring with "peculiarly dead, expressionless eyes."

And after her marriage to a tenant boy, Jerry Blackford, who had saved some money, she seemed to be approaching her ideal of owning a farm when the inevitable fate of all tenants began its working. Regular child-bearing, more mouths to feed, drought, death of stock, falling prices of tobacco, rising of living costs during the World War—always something ruined the good year that would have put the Blackfords ahead.

Under such a merciless Providence, Judy began to lose her old exuberance. Pregnancy sapped the vitality she needed for work in the fields and in the tobacco barn. The dullness that she felt creeping over herself, she discovered with horror in her children. "She saw already appearing traces of the look that she had learned to dread, a look that stamps itself upon the faces of those who for generations have tilled the soil in solitude, a heavy, settled, unexpectant look. . . ." Against sinking into the clod-like existence of other tenant women, Judy rebelled. Once, when pregnant, she tried to kill herself; for a time, she regained her joyousness in giving her body to a wild-eyed evangelist; and finally, she determined to have control of her body; she would be a brood-mare no longer. But her deserting Jerry's bed forced him to take a neighbor's wife. Only Uncle Jabez Moorhouse in the whole tenant community understood how Judy felt about things and what she was fighting against; he had her sensibility; and both knew it.

Sensibility and Realism

During the first influenza epidemic when Uncle Jabez died and her little girl came near doing so, Judy realized the growing morbidity of her life and came to a decision: "she was through with struggle and questioning"; "peace was better than struggle, peace and a decent acquiescence before the things which had to be."

Three years after *Weeds*, Elizabeth Madox Roberts repeated almost exactly the story and character of Judy in Ellen Chesser, also a tenant girl of the Kentucky tobacco fields, in her novel, *The Time of Man*. And yet these two versions of the poor-white show striking differences, mainly because of the methods employed by the two authors. Miss Roberts is primarily interested in the mind of Ellen Chesser as it is changed by touching the world about her; Miss Kelley in the brutal impact of that world on the mind of Judy Pippinger. Miss Roberts works more from the inside outward, Miss Kelley from the outside inward. Consequently, *The Time of Man* is more poetic and less harsh in sordidness of background than *Weeds*.

Ellen, even more than Judy, was endowed with sensibility, accentuated by her early life. While her parents led a roving existence with a trashy lot of wagoners, her lively imagination had been stimulated by brawls, thieving escapades, yarn-telling, queer books, and marvelous sights like the great church in Nashville, Tennessee. An only child, the sole survivor of seven, premature and precocious, she felt the shock of sexual knowledge with the usual repugnance of puberty. Her parents whispering and straining in the dark, one-room cabin; women in labor, screaming and pulling on the bed posts—all of it was "ugly and everything ugly, all the way back to the first as far as you can recollect. . . ."

Used to the excitement of the road, Ellen naturally rebelled when Henry Chesser, her father, again became a tenant. The "fear of fences that enclosed the land" made her so restless that she wandered about the open fields and woods. Like Judy, she hated the loose, dirty cabin and escaped to the meadows to play with the colts or the dogs: they were "animals of the road." It was a joy to put her face to a colt's forehead and talk to him, or sprawl upon the fragrant, new-mown clover and pile it over her.

As Ellen came into the quick womanhood of poor-white women, she contemplated her body with Narcissan awe: "It's no knowen," she murmured, "how lovely I am." Now, when she sang "Lord Lovel," the ballad world of milk-white steeds and tragic lovers came to her with a new poignance. Yet, from the same prideful feeling, Ellen, just as Judy, avoided marriage until her mother became distressed. When she finally pledged herself to Jonas Prather, her life of disillusionment began, for Jonas not only confessed his whoring with Jule Nestor among the river-bank trash but deserted Ellen for a doll-faced fool. The first urgency of sexual life had passed. The monotony of toil, ill luck, and moving from one tenant shack to another brought to her a stoical repose.

Not too long, however: Ellen married Jasper Kent, a powerful-bodied tenant farmer, and a new joy and a new struggle claimed her. Jasper, restless and persecuted by his false reputation as a barn-burner, moved often and each time to a worse place. After trying to make four different shacks livable, Ellen sank into the slatternly housekeeping of her sort: "It mattered much less to her now what country she lived in, here or there, or whether there was a tree in the yard or a well for water, or a stove for heat or a fireplace."

Still, she had not surrendered completely. After bearing five children, she rebelled at what seemed to her senseless breeding. Often she would whisper: "Out of me come people forever." Pregnant with her sixth child, Ellen so resented her condition and especially Jasper's naming his landlord as the father that she deliberately abused herself, and when her time came, locked the children in the kitchen and bore the child alone. This sickly boy lived some years and made such demands upon the family's affection that Ellen and Jasper came to a life-long understanding. And so, when Jasper, after having been wrongfully whipped by a mob for alleged barn-burning, wished to go away and return for her and the children, Ellen knew once and for all that apart from Jasper her life was meaningless. "No," she said, "I'd go with you, Jasper, wherever you see fitten to go. I couldn't nohow see my way to stay behind. I'd go where you go and live where you live, all my enduren life. If you need to go afore sunup, why then I need to go afore sunup too. I couldn't make out to live here with you gone. I'd have to go where you go and when."

No less interested than Miss Kelley and Miss Roberts in the tenant woman who strives toward a little beauty in life, Paul Green has given his version in three plays and one story. The one-act play, "Fixins" (1924), which he wrote with Erma Green, and "Tempered Fellow,"

(1928), a short story, present the conflict of the wife's desire for beauty with the man's passion for land. In the play, Lillie's especial longing was for some "fixins" or furnishings for the tenant cabin. After having returned from a visit in town and discovered that Ed, her husband, had again paid her cotton money on land, Lillie delivered a full-length tirade against him. "You don't care for nothin' but a mule to plow in the day time and a shuck mattress to sleep on at night—that you don't and always laying up for land, always a-talking about it, and lettin' me and everything I want go with never a thought." She accused him of killing their baby by refusing to pay for proper care and berated him for letting her prettiest geranium die while she had been away. "You see how it is, Ed? You kill things you tech!" With that, Lillie picked up the suitcase (it had not been unpacked) and left Ed for good.

In "Tempered Fellow," the same conflict between Ollie York and her husband, Eddie, terminated more violently. Since "they were both the children of tenant farmers, the grandchildren of tenant farmers, the great-grandchildren, and on back," Eddie vowed that he would one day pay taxes on his own land. But Ollie, a neat industrious housekeeper, was so beset with the love of fun and finery that she refused to co-operate in Eddie's ambition. Enraged at this, he struck her and off she went to Raleigh, North Carolina. Weeks later, when Eddie called for her in the city and she scorned him, he strangled her to death. The sheriff found "the tempered fellow" ready. "Poor fool, he was sitting on the porch dressed in his Sunday best with his head bent over his hands. The dishes were washed, the floor swept, the flowers watered, and all in order. He went away like a child and stayed so till the last day."

The one-act play, "The Picnic" (1928) and the full-length drama, *The House of Connelly* (1931), set forth the struggle of the ambitious poor-white girl against the prejudices of the aristocracy. In "The Picnic," Ed Roberts, plantation owner, always aloof from the plain people of the Little Bethel community, became lonely after the death of his proud mother. Naturally enough, he was attracted to his tenant's vivacious daughter, Nancy Nelson, "a raven-haired girl with a lithe, full figure," who had long revolved in her head plans for taking the queerness out of the young squire. At a picnic, they declared their love, but Ed hesitated and betrayed his fear of the social stigma involved in a marriage with Nancy. To prove the strength of her love and to discover his true mettle, she offered herself to Ed without demanding a promise of matrimony. But the aristocratic weakling ran away while Nancy cried after him: "Coward, fool. . . !"—and then wept.

But whereas Nancy Nelson failed to make a man of Ed Roberts, Patsy Tate, heroine of *The House of Connelly*, succeeded completely in reclaiming not only her landlord, Will Connelly, but his plantation as well. Patsy, even by aristocratic Evelyn Connelly's admission, was "about as pretty a poor-white girl" as one ever saw: "lithe, full-figured" and pink-cheeked, she had "cold and dark gipsy-like eyes" of command. But she was no less capable than fetching. Jesse Tate had trained her as if she had been his son, that is, to shoot straight and farm right. He had also made her covet the two thousand Connelly acres, which as a boy he had seen richly productive and to which he had now returned as tenant after a lifetime of wandering from one shack to another. But longing as he did to reclaim this now broken-down plantation, he despaired of ever owning a foot of it. "I'll die the other fellow's man—a tenant," he would say to Patsy; "you will too." Patsy, however, thought otherwise. By making Will Connelly love and seduce her, she gained control over him in spite of his family, and brought industry, prosperity, happiness, and herself as mistress to Connelly Hall.

Certainly, as Big Sis and Big Sue said, Patsy was one of those "scroughing and a-gouging po' white trash," "pushing up in de world—reaching and a-grabbing at de high place of de quality." And yet she had one attribute which counteracted the mercenary element in her nature: a natural sensibility that made her love the soil and the solemn beauty of the old mansion and that also caused her to love and shield the weak heir to the House of Connelly.

Judy Pippinger, Ellen Chesser, Lillie Robinson, Ollie York, Nancy Nelson, Patsy Tate—every one an exceptional tenant woman of sensitivity and some admirable traits. It has seemed feasible to sketch them fully, first, because Judy and Ellen are "literary events" in this history, and, second, because the succession of portraits reveals a degeneration of sensibility into sentimentality. When this happens, special pleading and the author's emotions supplant representation. Therefore, the degree to which these characters and several others of Mr. Green have been thus vitiated must be established.

The cause of this defect is not to be sought in igno-

Sensibility and Realism

rance of the poor-whites such as one expects in the note-taking local-colorist. Miss Kelley knows her tenant folk of Kentucky, and Paul Green his of eastern North Carolina to the very core. Their trouble is more fundamental and concerns their literary attitude. They pity their characters. That Miss Kelley fell into this error surprises one, especially since she steps out of her narrative to tell the reader that she will have none of Wordsworthian sentimentality about rustics. "There is an idea existing in many minds," she tells us, "that country folk are mostly simple, natural, and spontaneous, living in the light of day and carrying their hearts on their sleeves. There is no more misleading fallacy." And yet, by her manner of describing scrawny, little, "young-old" girls; angular, dried-up tenant wives; and the "sodden life of the soil," Miss Kelley pleads for pity—pity that Judy and her family are sinking into the deadening typicality of those about them. Nevertheless, despite this indirect sentimentalizing of the lot of Judy, the hard, clear outline of her being is not spoiled.

But this lapse, which in Miss Kelley is more implicit than actual, becomes in Paul Green pure and unabashed sentimentality. In "Fixins," Lillie has chopped and picked cotton until "her fingers drip blood," and in her five years of marriage has received hardly "a dozen sweet words" out of Ed. "God help me!" she cries, "who wouldn't get crazy for a sight of a town and purty things onct in a while?" How grievous Paul Green's sin of special pleading really is one can see by contrasting with "Fixins" the hard veracity of a play on exactly the same theme published two years earlier.

"Peggy," also a Carolina folk-play, by Harold Williamson, portrays in plain, hard manner the defeat of a tenant girl's naïve, romantic notion by the brutal necessity of tenant existence. Peggy Warren, after being flattered by Wes McDonald, her landlord's son, determined not to marry Jed, a farm laborer, but to get a job in a city five-and-ten-cent store. Her father, Will Warren, who suffered from heart trouble, died after a violent quarrel with Peggy over her new ambition. The landlord then informed the Warrens that they must give up the tenant house. Jed offered to take Will's place and thereby give the family a home. Peggy, realizing that escape to the city is impossible, agreed to marry Jed and take up the round of life followed by her mother.

In "The Picnic" and *The House of Connelly*, admiration for the capability of Nancy and Patsy vies for the ascendancy with pity; but in other pieces, the weakness of Mr. Green before the tragedy of tenant women comes out clearly in the ever-recurrent theme of the mother crying after her dead child. Both Lillie Robinson in "Fixins" and Mary Adams in "The Lord's Will," accused their husbands of infanticide. Lettie Weaver in the story, "The Humble Ones," wept in the barn and crawled under the house calling for her dead boy, "Little Chick." And in the *Laughing Pioneer* (1932), Edith Harkness had cried over the shoes and dresses of little Artis until she was "nothing but skin and bones." The author's preoccupation with this motif seems almost pathological.

Paul Green's sympathy for the poor-white woman explores even the lower depths of her lot. Through his drama, "The Field God" (1925), moves Lonie, a

stooped silent creature, in "heavy brogan shoes, an old
slat bonnet, and a man's ragged coat." Old Squire
Morgan had used her as his woman until she became
too old for that; then he "threw her off like a nigger's
shoe in a fence-jamb." When Lonie, now a sort of
animated carcass, says that "everybody has to give up
what they're a-doing someday and stop it," one thinks it
about her time to do so. But even a stronger use of the
pathetic may be observed in "The Woods Colt," a short
story about Beck Ragland, washerwoman and field hand,
who had been "wronged" by Squire Johnson and lived,
"soured on the world," with her poetic and consump-
tive bastard, Will. Even Joel Chandler Harris' Emma
Jane and Bud Stucky reach no such tearful depths.

In view of Mr. Green's complete knowledge of poor-
whites and his extensive writings about them, this lack
of austerity and detachment is important enough to
warrant an explanation. The truth is that Mr. Green,
as he says of himself, "started out very close to the dirt,
in the elemental"; even so, he has not traveled very
far from the post-bellum Southern viewpoint of romance
in his first play, "Surrender to the Enemy," a North-
South love tale of "practical reconciliation," written in
1917 while he was a college freshman. For in 1928 he
called upon his fellow tar heels to rouse themselves
from artistic lethargy and "do our duty before God and
man—the duty of building monuments in the name of
*what is finest and most beautiful in the lives of human
beings.*" To do this, he recommended the revival of a
spiritual consciousness very like that of the Victorians.
But when he laments the literary neglect of "the
romance of the farmer's life among his tobacco, his cot-

ton and corn,"[4] his literary position is clear. Mr. Green is a spiritual propagandist and is therefore allied to the Glasgow-Scarborough group as well as to the sensibilitists like Miss Kelley and Miss Roberts.

If, however, Mr. Green represents the perversion of sensibility in depicting the wistful tenant woman, Elizabeth Madox Roberts stands for another type of excess in this quality, but one employed with surer taste. Alva C. Bessie has said that all of Miss Roberts' characters "share her own hyper-sensitivity."[5] This being true of Ellen Chesser, she can no more be considered representative of the poor-white woman than the other tenant heroines from Judy Pippinger to Patsy Tate; they are all a-typical and intended to be so by their creators. What matters is not whether *The Time of Man* fits the spurious formula of average characters in average situations, but whether it has convincing probability and conveys a sense of veracity. Ellen and the tenant world in which she lives meet both qualifications.

No group of writers has made a richer contribution to the literary interpretation of the poor-white than this one. In the creation of types alone, it is pre-eminent, as a result mainly of the efforts of Paul Green. The most original of these creations is Danny Lawton, the hero of *Laughing Pioneer*, who marks the re-emergence of the picaresque poor-white, absent from fiction since Simon Suggs wandered Alabama. Original also is the social angle provided by the narrator, a bookish invalid who hates his trashy family with their "poor-white drawl."

4. "The Playmakers and Our Art," Carolina Folk-Plays (Third Series), ed. F. H. Koch, xxxii. Italics mine.

5. *Sat. Rev. of Lit.*, IX (Nov. 26, 1932), 270.

Sensibility and Realism

Danny was a jaunty cuss, footloose and fancy free. A tumbler, ballad-singer, and yarn-spinner, he has in him the wanderlust of Bliss Carmen's and Richard Hovey's vagabonds as well as that of Green's own "No 'Count Boy." And he came by his traveling itch honestly, for his mother had listened too long to a singing peddler.

When Danny with his old dirty cap and hair as "knotty as chinquapin burrs" turned up at the planter hall of Judge Lang, a decayed old Confederate and "hater of the poor white trash," trouble came with him. The melancholy Judge thought the vagrant funnier than a puppy or a little "coon," but he also thought unprintable things when his tall, spinster daughter, Miss Alice, also took a liking to the boy. "I don't think he likes poor white folks like me," Danny said. Yet after the Judge's death Alice came to love the tramp, who, amazingly enough, was reclaiming the tumble-down plantation; but she could not break down the class barrier between them. When a sort of K. K. K. dragged Danny into the night to whip the poor-white for the insolence of living in the same house with a gentlewoman, Alice rescued him but died later from the horror and exposure of the ordeal.

Danny's life then came to the crossways. The new owner of the plantation offered him the insult of one hundred dollars a year as hired man. The boy took to the road again, and the narrator joined him so that he also may escape the usual poor-white existence.

His volume of sketches, *Wide Fields* (1928), contains a section: "Little Bethel People," modeled on the *Spoon River Anthology*, which is to date the best representation available of poor-whites in the setting of an entire average Southern community. Like Faulkner in North Mississippi, Green is building a literary world in Little Bethel Neighborhood in Eastern North Carolina as Hardy created Wessex. In *Wide Fields*, "The Field God," *The House of Connelly*, and *The Laughing Pioneer*, we tramp familiar ground and meet old acquaintances ranging from aristocrats to poor-whites.

But the highest achievement in characterization belongs to Misses Kelley and Roberts: they were the first to bring alive the mind and body of the poor-white woman. Judy and Ellen have joined the motley company of their poor-white sisters in literature.

Noteworthy, also, are the aspects of poor-white life, hitherto neglected, which these authors have utilized. Of these, the most conspicuous, perhaps, is religion. Instead of writing out-worn *genre* pieces about camp-meetings, Miss Kelley and Miss Roberts have made us feel—indeed, for the first time—what "Sunday preaching" must mean in the dreary days of tenant mothers. And with Lem Banks in "The Lord's Will" (1922), Paul Green advanced beyond what had been done with rural religion and the poor-white. This trifling tenant-preacher, "a spindle-shanked fool . . . always dribbling gospel from his jaws" at brush revivals to "all the common trash in the neighborhood" until his crop and home come to ruin is a penetrating study of fanaticism and tenantry. The thesis of "The Lord's Will" and "The Field God" merely echoes the old contention of Walter Hines Page regarding protestantism in the rural South.

"As for the poor-white . . ." Green wrote in *Laughing Pioneer*, "the narrow moralism of the Scotch settlers has carried on in him, Methodist or Baptist, and he goes oppressed by the world and the straight-jacket of his religion. The juice and the comedy of living have been squeezed out and left him sour-souled, and the cramp of poverty, the clutch of ignorance and evil dreams have gnarled him into bitterness. And when sometimes the voice of song and poetry arises as an exception by his doorstep, he looks suspiciously upon it and most often thinks it fraught with the levity of the devil, the dark swamps and blasphemy against the Holy Ghost."

Here Green mistakes result for cause: the mournfulness of the whining songs in any ignorant backcountry church of the South is the tone of hard living and often of social hopelessness. Nor should this Sunday evidence of other-worldliness and fatalism be over-emphasized, especially among poor-whites, since probably most roving tenants and sharecroppers families take no such active part in religion as the upper classes of farmers. Neither ought one to forget Green's own Bible-mouthing, drunken tenant, Jacob Alford, in "The Field God," who finds "gospel for drinking" and glows with sanctimoniousness and superiority as one of the faithful praying for his "sinful" landlord, who has "et the fat of the land and fed us the husks and crumbs. God is hard on the poor harlings and tenants."

Nor should the technical innovations of these writers in expanding the range of poor-white portraiture be minimized. To Paul Green must be accredited the establishment of the tenant farmer in drama, for beginning when only one play, Williamson's "Peggy," had portrayed the type, he has used the "lost people" in six plays. One other mechanical contribution came from Miss Roberts:

the creation of a new dialect, characterized by archaic forms and inverted word-order. In it one seems to hear John M. Synge's Aran Islanders saying, "In the law again, he'll be, in jail, maybe" or to meet the dialogue of balladry, for example, after the play party in *The Time of Man* when a small boy calls after the heroine:

> *Could you sing me a song, Ellen Chesser?*
> *Sometime I will, Hank Seay.*
> *Could you sing now, Ellen Chesser?*
> *Sometime, Hank Seay.*

And although it has never been caught from the mouths of poor-whites by any other writer, it sounds plausible enough when spoken by a hyper-sensitive character like Ellen Chesser. Be it said, however, that this especial dialect and rhythm are used only for moments of a poetic sort.

The significance of the writings of Kelley, Roberts, and Green in the drift toward the work of Faulkner and Caldwell lies in the frank, and, at times, sordid elements: sex, filth, disease, violence, insanity—all of them, stock charges against the so-called "school of cruelty," can be found in the works of the sensibilitists. Sexual matters are recounted with an intimacy not met with before, especially in *Weeds*, wherein the philanderings of Judy, Jerry, and Het may be closely observed. Nor are we denied the child-birth in the solitary labor of Ellen Chesser. And though Paul Green from dramatic and other causes already indicated avoids the immediate act, he demonstrates the wages of promiscuity by the lives of Beck Ragland and Lonie. The shacks which

Sensibility and Realism

Ellen and Judy occupied always had yards inlaid with
the filth of other tenants. And no less dirty are other
details and practices such as the absent-minded pleasure of Ellen's mother in picking the seams of her dress
for fleas. The maladies of country people, especially
poor-white, which develop from neglect have been used
by Paul Green in his short story, "The Humble Ones."
In *Weeds*, because of the winter isolation of the mud-
bound tenants, Judy's friend, Uncle Jabez, lay a corpse
in his cabin for days before he was discovered. Nor is
violence unrepresented or without precedent, since
Ellen Glasgow in her earlier works was much addicted
to hammer-murders and the like. A tenant, numb from
cold, falls under his wagon wheels and is crushed; a mob
strips and flogs a man; a mule tramples a child to
pieces; a pregnant woman tries to drown herself. Such
incidents anticipate nearly everything in the later
naturalistic versions except the attitude of the other
characters toward them. Insanity, that mark of run-
down stock and often of solitude and overwork, appears
in tragic, sometimes comic, illustration in *Weeds*, *The
Time of Man*, and Paul Green's *Wide Fields* and "The
Field God."

These elements—arrows toward naturalism—will be
raised to major emphasis in the Faulkner-Caldwell
method.

VI. NATURALISTIC MODES: THE GOTHIC, THE RIBALD, AND THE TRAGIC: WILLIAM FAULKNER AND ERSKINE CALDWELL

AFTER the publication of William Faulkner's *As I
Lay Dying* in 1930 and of Erskine Caldwell's *Tobacco
Road* in 1932, the Southern poor-white became the

literary property of the naturalists. But the naturalism practiced by these authors does not conform exactly to the generally approved conception of this mode.

V. L. Parrington has formulated the best statement of the standard view.[1] Beginning with a definition of naturalism as "pessimistic realism," he enumerates six criteria: scientific objectivity; frankness about the whole man, hence the emphasis on three strong instincts: hunger, fear, and sex; amorality; deterministic philosophy; pessimism; and preference for three types of characters: physical brutes of strong desire, neurotics, and strong characters of broken will.

Contemporary Southern naturalism is marked off rather sharply in a few respects from the older method of Zola, Dreiser, and Norris. Faulkner in *As I Lay Dying*, while observing most of the naturalistic rules, has little to do with deterministic philosophy, which Parrington considered "the vital principle of naturalism, setting it off from realism"; in this book the Mississippi author is concerned almost exclusively with the mind-flow of low intelligence. Nor can the works of Faulkner and Caldwell about poor-whites be regarded as entirely pessimistic. Caldwell's Jeeter Lester in *Tobacco Road* and Ty Ty Walden in *God's Little Acre* are incurable optimists.

Despite such differences, these writers belong definitely to naturalism as much by virtue of their emphasis on the so-called animal instincts, particularly sex, as by their conventional lapses from the naturalistic formula. For example, in *Tobacco Road*, Caldwell drops the objective viewpoint by criticizing a landowner for

1. *Main Currents in American Thought*, III, 323-25.

unintelligent management and by advocating "co-opera-
tive and corporate farming" as a means of saving Jeeter
and other sharecroppers. This is propaganda as bald
as any in Dorothy Scarborough's *In the Land of Cotton*.

Creating in the naturalistic manner, William Faulkner
and Erskine Caldwell have brought about five culmina-
tions in the history of fiction about the poor-white:
(1) the frank and full representation of the sordid elements in these people, (2) the emphasis upon sex,
especially in comedy, (3) the exploration of stupid
poor-white minds, (4) the tragic concept of the poor-
white, and (5) the complete studies of poor-white men
to match those of women by Miss Roberts and Miss
Kelley. All of these are, in effect, variations of earlier
portraiture and all have definite connections with other
contemporary work.

With the appearance of Faulkner's *Sanctuary* in
1931, the interest of these Southerners in the sordid
evoked protest and distress in critical quarters. Henry
S. Canby tagged Faulkner and other naturalists, "the
School of Cruelty."[2] To some critics, the Mississippi
author's characters were "the dregs of humankind,"
"bad dreams of reality," and "creatures almost too sick
or too depraved to be called human." And one reviewer
thought that readers of Caldwell's *Tobacco Road* (1932)
would "probably finish it—with disgust and a slight
retching." But these Southern naturalists are merely
emphasizing a side of poor-white life that has existed
both in fact and in literature for two hundred years.
About 1728, William Byrd was amused at the squalor
of the North Carolina (?) lubbers; in 1834 Caruthers

2. *Sat. Rev. of Lit.*, VII (March 21, 1931), 673-74.

pitied a diseased tar heel family; twenty-two years later Mrs. Stowe displayed the evils of slavery in filthy, starving squatters; and from the thirties to the early fifties Simms found that poor-white degeneracy added to the viciousness of his villains. All of this before the Civil War. From the seventies through the nineties, the local-color period, addicted to the quaint and sweet, forgot about the brutalizing poverty of the po' buckra. And in the twentieth century, the sensibilities amplified some sordid details as impacts upon mind and heart.

Historically considered, the loudly condemned American sadism of Faulkner and Caldwell, as it applies to poor-whites, is merely a revival of the emphasis upon degradation, employed by Longstreet and a few others for humor, by the abolitionists for propaganda. Now it is used by these Southerners for fictional effects, both humorous and tragic.

And because of this difference in literary intention, Faulkner and Caldwell have created a poor-white world sharply set off from its earlier Northern prototype. The abolitionists were concerned with sandhiller depravity only for its social moral; in short, the same motive that produced E. C. L. Adam's recent sketches, "The Carolina Wilderness,"[3] which depict the hates, violence, and lawlessness of South Carolina Crackers. Caldwell and especially Faulkner have raised the baser aspects in the life of the "low-down people" from propagandist illustration to the level of horror, and thereby earned for themselves another tag, "The Southern Gothic School."[4]

3. *Scribner's Magazine*, LXXXIX (June, 1931), 611-16.
4. Ellen Glasgow, *Sat. Rev. of Lit.*, XII (May 4, 1935), 3-4.

Naturalistic Modes

The novel, *As I Lay Dying*, and the story, "The Hound," published in 1930 and 1931 respectively, may be taken as examples of Faulkner's Gothic mode in which his preoccupation with putrescence surpasses that of Shelley. The novel tells of the Bundren family's hauling the mother's corpse by wagon over forty miles to Jefferson, Mississippi. While they were fording a swelling stream, the coffin was soaked, the mules were drowned, and the leg of a son was broken. During the remainder of the journey, the corpse began to rot; buzzards wheeled on high; and the boy's leg became gangrenous. In "The Hound," Cotton, a murderer, jammed his victim's body head first into a hollow tree. Fearing detection from the howling at the tree of the dead man's hound and the buzzards' circling overhead, Cotton cut into the tree and pulled the body out— all except one leg, just as the sheriff arrested him. In jail, Cotton babbled wildly: "It would a' been all right, but it started coming to pieces. . . ."[5]

But even greater heights — or depths — of such writing were reached in the sordid burlesque, "Savannah River Payday" (1931),[6] by Caldwell. Around the Georgia sawmill, the countryside was foul with the carcasses of mules killed by overwork. Jake and Red started to town in a rattling Ford with the body of a Negro murdered on pay day. Stopping on a bridge for water, they noticed the Negro's gold teeth, and knocked them out with a wrench. But when Jake claimed these treasures, Red mauled him over the head; "a ball of skin and hair fell in the dust"; and Jake was dumped

5. *Harper's Magazine*, CLXIII (Aug., 1931), 70.
6. In *American Earth*, 85-97.

unconscious into the back seat. Later they stopped and chased a Negro girl whom Jake felled with a clod, but she escaped while her assaulters quarreled. Red seized the girl's hoe and sliced Jake's "ear off close to his face. Jake fell back and felt the side of his face and looked at the ear on the ground." Then he bandaged his head with his shirt sleeve. In town, their engine "killed" by rain, they went into a pool room, leaving the carcass behind. A dog snuffed the body; the town marshall sent word to move the Negro "before he stinks up the whole town." "Say," Jake said . . . "You go and tell that marshall that I said for him to take a long runnin' start and jump to hell. Me and Red's shootin' pool."

But a more important feature of the Southern naturalists' preoccupation with the animal nature of poor-whites is their emphasis upon sex, especially for comic purposes. But, again, as with bestiality and violence, this "careless love" of the trash has been neither invented nor newly found; it has been re-discovered. Early in the eighteenth century, Colonel Byrd recorded with Restoration delight the amorous tussles of lubber wenches with his surveyors; Joseph B. Cobb in *Mississippi Scenes* (1850) wrote of bawdy practical joking in the Lick-the-Skillet neighborhood; and in 1863, J. R. Gilmore showed us Mrs. Bony Mulock bartering away her husband's sexual services. But for nearly seventy years after Gilmore's slattern, no writer thought the sensual antics of the poor-whites funny—or was prepared to say so. Indeed, the local-color period was so prudish that in literature the prolific trash became sexless and largely remained so

222

until the twentieth century. From DeForest's lively bawds, Nancy Gile and Sally Hugg, in 1871 to Alice French's "Headlights," twenty years later, there was not a whisper to indicate that the tackies might sometimes play fast and loose. Only with the work of the Kelley-Roberts-Green school did the revival of this part of poor-white existence begin.

And although this sexual emphasis of Caldwell and Faulkner is the usual one of naturalists and, at the same time, owes much to the sanction of contemporary taste, as well as to the writings of Sherwood Anderson, Masters, and Joyce, it is historically the dramatization of poor-white sexual sins outlined by J. R. Gilmore about seventy years ago in his essay, "The Sum of the Whole."[7]

Yet contrary to the popular impression of Faulkner, in the small number of his works about poor-whites, sex is not very important. Dewey Dell Bundren in *As I Lay Dying*, pregnant because of a cotton-patch rendezvous, interrupts the wagon trip with her mother's corpse to buy illegal medicines. Also with child out of wedlock, Lena Grove in *Light in August* (1932) wandered from Alabama to Mississippi searching for her "sawdust Casanova." After giving birth to her child at Jefferson (Oxford), Mississippi, and setting out in a wagon to wander with a kind religious hill-man, until she can agree to marry him, Lena drawls in poor-white laconic fashion, "My, my. A body does get around. Here we ain't been coming from Alabama, but two months, and now it's already Tennessee." But Faulkner does not dramatize the sexual experience of these women.

7. *Among the Guerillas*, chap. ii.

The Southern Poor-White

Not so with Erskine Caldwell. He appears, to William Troy, so absorbed with sex or the "ecstacy of the animal" that his characters are divested of all things human: "What each of them is reduced to finally," he thinks, "is a kind of abstraction from the human to the animal and even farther . . . from the complete animal organism to the single instinct." This opinion can be maintained for some characters, but it is a short-range view. Historically, the important fact is that Erskine Caldwell has developed a long-neglected side of poor-white life, which, narrowed and bestialized by poverty, is of necessity strongly motivated by the instincts of sex, as well as of fear and hunger. And, in the second place, by writing of the sensuality of Georgia Crackers as comedy, he has added to American literature a sort of humor that Mark Twain might have written had he dared.

In this sex comedy of the poor-whites, two stories by Caldwell tell of promiscuity among itinerant field-hands, a theme and a group last used by Alice French, forty years ago, in her story, "The Mortgaging of Jeffy." But from this story, Caldwell's two narratives: "The Strawberry Season" (1931)[8] and "Picking Cotton,"[9] differ sharply. Whereas Miss French devotes herself to the wages of sin—just as Paul Green does today—Caldwell is interested in the easy sexual ways of these footloose farmhands as they affect the emotions of two small boys whom he makes the narrators. In "The Strawberry Season," the boy cannot forget how Fanny cried when he put a berry down the front of her dress and slapped

8. *American Earth*, 3-9.
9. *We Are The Living*, 89-94.

it hard. The adolescent in "Picking Cotton," enraged at Gertie for boasting of her end-of-the-row woods-trysts with men pickers and for her teasing him with sex riddles, beat her and crammed her mouth full of cotton. Both stories, strongly reminiscent of Sherwood Anderson's "I Want to Know Why," represent the gap between local-color like that of Miss French and the naturalistic mode.[10]

These sex stories, however, with the pathetic note of adolescence about them are not in Caldwell's characteristic vein—a vein which is marked by drollery and what Horace Gregory calls "idiotic gravity." Like Faulkner's Dewey Dell, Caldwell's tenant folk regard sex as irresistible. With them it is not a question of shall or shall not, but of when and how. Accepting the urgent necessity of sex, they are tolerant of others' philandering; oblivious of the inhibitions of more squeamish people, they, like the folk of the ages of Chaucer and of Charles II, can enjoy the game of sex without self-consciousness. By so representing the Georgia Cracker, Caldwell has been able to approximate the *fabliau* more closely than any other American writer.

The finest single example of this humor in Caldwell is the story, "Meddlesome Jack" (1933),[11] which Carl Van Doren, with justifiable enthusiasm, calls "a bawdy masterpiece."[12] It is a tall yarn about "the meanest looking jackass" that had ever been seen on a certain Georgia countryside and how his braying threw all things female into idiotic frenzy. White women, black

10. For example, with a modicum of the description used by Miss French, Caldwell gives both scene and poor-whites with far greater actuality.
11. *We Are The Living*, 95-114.
12. *Nation*, CXXXVII (Oct. 18, 1933), 445.

women, and mares all acted alike when the jack, galloping about, sawed the air with his rasping cry.

Long ago, European authors employed this theme of the sexual stimulation of human beings by the behavior of animals; but American taste has only recently altered enough to make possible Erskine Caldwell's rare tale of the poor-whites and the meanest looking jack. In 1926, Faulkner had written. "We have one priceless universal trait, we Americans. That trait is our humor. What a pity it is that it is not more prevalent in our art."[13] Such yarns as this one and others of Caldwell, along with Faulkner's own "Spotted Horses," have done much to return our humor to strong native channels.

But the "idiotic gravity" of the poor-whites, which only Gilmore in his portrait of Mrs. Bony Mulock and DeForest in his sketches of bureau life had caught, Caldwell has exaggerated and applied to sex with excellent effect. In *Tobacco Road*, Jeeter Lester, having sold his daughter, Pearl, to Lov for a wife, discussed sagely with his son-in-law the problem of the girl's refusal to sleep with her husband; Ty Ty Walden in *God's Little Acre*, watched raptly by lantern light his daughter, Darling Jill, and an albino in amorous toil; and Vic Glover in "August Afternoon" fumed and did nothing about his new wife sitting on the front steps and enticing a "yellow-headed sapsucker" who whittled confidently under a tree.[14]

This favorite comic scene of Caldwell—one in which a person watches sexual preliminaries—may be found

13. *Sherwood Anderson and Other Famous Creoles*, foreword.
14. *We Are The Living*, 143-57.

superbly written in Chaucer's *Troilus and Criseyde*.
There Pandarus leads his friend Troilus at night to the
bed of Criseyde. Troilus falls by the bed and prays
until Pandarus strips the timorous lover's shirt off and
hurls him into bed; Troilus faints. Pandarus and his
niece, Criseyde, revive him. Criseyde kisses and loves
Troilus into a passion. Uncle Pandarus, altogether
delighted, says that he should no longer hold the candle
to the rendezvous, but put it in the fireplace. Thus
Chaucer, a master of the lusty yarn or *fabliau*, used his
masterpiece of characterization, Pandarus, in the exact
situation employed by the Georgia author.

Through the poor-white by the hand of Caldwell the
fabliau accent has re-entered American literature.

The third important cumulation made in the depiction of the poor-white by the naturalistic method has
been the exploration of low-intelligences. Before the
studies of Faulkner and Caldwell almost nothing had
been done in this direction. The incidental use of woolhats in fiction made the probing of their minds super-
fluous. Ben Pickett's idiot daughter in Simms' *Richard
Hurdis*, half-witted Bud Stucky in Harris' "Azalia,"
and simple-minded Sion Alford in Green's *The Field
God*—all are merely objects to be seen and pitied. The
practice before the twentieth century had been either
to stay outside the Cracker's mind or to attribute to
him thoughts and emotions suitable for almost anyone.
For instance, Thomas Nelson Page provided Little
Darby with the mental equipment of any high-souled
Virginian. And the sensibilitists in the twentieth
century have concerned themselves primarily with the
sensitive minds of exceptional tenant women.

The Southern Poor-White

Thus it remained for Faulkner to study fully the slow, dull wits of poor-whites in a series of inner-monologues which make up his novel, *As I Lay Dying*. Four years before the publication of this novel, E. J. O'Brien had noticed the beginning of a shift in the story to the "more difficult task of eliciting and defining the inarticulate emotions of those who have been dimly defeated by American life." In Faulkner's book, for the first time, we follow the twilight minds of an entire family: Mrs. Addie Bundren, the dying woman, who had been decent before marrying a poor-white; Anse, her lazy, stupid husband; and four children: Cash, simple but capable with tools; Darl, an idiot; Dewey Dell, a slow-witted, sensuous girl; Vardaman, a normal child; and Jewell, the result of Addie's illicit relation with a preacher, and, therefore, a brighter person than the other children.

But Faulkner's method of revealing the stream-of-consciousness in such inarticulate human beings is not the usual one of childish vocabulary and naïvete. Witness the feelings of the young boy, Vardaman, described in words like "integrity" or "co-ordinated whole." Much of the content of these inner monologues is undoubtedly modernistic trickery; but, on the other hand, Faulkner has made an attempt to convey a sense of the callousness, limitation, and, at times, the strange acuteness of poor-white minds. And so well has he succeeded that through the thoughts of various persons the character and story of Anse merge with uncommon reality. He was the first important Southern poor-white to appear in contemporary American fiction, even though he is far less completely realized than Caldwell's Jeeter and Ty Ty.

Anse was a sight to behold: his collapsed, toothless face had the "appearance that old dogs have," and his eyes were "like pieces of burnt-out cinder." A shiftless procrastinator, he had brought his wife to her deathbed from field-work and from worry over his laziness. Now as she was dying, Anse cursed his ill luck, the hardness of God's ways, and longed for a set of false teeth. When Addie finally stopped breathing, Anse thought: "God's will be done. . . . . Now I can get them teeth." Yet Addie had dominated his weak mind for so long that he could not deny her last request to be buried at Jefferson, forty miles away. This sworn duty to the dead so possessed him that he mortgaged everything he had to complete the journey. Once Addie— already somewhat rotten—had been put underground, Anse quickly got his false teeth and then another wife before the family started homeward. Since this was Anse's first trip to town in twelve years, he thought best to provide for the future.

The life of Anse suggests several aspects of poor-white mentality as presented by both Faulkner and Caldwell: first, the tendency of limited minds to obsessions; second, a marked insensitivity; and third, a somewhat paradoxical acuteness, perhaps better—sensibility. Anse Bundren can think only of getting Addie buried and Cash of nothing except carpentering. Caldwell's Jeeter Lester has a mind overwhelmed by the longing to farm; and gold-fever causes Ty Ty Walden to dig his farm full of deep pits.

The deadening of normal emotions from dire poverty

The Southern Poor-White

receives its most extreme illustration in *Tobacco Road*. Not only are the Lesters without family feelings or sympathies; they show a queer insensitivity toward people physically deformed. Ellie May Lester, a hare-lipped girl, cried and ran when the other Lesters talked about her slit mouth. And Bessie, the cracked-brained preacher, whose nose had no bone in it, was forever clapping her hand over her wide-open nostrils, for "Dude had once said that when he looked at her nose it was like looking down the end of a double-barrel shotgun."

This callousness in ordinary human relations, however, is balanced somewhat by a paradoxical sensibility in both Jeeter and Ty Ty, which relates them to the characters of Miss Roberts and her sort. As dead as Jeeter's emotional nature is in some respects, he has a fine, primitive sense of the ground not inferior to that of Ellen Chesser or of Miss Cather's Alexandra Bergson in *O Pioneers* (1913). And Ty Ty possesses a sort of mystical knowledge of the living beauty in man. It is from these virtues that the ironic tragedy of these two Crackers springs.

To present adequately the last two contributions of the naturalistic mode, the tragic concept and the remaining pair of full-length studies of poor-white men, the characterizations of Jeeter Lester and Ty Ty Walden must be placed in historical perspective.

It has taken two hundred years of writing about the poor-white to produce Jeeter Lester. In 1932, when he appeared as the chief character in *Tobacco Road*, there was no completely adequate portrait of a man from his class in American literature. Longstreet's Ransy Sniffle and Taliaferro's Ham Rachel we glimpse for only a short

Henry Hull as Jeeter Lester in the Play, *Tobacco Road*

while in their sorry careers; Smith's life of Bill Arp is anecdote and synopsis rather than a complete fictional re-creation; and Miss Glasgow's Nick Burr and Abel Revercomb rise out of their poor-white world by early manhood. But not so with Jeeter; for, although Caldwell concerns himself with only the last few weeks of this Cracker's existence, by cut-backs in the story he has been able to relate the history of three generations of Lesters from the time of the original settlement on Tobacco Road to the death of Jeeter. And in *God's Little Acre* (1933), Ty Ty Walden, the second life-sized creation of the trashy Cracker, established Caldwell as the foremost interpreter of the poor-white.

But not only were Jeeter and Ty Ty the first satisfactory novelistic "heroes" from the trash; they were the first tragic poor-whites. Before them, there was merely the pathetic and the near tragic. Caruthers had drawn his still-life of a destitute tar heel family with pity; Trowbridge's heart went out to weak Dan Pepperill in his sufferings in *Cudjo's Cave;* and R. M. Johnston in "A Surprise to Mr. Thompson Byers"[15] wrote with moist eye of the idiot boy, Sandy. These and many other writers, North and South, before and after the war, came no nearer the tragedy of poor-white life than to pity its miseries. Just one Southerner in one story went further. In the life of Mrs. Feratia Bivens in "Mingo" (1880), Joel Chandler Harris realized that he had tragedy, but he apologized for this old crone as a tragic figure and lapsed into sentiment. The creator of Uncle Remus was all heart.

Much nearer the tragic conception of Caldwell was

15. *Lippincott's Magazine,* XLVIII (July, 1891), 74-82.

The Southern Poor-White

the work of the Northern writer, John W. DeForest. In his story, "The Independent Ku Klux" (1872), he conceived his poor-white, Selnarten Bowen, in burlesque and irony. For Selnarten, initiated into the K.K.K. in mock ceremony, started on a career of comic thievery which ended in murder and surrender to the law. In this yarn, DeForest used elements that with starker handling, more sympathy, and less burlesque, were to be used by Caldwell in creating his two master portraits. Besides these nineteenth-century hints toward tragedy, in the present century Miss Glasgow and Miss Scarborough preceded Caldwell with their stories of self-made heroes in defeat. But these were hardly anticipations; only the romantically diluted determinism of Miss Scarborough pointed toward *Tobacco Road*. And the hankering after something higher in the works of Paul Green and the other sensibilitists has little in common with the longings of Jeeter and Ty Ty.

The truth of the matter, then, seems to be that Erskine Caldwell's tragic conception of his Georgia Crackers is original. For, in it, he has compounded all of the elements used before his time and given to the fusion the peculiar marks of his talent and of the naturalistic licenses of the time. And so, over two centuries after Colonel William Byrd had watched the lubber leaning on his snake-fence, Caldwell introduces us to Jeeter Lester on Tobacco Road, not to ridicule him as the Virginian would have done, but to show the irony and tragedy of his lot. The story of this old Cracker is one of determinism, both hereditary and economic.

In Georgia, Jeeter Lester was starving to death on

232

Naturalistic Modes

the wornout sandhills of Tobacco Road. For nearly eight years he had not farmed. That meant no credit for rations or snuff. And now that his cow had died and his old Ford would no longer rattle to Augusta with a load of almost unsalable blackjack wood, he was desperate. People watched him so closely that stealing food seemed impossible. As a result of all these things, Jeeter and his family had existed for the past several days on boiled meat rinds and corn pone.

Nor was there any hope of farming or of getting work to do along Tobacco Road, because the whole section was an agricultural graveyard, the ghost-land of two crops. At present, many years after it had been exhausted by tobacco, it was abandoned by the absentee owner as unfit for cotton. Out of pity, the landlord allowed Jeeter and other sharecroppers to remain in the shacks rent-free until the miserable hovels should rot down. Across the field, grown up in broomsedge and scrub pines, could be seen wrecks of long-unused tobacco barns and deserted tenant houses. And everywhere red gullies cut the land and even Tobacco Road.

Still Jeeter would not move elsewhere: he expected any day to borrow a mule, find credit for guano, and start a cotton crop. But meanwhile, the Lesters in their struggle to escape starvation sank to the lowest poor-white level. Even the Negroes passing along Tobacco Road stared, silent and amazed, at the Lesters as if seeing some new form of life.[16] Nor did the blacks ever lower themselves by speaking; and they knew "white folks." Certainly, the Lesters were a simple, if not

16. That there were and are plenty of originals of the Lesters in Jefferson County, Georgia, between Wrens and Keysville (Tobacco Road Country), the survey of the *Chronicle* (Augusta, Ga.), clearly proved. See *Time*, March 25, 1935, "Letters."

weak-minded lot. Jeeter had few brains, and his wife
Ada had fewer. Indeed, during most of her married
life of forty years, she had been silent. Dude, Ellie May
—perhaps all of the seventeen Lester children were
hare-brained. And not one of them could read or write.

With so little of brain to provide either will or fore-
sight, Jeeter, along with his family, in the struggle to
eat became a beast, driven by hunger to live and then
by sex to "pleasure himself." In such a dog-eat-dog
existence, he had lost all morality and family sense.
He sold Pearl, his twelve-year-old daughter, to Lov for
a wife; the price was seven dollars, a gallon of cylinder
oil, and some quilts. Jeeter hated his mother, a pel-
lagra-ridden sack of bones, for living so long. To him she
was "nothing more than a door-jamb," and whenever
he could keep her from eating he did so. Nor did Jeeter
have a mite of fatherly kindness. Through the years,
he had sworn that he would have Ellie May's hare-lip
sewed up. Now he faulted God and made the girl cry
by his talk. "I don't believe He done the right thing by
her," Jeeter said, "when He opened her lip like that. . . .
What use is a slit like that for? You can't spit through it,
and you can't whistle through it, now can you? It was
just meanness on His part when He done that. That's
what it was—durn meanness."

Cut off by poverty and degeneracy from the countryside diversions of decent folk, he found little delight
except in sex. Rebuked for his bawdy life by the bawdier
preacher, Sister Bessie, Jeeter at once dilated. "I used to
be a powerful sinful man in my time. I reckon I was at
one time the most powerful sinful man in the whole
country. Now, you take them Peabody children over

across the field. I reckon clear near about all of them is half mine, one way or the other."

Just as the Lester shack could not rot and sag further without falling, so Jeeter and his family could not sink lower and live. How he had fallen to such degradation was the story of the Lesters over a hundred years. The whole section around Tobacco Road had been owned and cleared by Jeeter's grandfather, a prosperous grower of the weed. Half of this original tract was willed to Jeeter's father, who quickly lost most of it, because he raised only cotton—and less of that every year. Then Jeeter inherited what land there was, debts, and a mortgage. The few acres left after the settlement slipped away from Jeeter, for, he, too, was a one-crop farmer, pouring into the loose, sandy land more and more guano that the rains promptly washed out. Thereafter, a share-cropper on the old Lester land, he farmed in the same way, until the discouraged owner sold the stock and left him to starve.[17] This decline through two generations of the cotton-growing Lesters constitutes a Southern type-history, a parable of the poverty crop. It is also a naturalistic sequence of economic and hereditary determinism. Stupid, undiversified farming produced poverty; poverty brought filthy living and ignorance; ignorance and filthy living caused depravity, both physical and moral.

But this is neither *all* of the parable nor *all* of Jeeter's story. Despite this old Cracker's degeneracy, he had

17. This entire chronicle is placed into the novel as an interlude of propaganda. J. D. Wade's opinion that "the protracted economic depression of the Southern farmer is in each of the Caldwell books set morally somewhere distressingly close to Wall Street's own front doorstep" is simply not true (*Southern Review*, I, Winter, 1936, 457).

one redeeming passion that, properly guided, might have saved him: he was a fool about farming. He scorned being a "durn woodchopper," and as for moving to the cotton mills as many another sharecropper was doing:

"No! By God and by Jesus, no!" Jeeter had said. "That's one thing I ain't going to do! The Lord made the land, and He put me here to raise crops on it. I been doing that, and my daddy before me, for the past fifty years, and that's what's intended. Them durn cotton mills is for the women folks to work in."

And the county poor farm—that place would never see him.[18] He would rather starve than leave the Lester farm—"my land," he called it. And home ground it was, only more; it was to Jeeter "the good earth." For he had an acute awareness of the power in the soil. In the spring, his nose was the first to catch the smell of plowed fields miles away, and he loved to feel the winds off them "going down inside of his body."

Yet this one redeeming passion of the old Cracker was denied; he had nothing with which to farm. Hence, late February days, when fields were to be burned over for plowing, made Jeeter restless and miserable. "I sort of want to cry . . ." he said. "The smell of that sedge-smoke this time of year near about drives me crazy. Then pretty soon all the other farmers will start plowing. That's what gets under my skin worse. When the smell of new earth turning over behind the plows strikes me, I get all weak and shaky." This longing he could not down, so that every year he had burned over his land, hoping that somehow he could break ground.

18. This queer pride of the Southern poor-white J. W. DeForest noted nearly seventy years ago.

Naturalistic Modes

One February after firing his fields, Jeeter went to bed, "smelling the aroma of pine and broomsedge smoke in the night" and swearing that he would get up the next morning, borrow a mule, and plow his land for the first time in eight years. Before sun-up the wind shifted, blowing the flames toward his dry tar-dripped cabin. At mid-morning he and Ada were two charred corpses in a bed of hot ashes.

Ironically enough, the good in Jeeter had led to his destruction. In his love of farming (no matter that it was stupid farming) and in his hatred of cotton mills, Jeeter represents the last stand of the old agrarian stock against the exodus to the cotton mills. "It would be difficult to explain to a stranger," wrote Edwin de Leon in 1874, "the horror the Southern men and women . . . entertained for the cotton factory and its life and labors."[19] Yet by the twentieth century fewer and fewer poor-whites were willing to starve and say to mill-hill with Jeeter, "No! By God and by Jesus, no!"

Ty Ty Walden in *God's Little Acre* has much in common with Jeeter. Both are dominated by obsessions: Jeeter to farm, Ty Ty to find gold. For "close on to fifteen years," Ty Ty had been digging his farm full of pot-holes, and the gold-fever still had him steaming. Like Jeeter before forced to stop sharecropping, he was a trifling farmer. Instead of cultivating his land, he kept his two sons deep in the red-clay gold pits, while two lazy Negro croppers made sorry cotton. Completely absorbed in digging, Ty Ty forgot to feed his workers until Black Sam threatened to eat his landlord's mule to keep from starving. Once Ty Ty and his family

19. *Southern Magazine*, XIV (June, 1874), 568.

barely escaped starvation by securing a loan from his son, Jim Leslie, who had prospered in a mill town nearby. Known far and wide as a gold fanatic and shabby farmer, Ty Ty was no longer respected, not even by Jim Leslie, whose pocketpook he was forever trying to open. Moreover, in his sexual nature, he is even closer to Jeeter. The naughty curiosity of an old lecher, past his days of potency, afflicted them both. And their code of sex is the same as that of the Negroes which in turn was very nearly that of the dogs.

Nevertheless, Ty Ty is not another Jeeter. Even the traits which they share are somewhat different, and in others Ty Ty is sharply set off from his predecessor. He is honest, humane, and religious according to his lights. Had he not set aside "God's Little Acre" for his Lord? And while both he and Jeeter are obsessed by sex, Ty Ty possesses a mystical sense of its beauty. Simple and foolish old Cracker though he is, Ty Ty, like Whitman and D. H. Lawrence, knew the cleanness and beauty of the procreative act as a living principle in man. And his joy in this certainty brought about his tragedy.

Confident that he had the key to man's happiness, Ty Ty evolved a way of living which was a queer jumble of mysticism and free love. He would have none of the preacher's doctrine of duality: God against the flesh and the devil. "A man," he claimed, "has got God in him from the start." And this divinity in man the old Cracker thought he recognized in sexual love. "If there's anything in the world He's crazy about," he declared, "it's seeing a man and a woman fools about each other. He knows then that the world is running along slick as grease." To try to keep a man or a woman "all for yourself" is to invite "trouble and sorrow the rest of your days." Hence, it is a man's duty, as he told his prospective son-in-law, Pluto Swint, to make Darling Jill "so pleased she'll leave off with everybody but you."

In his glorification of what to him was the beauty in life, Ty Ty lauded the prowess of his family, vowing that "it takes a Walden to make the girls all wrought up." He was thankful that the good Lord had blessed him with three of the prettiest girls a man ever had in his house. But his pride in the beauty of his daughter-in-law, Griselda, brought about his tragedy. Her perfect body so amazed old Ty Ty that he spent all his spare time snooping about to spy on her. And whenever possible, he launched into a paean of her loveliness. "It's a wonder," he mumbled, "that God ever put such prettiness in the house with an onery old cuss like me." But when Ty Ty went with Griselda to borrow money from his son in Augusta, he praised her to the wrong man. Jim Leslie had a diseased wife who "looks like she's all mashed down on the chest and can't rise up." Later, Jim Leslie came to take Griselda by force out of his father's house and was shot by the girl's husband. To foolish old Ty Ty had come the thing he dreaded most of all. "I reckon," he once said, "I'd just fold up and die if I saw blood spilled on my land. I'd never be able to get over the sight of it." It was also tragic irony that his praising Griselda's beauty had caused one son to kill another, nor merely on his land, but on God's Little Acre. Therefore, the immediate tragedy of Ty Ty came from perverted idealism, the product of his weak, gentle mind, not from economic pressure as was the case with Jeeter. By mixing God and poor-white promiscuity into a sort of private religion and by becoming the evangel of it, he destroyed his own happiness.

Finally, what may be said of the naturalistic contribution? By virtue of their additions to the literary chronicle of the lowest Southerners, Faulkner and Caldwell have given these folk their most important literary existence. The creation of Jeeter would alone warrant such a verdict, for thereby the Southern poor-white became established in contemporary literature alongside of Babbitt and other American types. Jeeter Lester is to the poor-whites what Uncle Remus is to the Negroes—a name for his class.

CONCLUSION

BACKWARD GLANCE OVER THE POOR-WHITE'S STORY

THROUGH SOMEWHAT OVER TWO CENTURIES — from William Byrd's "History of the Dividing Line" (1728) to Erskine Caldwell's *Tobacco Road* (1932) —the literary history of the Southern poor-white has been tracked and explained in four periods.

In the Colonial era, Byrd recorded humorously the origin of the poor-white as frontier lubber along the Virginia-North Carolina border—an indolent, shiftless wretch, bedevilled by vermin, agues, and the "country distemper" from eating unsalted pork.

From the early 1800's to the Civil War, the lubber emerged in literature as the poor-white, variously dubbed Cracker, woolhat, dirt-eater, or tacky. Having received the attention of only travel writers and historians in the eighteenth century, he now was placed in novels as a minor character and in short sketches of humor as "the whole show." The Southern novelists in the plantation tradition largely ignored him, although Caruthers in the *Kentuckian in New York* (1834) pitied him and Simms used him as a villain, achieving the notable portrait of Bostwick. Humorists in the South, however, from Longstreet to Charles H. Smith, employed the trashy Cracker with excellent effect and produced the most important interpretation before the twentieth century. In fiction, the major treatment of him occurred in the North, where abolitionists displayed him in minor rôles as a living indictment, economic and moral, of the planter class.

During the local-color age (*ca.* 1870-1900), the poor-white came into the main rôle of short stories and general consideration in one novel, Cable's *Bonaventure* (1888). Besides this gain in fiction, the range of literature about the po' buckra was expanded both in geographical setting and in types. Indeed, the work of authors like Thomas Nelson Page, Joel Chandler Harris, and Cable so firmly established him as a pathetic regional type, worthy of understanding, that the tradition of the Cracker was passed on vividly to the twentieth century for yet another literary emphasis.

Beginning around 1900, the swelling stream of writing about the sorriest Southerner, once a lubber, then a poor-white, and now a tenant or sharecropper, reached a crest in the vogue of the twenties and early thirties. In Miss Glasgow's fiction during the early years of the century, he entered the main rôles of novels; by 1923, the poor-white woman had at last the same consideration in Edith S. Kelley's *Weeds;* and with Harold Williamson's *Peggy* (produced 1919, published 1922), closely followed by the work of Paul Green, the lowest tar heels came into drama. The profusion of sketches, short stories, novels, plays—everything except poems— was so varied that nearly every sort of previous writing about the trash re-appeared with time-differences. There were, however, two outstanding advances in the fiction of sensibility and naturalism—modes which have apparently exhausted the literary possibilities of the tenant farmer as he now exists. Through these two schools, the mind, degeneracy, and tragedy of the poor-white were completely presented.

But in addition to such a running account of the steadily augmenting literature about poor-whites, a view of these characters from all over the South moving down to our time will, more than any other means of presentation, reveal the variety, continuity, and near-completeness of this American chronicle.

In 1728, Col. Byrd watched the lubber—the original poor-white—resting his lazy life away along the Dividing Line. Just after the Revolution, Bostwick, squatter and "white Indian," did the dirty work for Tory Negro stealers during South Carolina's first reconstruction; and later in the great days before the Civil War, Nancy Gile and Sally Hugg gave "treats" in their old-field cabin to which planters went when on the loose. Up in the Old North State, Mrs. Bony Mulock, who had a "durn sight d'ruther chaw," was blackmailing her husband into a cash settlement. At Georgia musters, Bill Arp and O. J. G. stamped about, the crowing bullies of the drill ground; and once the gouging and fighting got under way, the dirt-eater, Ransy Sniffle, began whooping it up and tearing about like a "fice" dog. Down in Mississippi, Bob Bagshot was such an amorous and violent cut-up that his pranks kept the whole Lick-the-Skillet neighborhood in a stew. That lanky sharper, Simon Suggs, wandered and swindled in Alabama, while Ham Rachel staggered home from Eufaula to his "diggins" with two jugs of the "good critter" slung over his shoulder. At his lonely Virginia cross-roads shack, Jimmy Gordon stealthily traded liquor to slaves for stolen goods.

The Southern Poor-White

Then came the Civil War. Some of the Crackers delighted in playing war; but Tim Mills got tired of the game and hied back to Holetown in the Virginia piney-woods. There he skulked about the woods as Long John was doing in Florida. But "Little Darby," a sorrier Crockett of the Old Dominion, discovered his true forte in battle and died a hero's death. Across the mountains in the Tennessee foothills, weak Dan Pepperill tried to remain neutral while helping a Union family secretly, only, after being flogged, to weaken and join the C. S. A. Far to the South the illiterate Cajuns were hauled off to a war and a world they knew not of.

After the surrender, when Ku Kluxery was abroad, Selnarten Bowen, a pigstealer, tried to join the Klan to carry on his thievery. Later, one picnic day in Georgia, Mrs. Feratia Bivins poured out to her guest the bitter story of her sufferings at the hands of an aristocratic planter family. In the same state, Emma Jane Stucky and her half-wit son, Bud, hovered around the village of Azalia depending upon charity for the meager existence of their kind. About the Black River country in Arkansas, "Headlights" roved with her band of wandering cotton-pickers, carousing and fighting. While in Louisiana, the sorry Cajun, Arsène, wheedled his perique tobacco and *café noir* from the planter's store and forgot about his crop. But not all of the poor-whites were trash. Once the South began to be developed commercially and business broke down class lines somewhat it was possible for Nick Burr to become a Virginia Lincoln and occupy the governor's mansion of his state.

By the twentieth century the tenant system of the South was pressing all hope out of the descendants of happy Crackers like Ham Rachel and Bill Arp. Year after year in Kentucky tobacco fields, Judy Pippinger and Ellen Chesser slaved to no purpose and found peace only in a stoical acceptance of their lot as tenant wives. Likewise, Peggy Warren's dreams of escaping North Carolina cotton fields and tenant cabins and going to the city were blasted. Deep in the Florida wilds, the "white Indian" Mart was at last overtaken by society; the squatter and trapper could no longer hide out from the world. Across forty miles of Mississippi roads, simple, degenerate old Anse Bundren hauled and finally buried the corpse of his wife. But on Tobacco Road in Georgia, Jeeter Lester reached the dead end of the sharecropper's row.

BIBLIOGRAPHY

BIBLIOGRAPHY

I. BIBLIOGRAPHY

Boyd, William K. and Brooks, Robert P. *Selected Bibliography and Syllabus of the History of the South, 1584-1876.* University of Georgia Bulletin, Vol. XVIII, No. 6 Athens, Ga.: McGregor Co., 1918.

Cappon, Lester J. *Bibliography of Virginia History Since 1865.* University, Va.: Institute for Research in the Social Sciences, 1930.

Engstfeld, Caroline P. *Bibliography of Alabama Authors.* Howard College Bulletin, Vol. LXXXI. Birmingham, Ala.: Howard College, 1923.

Hart, Bertha S. *Introduction to Georgia Writers.* Macon, Ga.: J. W. Burke Co., 1929.

Longmire, Rowena. *Dictionary Catalogue of the Short Stories of Arkansas, Missouri, and Iowa from 1869-1900.* Unpublished Master's thesis, Department of English Language and Literature, University of Chicago, 1932.

McVoy, Lizzie C. and Campbell, Ruth B. *Bibliography of Fiction by Louisianians and on Louisiana Subjects.* Baton Rouge, La.: Louisiana State University Press, 1935.

Ray, Frank J. *Tennessee Writers: A Bibliographical Index.* Unpublished Master's thesis, Department of English, University of Tennessee, 1929.

Rothert, Otto A. *Local History in Kentucky Literature.* Paper read before the Louisville Literary Club, Louisville, Ky., September 27, 1915.

II. BOOKS OF HISTORY AND CRITICISM

Agar, Herbert. *The People's Choice.* Boston: Houghton Mifflin Co., 1933.

Andrews, Sidney. *The South since the War.* Boston: Ticknor and Fields, 1866.

The Southern Poor-White

Baldwin, Charles C. *The Men Who Make Our Novels*. New York: Dodd, Mead and Co., 1924.

Ball, William W. *The State That Forgot, South Carolina's Surrender to Democracy*. Indianapolis: Bobbs-Merrill Co., 1932.

Barbour, George M. *Florida for Tourists, Invalids, and Settlers. . .* New York: D. Appleton and Co., 1882.

Bassett, John S. *Slavery in the State of North Carolina*. Baltimore: Johns Hopkins Press, 1899.

Beard, Charles and Mary R. *The Rise of American Civilization*. Revised edition; New York: Macmillan Co., 1934.

Beard, James. *Ku Klux Klan Sketches*. Philadelphia: Claxton, Remsen, and Haffelfinger, 1877.

Beatty, Richmond C. *William Byrd of Westover*. Boston: Houghton Mifflin Co., 1932.

Beverley, Robert. *History of Virginia*. London: F. Fayram and J. Clarke, 1722. First published 1705.

Bissell, Benjamin J. *The American Indian in English Literature of the Eighteenth Century*. New Haven: Yale University Press, 1925.

Bond, Marjorie. *Below the Potomac*. University of North Carolina Bulletin, Vol. X, No. 7. Chapel Hill: Extension Division, University of North Carolina, 1933.

Bowers, Claude. *The Tragic Era*. Cambridge, Mass.: Houghton Mifflin Co., 1929.

Brown, William G. *The Lower South in American History*. New York: Macmillan Co., 1902.

Bruce, Philip A. *Virginia Plutarch*. Chapel Hill: University of North Carolina Press, 1929. Vol. I.

Bryant, William C. *Letters of a Traveller*. New York: Geo. P. Putnam, 1851.

Byrd, William, Fitzwilliam, R., and Dandridge, H. "A Journal of the Proceedings of the Commission. . . ." *Colonial Records of North Carolina*, ed. W. L. Saunders. Raleigh, N. C.: P.M. Hale, 1886. Vol. II.

Canby, Henry S. *The Short Story in English*. New York: Henry Holt and Co., 1909.

Bibliography

Cason, Clarence. *90° in the Shade*. Chapel Hill: University of North Carolina Press, 1935.

Clark Barrett H. *Paul Green*. New York: Robert M. McBride and Co., 1928.

Clark, Emily. *Innocence Abroad*. New York: Alfred A. Knopf, 1931.

Couch, William T. (ed.). *Culture in the South*. Chapel Hill: University of North Carolina Press, 1934. A. N. J. Den Hollander, "The Tradition of the 'Poor Whites.' "

Coulter, Ellis M. *A Short History of Georgia*. Chapel Hill: University of North Carolina Press, 1933.

Dabney. Virginius. *Liberalism in the South*. Chapel Hill: University of North Carolina Press, 1932.

Deland, Margaret. *Florida Days*. Boston: Little, Brown and Co., 1889.

Dennett, Daniel. *Louisiana As It Is*. . . . New Orleans: Eureka Press, 1876.

Dibble, Roy F. *Albion W. Tourgée*. New York: Lemcke and Buecher, 1921.

Ditchy, Jay K. *Les Acadiens Louisianais et leur parler*. Paris: Librairie E. Droz, 1932.

Dwight, Timothy. *Travels in New England and New York*. New Haven: Timothy Dwight, 1821. Vol. II.

Ellinger, Esther. *Southern War Poetry of the Civil War*. Hersley, Penna.: Hersley Press, 1918.

Faulkner, William. *Sherwood Anderson and Other Famous Creoles*. A Gallery of Contemporary New Orleans. Drawn by William Spratling and Arranged by William Faulkner. New Orleans: Pelican Bookshop Press, 1926.

Field, Henry M. *Blood is Thicker Than Water: A Few Days Among our Southern Brethren*, New York: Geo. Munro Publisher, 1886.

Fields, Annie. *Life and Letters of Harriet Beecher Stowe*. Boston: Houghton Mifflin and Co., 1897.

Fleming, Walter L. *Civil War and Reconstruction in Alabama*. New York: Columbia University Press, 1905.

Fleming, Walter L. (ed.). *Documentary History of Reconstruction—*. Cleveland, Ohio: A. H. Clark Co., 1907.

The Southern Poor-White

Fortier, Alcée. *Louisiana Studies*. New Orleans: F. F. Hansell and Brothers, 1894.

Gaines, Francis P. *The Southern Plantation*. New York: Columbia University Press, 1924.

Hamilton, J. G. DeR. *Reconstruction in North Carolina*. New York: Columbia University Press, 1914.

Harris, Joel C. (ed.). *Life of Henry W. Grady, including his Writings and Speeches*. New York: Cassell Publishing Co., 1890.

Harris, Julia (ed.). *Joel Chandler Harris, Editor and Essayist*. Chapel Hill: University of North Carolina Press, 1931.

Harris, Julia. *Life and Letters of Joel Chandler Harris*. Boston: Houghton Mifflin Co., 1918.

Hart, Albert B. *The Southern South*. New York: D. Appleton and Co., 1910.

Hawk, Emory Q. *Economic History of the South*. New York: Prentice-Hall Co., 1934.

Hazard, Lucy L. *The Frontier in American Literature*. New York: Thomas Y. Crowell Co., 1924.

Hendrick, Burton J. *The Training of an American: The Earlier Life and Letters of Walter H. Page, 1855-1913*. Boston: Houghton Mifflin Co., 1928.

Holladay, Alexander Q. *Social Conditions in Colonial North Carolina*. Raleigh, N. C.: E. M. Uzzell and Co., 1904.

Hollander, A. N. J. den. *De Landelijke arme Blanken in het zuiden der Vereenigde Staten*. Gronigen: J. B. Wolters' nitgevers-maatschapij, 1933.

Howells, William D. and Alden, Henry M. (eds.). *Southern Lights and Shadows*. New York: Harper and Bros. 1894.

Hundley, Daniel R. *Social Relations in our Southern States*. New York: H. B. Price, 1860.

Ingraham, Joseph H. *The Southwest*. New York: Harper and Bros., 1835. Vol. II.

Jones, Howard M. *Contemporary Southern Literature*. University of North Carolina Bulletin, Vol. VIII, No. 3. Chapel Hill: Extension Division, University of North Carolina, 1928.

Jones, Hugh. *Present State of Virginia*. Sabin's Reprints, No. 5.

Bibliography

New York: Reprinted for Joseph Sabin, 1865. First published 1724.

King, Edward. *The Great South*. Hartford, Conn.: American Publishing Co., 1875.

King, Joseph L., Jr. *Dr. George W. Bagby, A Study of Virginian Literature, 1850-1880*. New York: Columbia University Press, 1927.

Koch, Sigfrid Von. *Farmertypen nach dem Amerikanischen Roman*. Hamburg: Schimkus, 1933.

Lawson, John. *History of Carolina*. ed. Fred A. Olds. Charlotte, N. C.: Observer Printing House, 1903. First published 1714.

Lonn, Ella. *Reconstruction in Louisiana*. New York: G. P. Putnam's Sons, 1918.

Lyell, Sir Charles. *Second Visit to the United States of America*. London: John Murray, 1849. Vol. II.

Mesick, Jessie L. *English Traveller in America, 1785-1835*. New York: Columbia University Press, 1922.

Moore, Albert B. *Conscription and Conflict in the Confederacy*. New York: Macmillan Co., 1924.

Morais, Herbert M. *Deism in Eighteenth-century America*. New York: Columbia University Press, 1934.

Newton, L. W. *Americanization of French Louisiana*. Chicago, 1929. Unpublished Doctor's thesis, Department of History, University of Chicago. This work contains various citations of illiteracy in Louisiana from 1803 to 1870.

Nordhoff, Charles. *The Cotton States in the Spring and Summer of 1875*. New York: D. Appleton and Co., 1875.

Odum, Howard W. *An American Epoch*. New York: Henry Holt and Co., 1930.

———— (ed.). *Southern Pioneers in Social Interpretation*. Chapel Hill, University of North Carolina Press, 1925.

————. *Southern Regional Study Tables*. Chapel Hill, University of North Carolina Press, 1933.

Olmsted, Frederick L. *A Journey in the Back Country in the Winter of 1853-54*. New York: G. P. Putnam's Sons, 1907. First published in 1860.

The Southern Poor-White

Overton, Grant. *The Women Who Make Our Novels*. New York: Moffatt, Yard and Co., 1922.

Page, Rosewell. *Thomas Nelson Page*. New York: Chas. Scribner's Sons, 1923.

Page, Walter H. *Rebuilding of Old Commonwealths—*. New York: Doubleday, Page and Co., 1926.

Parrington, Vernon L. *Main Currents in American Thought*. Vol. I, *The Colonial Mind*; Vol. II, *The Romantic Revolution in America*; Vol. III, *Beginnings of Critical Realism in America, 1860-1900*. New York: Harcourt, Brace and Co., 1921, 1927, 1930.

Pattee, Frederick L. *Development of the American Short Story*. New York: Harper and Bros., 1923.

Phillips, Ulrich B. *Life and Labor in the Old South*. Boston: Little, Brown and Co., 1929.

Purcell, James S., Jr. *The Southern Poor White in Fiction*. Durham, N. C. 1938. Unpublished Master's Thesis, Department of English, Duke University.

Ralph, James. *Dixie, or Southern Scenes and Sketches*. New York: Harper and Bros., 1896.

Rankin, Daniel S. *Kate Chopin and Her Creole Stories*. Philadelphia: University of Pennsylvania Press, 1932.

Ransom, John C. *et al. I'll Take My Stand*. By Twelve Southerners. New York: Harper and Bros., 1930.

Reid, Whitelaw. *After the War, A Southern Tour, May 1, 1865 to May 1, 1866*. London: Sampson, Son, and Marston, 1866.

Rourke, Constance. *Davy Crockett*. New York: Harcourt, Brace and Co., 1934.

Schurz, Carl. *Reminiscences*. New York: Doubleday, Page and Co., 1917. Vol. III.

Simkins, Francis B. *The Tillman Movement in South Carolina*. Durham, N. C.: Duke University Press, 1926.

Smith, Rebecca. *The Civil War and its Aftermath in American Fiction, 1861-1899*. Unpublished Doctor's thesis, Department of English Language and Literature, University of Chicago, 1932.

Stowe, Harriet B. *A Key to Uncle Tom's Cabin*. Boston: John P. Jewett and Co., 1853.

Bibliography

Street, James H. *Look Away!* New York: Viking Press, 1936.

Sullivan, Mark. *Our Times.* New York: Charles Scribner's Sons, 1930. Vol. III.

Tandy, Jeanette. *Crackerbox Philosophers in American Humor and Satire.* New York: Columbia University Press, 1925.

Tannenbaum, Frank. *Darker Phases of the South.* New York: G. P. Putnam's Sons, 1924.

Trent, William P. *William Gilmore Simms.* Boston: Houghton Mifflin Co., 1892.

Trowbridge, John T. *A Picture of the Desolated States. . . .* Hartford, Conn.: L. Stebbins, 1868.

Turner, Lorenzo D. *Anti-slavery sentiment in American Literature prior to 1865.* Washington, D. C.: Association for the Study of Negro Life and History, Inc., 1929.

Vance, Rupert B. *Human Geography of the South.* Chapel Hill: University of North Carolina Press, 1935.

Wade, John D. *Augustus Baldwin Longstreet.* New York: Macmillan Co., 1924.

Watterson, Henry *Compromises of Life.* New York: Duffield and Co., 1906.

Wertenbaker, Thomas J. *The Planters of Colonial Virginia.* Princeton, N. J.: Princeton University Press, 1922.

———. *Patrician and Plebeian in Virginia.* Charlottesville, Va.: author, 1910.

Weston, George M. *Poor Whites of the South.* Washington, D. C.: Buell and Blanchard, 1856.

Wiggins, Robt. L. *Life of Joel Chandler Harris.* Nashville, Tenn.: Publishing House Methodist Episcopal Church, South, 1918.

III. ARTICLES OF HISTORY AND CRITICISM

Angoff, Charles and Mencken, Henry L. "The Worst American State: Part III," *American Mercury*, XXIV (November, 1931), 355-71.

Atherton, Gertrude. "Geographical Fiction," *Lippincott's Magazine*, L (July, 1892), 112-14.

The Southern Poor-White

Borst, H. W. "Social Work in Acadia," *Survey*, XLIV (April 3, 1920), 9-12.

Bradford, J. S. "Crackers," *Lippincott's Magazine*, VI (November, 1870), 457-67.

Brewer, William M. "Poor Whites and Negroes in the South since the Civil War," *Journal of Negro History*, XV (January, 1930), 26-37.

Brickell, Herschel. "The Literary Awakening in the South," *Bookman*, LXVI (October, 1927), 138-43.

Buck, Paul H. "The Poor Whites of the Antebellum South," *American Historical Review*, XXXI (October, 1925), 41-54.

Canby, Henry S. "School of Cruelty," *Saturday Review of Literature*, VII (March 21, 1931), 673-74.

Carpenter, C. T. "King Cotton's Slaves," *Scribner's Magazine*, XCVIII (October, 1935), 193-99.

Coleman, Charles W. "The Recent Movement in Southern Literature," *Harper's Magazine*, LXXIV (May, 1887), 837-55.

Crane, Verner W. "A Lost Utopia of the American Frontier," *Sewanee Review*, XXVII (January-March, 1919), 48-61.

Craven, Avery O. "Poor Whites and Negroes in the Antebellum South," *Journal of Negro History*, XV (January, 1930), 14-25.

Davis, Rebecca H. "Here and There in the South, IV: In Attakapas," *Harper's Magazine*, LXXV (November, 1887), 914-25.

DeForest, John W. "The Low-Down People," *Putnam's Magazine*, new series, I (June, 1868), 704-16.

————. "Drawing Bureau Rations, I: The Applicants," *Harper's Magazine*, XXXVI (May, 1868), 792-99.

De Leon, Edwin. 'The Bayou Teche," *Fraser's Magazine*, XI (January, 1875), 27-39.

Dickson, Harris. "Waifs of the Winding River: Shantyboat Folks," *Collier's Magazine*, XCII (September 16, 1933), 16, 29-30.

Dunning, Charles. "In a Florida Cracker's Cabin," *Lippincott's Magazine*, XXIX (April, 1882), 367-74.

"The Farm and the Novel," *Saturday Review of Literature*, VI (July 27, 1929), 1, 4.

"Florida 'Crackers,' " *Littell's Living Age*, CLIX (December, 1883), 624-29.

Bibliography

Fortier, Alcée. "The Acadians of Louisiana and Their Dialect," *Publications of the Modern Language Association*, VI (1891), 64-94.

French, Alice ("Octave Thanet"). "Plantation Life in Arkansas," *Atlantic Monthly*, LXVIII (July, 1891), 32-49.

———. "The Farmer in the South," *Scribner's Magazine*, XV (April, 1894), 402-9.

Gilmore, James R. "Poor Whites of the South," *Harper's Magazine*, XXIX (June, 1864), 115-24.

Glasgow, Ellen. "Heroes and Monsters," *Saturday Review of Literature*, XII (May 4, 1935), 3-4.

Gordon, Clarence. Mr. DeForest's Novels," *Atlantic Monthly*, XXXII (November, 1873), 611-21.

Haardt, Sara. "Ellen Glasgow and the South," *Bookman*, LXIX (April, 1929), 133-40.

Harris, Joel C. "An Accidental Author," *Lippincott's Magazine*, XXXVII (April, 1886), 417-20.

Higginson, Thomas W. "The Local Short Story," *Independent*, XLIV (November 3, 1892), 1544-45.

Holmes, George K. "The Peons of the South," *Annals of the American Academy of Political and Social Science*, IV (September, 1893), 265-74.

Howells, William D. "Harben's Georgia Fiction," *North American Review*, CXCI (March, 1910), 356-63.

———. "Some Heroines of Fiction," *Harper's Bazaar*, XXXV (October, 1901), 538-44.

Johnston, Richard M. "Middle Georgia Rural Life," *Century Magazine*, XLIII (March, 1892), 737-43.

Landrum, Grace W. "Sir Walter Scott and His Literary Rivals in the Old South," *American Literature*, II (November, 1930), 256-76.

Lanier, Sidney. "The New South," *Scribner's Magazine*, XX (October, 1880), 840-51.

"Life of the Georgia Cracker," *Current Literature*, XXVII (January, 1900), 30-31.

"Literature in the South," *Critic*, X (June 25, 1887), 322-24.

Marshall, Dexter. "The River People," *Scribner's Magazine*, XXVIII (July, 1900), 101-11.

Masterson, James R. "William Byrd in Lubberland" *American Literature*, IX (May, 1937), 153-70.

"New South," *Saturday Review of Literature*, VI (October 26, 1929), 309-10.

Ormond, J. R. "Recent Products of the New School of Southern Fiction," *South Atlantic Quarterly*, III (July, 1904), 285-89.

Page, Thomas N. "Literature of the South since the War," *Lippincott's Magazine*, XLVIII (December, 1891), 740-56.

Page, Walter H. "The Hookworm and Civilization," *World's Work*, XXIV (September, 1912), 504-18.

Pinckney, Josephine, "Southern Writers in Congress," *Saturday Review of Literature*, VIII (November 7, 1931), 266.

"Planters and Mean Whites," *Galaxy*, IV (October, 1867), 752-53.

Poe, Edgar A. "Simms's The Wigwam and the Cabin," *Works*. Eds. Edmund C. Stedman and George E. Woodberry. New York: Chas. Scribner's Sons, 1914. Vol. VIII. Published in the *Broadway Journal*, October 4, 1845.

Powers, Stephen. "With the Yam-Eaters," *Lippincott's Magazine*, IV (December, 1869), 624-29.

Redpath, James. "The New Ruling Class of the South," *Nation*, I (August 7, 1865), 605-7.

Seabrook, E. B. "Poor Whites of the South," *Galaxy*, IV (October, 1867), 681-90.

"Southern Literature," *Literary World* (Boston), XVIII (June 25, 1887), 200.

Stedman, Edmund C. "Literary Estimate . . . of Richard Malcolm Johnston," *Publications of the Southern History Association*, II (October, 1898), 315 ff.

Stowe, Harriet B. "Our Florida Plantation," *Atlantic Monthly*, XLIII (May, 1879), 641-49.

"Studies in the South, I," *Atlantic Monthly*, XLIX (January, 1882), 76-91.

Tait, John L. "Shanty-boat Folks," *World Today*, XII (May, 1907), 473-78.

Tandy, Jeannette. "Pro-slavery Propaganda in American Fiction

Bibliography

of the Fifties," *South Atlantic Quarterly*, XXI (April, 1922), 41-50.

Tate, Allen. "Regionalism and Sectionalism," *New Republic*, LXIX (December 23, 1931), 158-61.

Taylor, Mortimer F. "The Turning-point in American Literature," *Southern Magazine*, XI (September, 1872), 323-27.

Thorpe, Thomas B. "Remembrances of the Mississippi Basin," *Harper's Magazine*, XII (December, 1855), 323-27.

Tourgée, Albion W. "The South as a Field for Fiction," *Forum*, VI (December, 1888), 404-13.

Van Doren, Carl. "Made in America: Erskine Caldwell," *Nation*, CXXXVII (October 18, 1933), 443-44.

Wade, John D. "Sweet are the Uses of Degeneracy," *Southern Review*, I (Winter, 1936), 449-66.

Warner, Charles D. "The Acadian Land," *Harper's Magazine*, LXXIV (February, 1887), 234-54.

Waud, A. R. "Acadians of Louisiana," *Harper's Weekly*, X (October 20, 1866), 670.

Wells, Benjamin W. "Southern Literature of the Year," *Forum*, XXIX (June, 1900), 501-12.

Wilson, Robert. "In the Pineland," *Lippincott's Magazine*, XVI (October, 1875), 441-49.

IV. LITERATURE

Adams, Edward C. L. "The Carolina Wilderness," *Scribner's Magazine*, LXXXIX (June, 1931), 611-16.

Alderman, Edwin A. *et al.* (eds.). *Library of Southern Literature.* Atlanta: Martin and Hoyt and Co., 1907. Vols. IV, IX.

Bird, Robert M. *Nick of the Woods.* New York: Vanguard Press, 1928.

Boyd, William K. (ed.). *William Byrd's Histories of the Dividing Line Betwixt Virginia and North Carolina.* Raleigh: North Carolina Historical Commission, 1929.

Burke, Thomas A. (ed.). *Polly Peablossom's Wedding.* Philadelphia: T. B. Peterson, 1851.

Burman, Ben L. "Minstrels of the Mist," *Best Short Stories of 1927.*

Edited by Edward J. O'Brien. New York: Dodd, Mead and Co., 1928.

———. *Mississippi*. New York: Cosmopolitan Book Corp., 1929.

———. *Steamboat Round the Bend*. Boston: Little, Brown and Co., 1935. Published 1933.

Burton, William E. (ed.). *Cyclopaedia of Wit and Humor*. New York: D. Appleton and Co., 1858. Vol. I.

Cable, George W. *Bonaventure*. New York: Chas. Scribner's Sons, 1888.

Caldwell, Erskine. *American Earth*. New York: Chas. Scribner's Sons, 1931.

———. *God's Little Acre*. New York: Modern Library, 1934. Published 1933.

———. *Tobacco Road*. New York: Crosset and Dunlap, 1934. Published 1932.

———. *We Are the Living*. New York: Viking, 1933.

Caruthers, William A. *The Kentuckian in New York*. New York: Harper and Bros., 1834. 2 vols.

Carver, Ada J. "Cajun," *American Scene*. Edited by Barrett H. Clark and Kenyon Nicholson. New York: D. Appleton and Co. 1930.

Chopin, Kate. *Bayou Folk*. Boston: Houghton-Mifflin Co., 1894.

———. *A Night in Acadie*. Chicago: Way and Williams, 1897.

Cobb, Irvin S. "Snake Doctor," *O. Henry Memorial Award Prize Stories of 1922*. Garden City, N. Y.: Doubleday, Page and Co., 1923.

Cobb, Joseph B. *Mississippi Scenes*. Philadelphia: A. Hart, 1851.

Crevecoeur, St. Jean de. *Letters from an American Farmer*. Edited by Ludwig Lewisohn. New York: Fox,Duffield and Co., 1904.

Crockett, David. *Autobiography*. Edited by Hamlin Garland. New York: Chas. Scribner's Sons, 1923.

Davis, Mary E. M. *An Elephant's Track and Other Stories*. New York: Harper and Bros., 1897.

DeForest, John W. "Kate Beaumont," *Atlantic Monthly*, XXVII (January-June, 1871), 70-92; 184-201; 298-321; 446-62; 573-89; 726-43; XXVIII (July-December, 1871), 45-63; 189-206; 289-306; 483-99; 546-63; 660-77.

Bibliography

————. "An Independent Kuklux," *Galaxy*, XIII (April, 1872), 480-88.

Earl, Mary T. "The Man Who Worked for Collister," *Century Magazine*, LIII (March, 1897), 728-32.

Edwards, Harry S. *Two Runaways and Other Stories*. New York: Century Co., 1904.

Faulkner, William. *As I Lay Dying*. New York: H. Smith, 1930.

————. *Doctor Martino and Other Stories*. New York: H. Smith and R. Haas, 1934.

————. *Light in August*. New York: H. Smith and R. Haas, 1932.

————. "Lizards in Jamshyd's Courtyard," *Saturday Evening Post*, CCIV (February 27, 1932), 12-13, 52, 57.

————. "Spotted Horses," *Scribner's Magazine*, LXXXIX (June, 1931), 585-97.

Fort, John. *God in the Straw Pen*. . . . New York: Dodd, Mead and Co., 1931.

French, Alice. *Expiation*. New York: Chas. Scribner's Sons, 1901. Published 1890.

————. *Knitters in the Sun*. Boston: Houghton Mifflin Co., 1887.

————. *Otto The Knight and Other Trans-Mississippi Stories*. Boston: Houghton Mifflin Co., 1891.

Gilmore, James R. *Among the Guerillas*. New York: G. W. Carleton, 1866.

————. *My Southern Friends*. New York: G. W. Carleton, 1863.

Glasgow, Ellen. *Barren Ground*. Garden City, N. Y.: Doubleday, Page and Co., 1925.

————. *The Deliverance*. New York: Doubleday, Page and Co., 1904.

————. *The Descendant*. New York: Harper and Bros., 1905. First published in 1897.

————. *The Miller of Old Church*. Garden City, N. Y.: Doubleday, Page and Co., 1911.

————. *The Voice of the People*. Garden City, N. Y.: Doubleday, Page and Co., 1900.

Green, Erma and Paul. "Fixins, The Tragedy of a Tenant-Farm Woman," *Carolina Folk-plays*. Edited by Frederick H. Koch.

Second and Third Series; New York: Henry Holt and Co., 1924, 1928.

Green, Paul. *The Field God and In Abraham's Bosom.* New York: Robert M. McBride and Co., 1927.

——. *The House of Connelly and Other Plays.* New York: Samuel French, 1931.

——. *In the Valley and Other Carolina Plays.* New York: Samuel French, 1928.

——. *The Laughing Pioneer.* New York: R. M. McBride and Co., 1932.

——. "The Lord's Will," *Poet Lore*, XXXII (Autumn, 1922), 366-84; *The Lord's Will and Other Carolina Plays.* New York: Samuel French, 1927.

——. *Wide Fields.* New York: R. M. McBride and Co. 1928.

Green, Frederick S. "The Cat of the Cane-brake," *Best Short Stories of 1916.* Edited by E. J. O'Brien. Boston: Small, Maynard and Co., 1917.

Griswold, Rufus (ed.). *Prose Writers of America.* Philadelphia: Carey and Hart, 1847.

Haliburton, Thomas C. (ed.). *Americans at Home, or, Byeways, Backwoods, and Prairies.* London: Hurst and Blackett Publishers, 1854. 3 vols.

——. *Traits of American Humor by Native Authors.* London: Colburn and Co., 1852. 3 vols.

Harben, Will N. *Northern Georgia Sketches.* Chicago: A. C. McClurg and Co , 1900.

Harris, Joel C. *Balaam and His Master.* Boston: Houghton Mifflin Co., 1899. First published in 1891.

——. *Free Joe and Other Georgia Sketches.* New York: Chas. Scribner's Sons, 1887.

——. *Mingo and Other Sketches in Black and White.* Boston: James R. Osgood and Co., 1884.

——. *On the Wing of Occasions.* New York: Doubleday, Page and Co., 1900.

——. *On the Plantation.* New York: D. Appleton and Co., 1892.

——. *Stories of Georgia.* New York: American Book Co., 1896.

Bibliography

Haynes, William. *Sandhills Sketches*. New York: D. O. Haynes and Co., 1916.

Hildreth, Richard. *The Slave, or, Memoirs of Archy Moore*. 2d. ed.; Boston: Whipple and Damrell, 1840. First published 1836.

Hooper, Johnson J. *Simon Suggs' Adventures*. . . . Americus, Ga.: Americus Book Co., 1928. Published in part 1846.

Hungerford, James W. *The Old Plantation and What I Gathered There*. New York: Harper and Bros., 1859.

Johnston, Mary. *Prisoners of Hope*. Boston: Houghton Mifflin Co., 1900. Published 1899.

Johnston, Richard M. *Autobiography of Col. Richard Malcolm Johnston*. Washington, D. C.: Neale Co., 1900.

———. *Dukesborough Tales*. New York: D. Appleton and Co., 1892. First published as *Georgia Sketches* (1864); editions under second title in 1871, '74, '83, '92.

———. *Old Times in Middle Georgia*. New York: Macmillan Co., 1897.

———. *The Primes and their Neighbors*. New York: D. Appleton and Co., 1891.

———. "The Various Languages of Billy Moon," *Harper's Magazine*, LXII (August, 1881), 395-99.

Kelley, Edith. *Weeds*. New York: Harcourt, Brace and Co., 1923.

Kennedy, John P. *Swallow Barn*. New York: Geo. P. Putnam, 1851. First published 1832.

Kroll, Harry H. *Cabin in the Cotton*. New York: R. Long and R. R. Smith, 1930.

Lane, Rose W. "Innocence," *O. Henry Memorial Award Prize Stories of 1922*. Garden City, N. Y.: Doubleday, Page and Co., 1923.

Lanier, Sidney. *Poems*. New York: Chas. Scribner's Sons, 1923.

Lee, Addie McG. *Playing 'Possum and Other Pine Woods Stories*. Baton Rouge, La.: Truth Book and Job Office, 1895.

Lewis, Henry C. *Louisiana Swamp Doctor*. By Madison Tenses, M. D. Philadelphia: T. B. Peterson and Bros., 1881. First published *ca.* 1843.

Longstreet, Augustus B. *Georgia Scenes, Characters, Incidents, etc.*,

The Southern Poor-White

in the First Half Century of the Republic. By a Native Georgian. Augusta: S. R. Sentinel Office, 1835.

McClelland, Mary G. "A Self-Made Man," *Lippincott's Magazine*, XXXIX (January, 1887), 195-284.

McNeil, John C. *Lyrics from Cotton Land*. Charlotte, N. C.: Stone and Barringer Co., 1907.

Meine, Franklin J. (ed.). *Tall Tales of the Southwest*. New York: Alfred A. Knopf, 1930.

Milward, Maria G. "Country Annals," *Southern Literary Messenger*, VII (January, 1841), 37-48; (February, 1841), 199-22.

Nott, Henry. *Novellettes of a Traveller.* . . . New York: Harper and Bros., 1834.

Page, Thomas N. *Burial of the Guns*. New York: Chas. Scribner's Sons, 1912.

———. *Works*. New York: Chas. Scribner's Sons, 1908. Vol. XI.

Page, Walter H. "The Autobiography of a Southerner Since the Civil War" by "Nicholas Worth." *Atlantic Monthly*, XCVIII (July, 1906), 1-12; (August, 1906), 157-76; (September, 1906), 311-25; (October, 1906), 474-88.

Paulding, James K. *Westward Ho!* New York: J. and J. Harper, 1832. 2 vols.

Pendleton, Louis. *In the Wire-grass*. New York: D. Appleton and Co., 1889.

Porter, William T. (ed.). *The Big Bear of Arkansas and Other Sketches—*. Philadelphia: T. B. Peterson and Bros., 1843.

———. (ed.). *Major Thorpe's Scenes in Arkansas*. Philadelphia: T. B. Peterson and Bros., 1858.

Rawlings, Marjorie K. "A Plumb Clare Conscience," *Scribner's Magazine*, XC (December, 1931), 622-26.

———. "Cracker Chidlings: Real Tales from the Florida Interior," *Scribner's Magazine*, LXXXIX (February, 1931), 127-34.

———. "Jacob's Ladder," *Scribner's Magazine*, LXXXIX (April, 1931), 351-66, 446-64.

———. *South Moon Under*. New York: Chas. Scribner's Sons, 1933.

Read, Opie. *An Arkansas Planter*. Chicago: Rand, McNally and Co., 1896.

Bibliography

Roberts, Elizabeth M. *The Time of Man.* New York: Grosset and Dunlap, 1928. First published 1926.

Rogers, John W. "Bumblebuppy" (1926), *American Scene.* Edited by Barrett H. Clark and Kenyon Nicholson. New York: D. Appleton and Co., 1930.

Scarborough, Dorothy. *In the Land of Cotton.* New York: Macmillan Co., 1923.

———. *Can't Get a Red Bird.* New York: Harper and Bros. 1929.

Seaworthy, Gregory. *Bertie, or, Life in the Old Field.* Philadelphia: A. Hart, 1851.

Shelby, Gertrude M. and Stoney, Samuel G. *Po' Buckra.* New York: Macmillan Co., 1930.

Simms, William G. *Guy Rivers.* New York: A. C. Armstrong and Son, 1882. All novels of this edition. *Guy Rivers* first published 1834.

Simms, Wm. G. "Home Sketches—," *Literary World* (New York), X (February 7, 1852), 107-10.

———. *Mellichampe.* First published 1836.

———. *The Partisan.* First published 1835.

———. *Poems.* New York: Redfield, 1853. Vol. II.

———. *Richard Hurdis.* First published 1838.

———. *Wigwam and Cabin.* First published 1841-'43.

———. *Woodcraft, or Hawks about the Dovecote.* First published as *The Sword and the Distaff* (Charleston, 1852).

Sketches and Eccentricities of Col. David Crockett of West Tennessee. 11th ed.; Louisville, Ky.: Morton and Griswold, no date. First published 1833.

Smith, Charles H. ("Bill Arp"). *Bill Arp's Scrap Book.* Atlanta: J. P. Harrison and Co., 1884.

———. *Bill Arp, So Called.* A Side Show of the Southern Side of the War. New York: Metropolitan Record Office, 1866.

———. *Farm and the Fireside.* Atlanta: Constitution Publishing Co., 1892.

———. *From the Uncivil War to Date, 1861-1903.* Atlanta: Hudgins Publishing Co., 1903.

Southern Chivalry, The Adventures of G. Whillikens, C. S. A., Knight of the Golden Circle and of Guinea Pete, his negro Squire. An Epic

Doggerel in Six Books. By a Citizen of the Cotton Country. Philadelphia: For Sale by all Booksellers, 1861.

Spears, Raymond S. *The River Prophet*. New York: Doubleday, Page and Co., 1920.

Stowe, Harriet B. *Dred*. Boston: Houghton Mifflin Co., 1884. First published 1856.

Stribling, Thomas S. *The Store*. Garden City, N. Y.: Doubleday, Doran and Co., 1932.

Stuart, Ruth McE. "Bud Zant's Mail," *Harper's Magazine*, LXXXVIII (December, 1893), 58-70.

Sutherland, Evelyn G. *Po' White Trash and Other One-act Dramas*. Chicago: Herbert S. Stowe and Co., 1900.

Taliaferro, H. E. ("Skitt"). *Fisher's River (North Carolina), Scenes and Characters—*. New York: Harper and Bros., 1859.

————. "Parson Squint," *Southern Literary Messenger*, XXXII (January, 1861), 50-52.

Thompson, Maurice. *Stories of the Cherokee Hills*. Boston: Houghton Mifflin Co., 1900. First published 1898.

Thorpe, Thomas B. *The Master's House*. New York: L. L. McElrath and Co., 1854.

————. *Mysteries of the Backwoods*. Philadelphia: Carey and Hart, 1846.

Tourgée, Albion W. *Bricks Without Straw*. New York: Fords, Howard and Hulbert, 1880.

————. *The Fool's Errand*. New York: Fords, Howard, and Hulbert, 1879.

————. *John Eax*. New York: Fords, Howard, and Hulbert, 1882.

Trowbridge, John T. *Cudjo's Cave*. Boston: Lothrop, Lee and Shepard Co., 1891. First published 1864.

Tucker, George. *The Valley of the Shenandoah—*. New York: Chas. Wiley, 1824. 2 vols.

Tucker, Nathaniel Beverley. *George Balcombe*. New York: Harper and Bros., 1836. 2 vols. in one.

Uhler, John E. *Cane Juice*. New York: Century Co., 1931.

Underwood, Francis H. *Lord of Himself*. Boston: Lee and Shepard, 1874.

Wall, Evans. *No-nation Girl*. New York: Century Co., 1929.

Bibliography

Watterson, Henry (ed.). *Oddities in Southern Life and Character.*
Boston: Houghton Mifflin Co., 1883.

Williamson, Harold. "Peggy, A Tragedy of the Tenant Farmer,"
Carolina Folk-plays. Edited by Frederick H. Koch. First series:
New York: Henry Holt and Co., 1922.

Wilt, Napier (ed.). *Some American Humorists.* New York: Thos.
Nelson and Sons, 1929.

Woolson, Constance F. *Rodman the Keeper, Southern Sketches.*
New York: Harper and Bros., 1886. First published 1880.

INDEX

INDEX

ABOLITIONISTS, xxiii, 19, 24, 33, 47, 74, 88-89, 190
Adams, E. C. L., 220
Agar, Herbert, 165 n.
Alabama. xxi, 24, 42, 52, 56, 86, 137, 176, 194
American Revolution, 27, 28, 30
Arkansas, xvii, 42, 47, 55, 104, 154, 168, 177

BAGBY, George W., 43-44, 69, 103
Ball, W. W., 82 n., 168
Beale, R. C., xv n. 107 n.
Beard, Charles and Mary, 76 n.
Bethea, Jack, 193-94
Beverley, Robert, 12
Bishop, John Peale, 164
Bowers, Claude, 84 n.
Bradford, J. S., xvi n. xx n.
Brickell, Herschel, 169
Brown, William G., 166
Bryant, William Cullen, 102
Buck, Paul H., 74 n., 172
Burman, Ben Lucien, 179-80
Byrd, William, xxiii, 8, 22, 59, 219, 232

CABLE, George W., 105, 198
Caldwell, Erskine, xiv, 39, 100, 156, 219
Canby, Henry Seidel, 160 n., 219
Carolina Playmakers, 173

Caruthers, William A., 21-23, 184, 219-20
Carver, Ada Jack, 178
Cather, Willa, 200, 230
Charleston, S. C., 42, 122, 167-68
Chaucer, Geoffrey, 226-27
Civil War, xiv, 36-37, 66, 72, 74, 121-23, 125-27
Classes of southern society, xiv, 21-22, 36-38
Climate of South, xx-xxi, 177-78
Cobb, Irvin S., 176-77
Cobb, Joseph B., 43, 54-55, 72, 222
Cooke, John Eston, 43
Creoles, xv, 109, 143
Crockett, David, 44-48

DABNEY, Virginius, 167 n.
Davis, Rebecca H., 140, 145
DeForest, John W., xiii n., 81 n., 85 n., 86 n., 96, 231-32
Deland, Margaret, 135-36, 137
Dennett, Daniel, 146
Determinism, 218, 235
Ditchy, Jay K., 139
Dwight, Timothy, xix

FAULKNER, William, 164
Fleming, Walter L., 78 n., 81 n., 83 n.
Florida, 78-79, 104, 135

Fortier, Alcée, 139
Freedman's Bureau, 81, 85
French, Alice ("Octave Thaney"), 138, 224, 225
Frontier influences, xvii, xix-xxii, 8, 31, 47, 181
Frost, Robert, 200
Fugitive group (Nashville), 170

GAINES, Francis P., 24 n., 33 n.
Georgia, 22, 28, 49, 52-54, 63, 128, 133, 137
Gilmore, James R., 37-39
Glasgow, Ellen, 172, 217, 232
Grady, Henry W., 101, 102-3, 113, 164-65
Green, Paul, 224, 227, 232
Greene, Frederick S., 176
Gregg, William, xxii-xxiii, 102
Griswold, Rufus, 26 n., 43
Growth of social studies in South, 172-73

HALIBURTON, Thomas C., 52
Harben, Will N., 161
Harris, Joel Chandler, xiv, 75-76, 107, 130, 161
Hart, A. B., 167 n.
Hayne, Paul Hamilton, 105
Haynes, William, 174-75
Hazard, Lucy L., 7 n., 44 n.
Hildreth, Richard, 32-33
Hollander, A. N. J. Den, 172
Hooper, Johnson J., 48-49, 71-72
Howe, Ed W., 112
Howells, William Dean, 93, 128

Hundley, Daniel R., xxii n., 67 n.
Hungerford, James, 20

INDIANS, 6-7, 28, 31
Ingraham, Joseph H., 56 n.
Interest in the South, 106 n.
Irving, Washington, 101

JOHNSTON, Richard Malcolm, 42 n., 63, 110, 231
Jones, Hugh, xxiii, 4, 5, 9, 13 n.

KENNEDY, John Pendleton, 18, 19
Kentucky, 21, 104, 201, 203
King, Edward, 82 n., 100, 139
Kroll, Harry H., xiii n., 197-98
Ku Klux Klan, 83, 96-99

LANE, Rose Wilder, 177
Lanier, Sidney, 101, 162
Lawson, John, 7 n., 13
Lewisohn, Ludwig, 167-68
Lincoln, Abraham, xvii
Longstreet, Augustus Baldwin, 49-51, 55, 57-59, 230
Louisiana, xvii, 23, 138-40, 178
Lyell, Charles, 59 n.

McNEIL, John Charles, xx n.
Mesick, Jessie L., xxi n.
Mississippi, 54, 56, 136
Moore, A. B., 77 n. 78 n.
Mountaineers, xxiv-xxv, 78, 102, 109

Index

NORDHOFF, Charles, 83 n., 84
n., 100, 102
North Carolina, xiv-xv, 22-23,
24, 36, 38, 175, 206, 209, 214

ODUM, Howard W., 112 n., 172
n.
Outrage mongers, 107
Overseers, xxii, 35, 187, 189

PAGE, Thomas Nelson, xiii, 76
n., 77, 79, 87 n., 105, 106
Page, Walter Hines, 101, 192,
214
Parrington, Vernon L., 218
Pendleton, Louis, xv n., 133-34,
138
Phillips, Ulrich B., xv n.
Planters, xv, xvii, 16, 17, 24, 34,
82, 167
Poor-whites:
  amusements, 35, 66-69
  appearance, 13-14, 22, 52, 56,
    57-58, 94-95
  crime, 29, 35, 81, 83 n., 98
  definition of the class, xvi-
    xviii
  diseases, xviii, 13-14, 59, 165-
    66, 170-71
  food, xx, 166
  habitats, 135, 163-64, 180,
    182
  illiteracy, 30, 89, 144-46, 171
  immorality, xviii, 28, 38-39,
    85, 158, 184, 188, 222-27
  laziness, 11-13, 146-47

and Negroes, xiii, xxiii, 33, 35,
  83, 84, 166-67, 168
nicknames, xiii-xvi
origins, xviii-xxiv
politics, 24, 33, 34, 47, 72-74,
  84, 147, 167-68, 172
pride, 86, 236 n.
religion, 5-6, 145, 214, 238
work, 34, 35, 86
Porter, William T., 47 n.

RALPH, James, 143
Rawlings, Marjorie K., 180,
  183-84
Redpath, James, 137
Reid, Whitelaw, 88
Roberts, Elizabeth Madox, 219,
  230
Rogers, John W., 177-78
Rourke, Constance, 45 n.

SCARBOROUGH, Dorothy, 195-
  97, 219
Schurz, Carl, 78, 82 n., 86
Shelby, G. M. and Stoney, S.
  G., xiii n.
Simms, William Gilmore, 25-32,
  44, 155, 227
Smith, Charles H. ("Bill Arp"),
  xvi, 62-66, 231
South Carolina, xiii, xxi, 21, 25,
  90, 94, 220
Southern literature, 17-18, 42-
  44, 87-88, 105-6, 110-11, 128,
  149, 159-62
Southern literary taste, 17-19,
  41-44, 74, 88

Southern Tenant Farmers Union, 168
Stedman, Edmund Clarence, 106, 129
Stiles, C. W., 170
Stowe, Harriet Beecher, 34, 35, 36, 77 n., 78-79
Street, James H., xiv n.
Stribling, T. S., 194-95
Stuart, Ruth McEnery, 161 n.

Taliaferro, H. E. ("Skitt"), 44, 56, 60-62, 230
Tandy, Jeannette, 41 n., 74 n.
Tannenbaum, Frank, 171 n.
Taylor, Mortimer F., 129 n.
Taylor, Richard, 144-45
Tennessee, 36, 80, 104, 173
Texas, 103, 132, 135
Thompson, William Tappan, xxiv, 59-60
Thorpe, Thomas B., 23-25, 55 n.
Tourgée, Albion W., 82 n., 173, 184

Trent, W. P., 26 n., 30 n., 31 n.
Trowbridge, John T., 34 n., 36, 88
Tucker, George, 20-21, 56
Tucker, Nathaniel Beverley, 23

Underwood, Francis H., 99 n.

Van Doren, Carl, 225
Vance, Rupert B., xvii, 57 n., 166 n.
Virginia, xvii, 4, 12-13, 37, 103-4, 125, 184 passim

Wagoners, 21, 55-57
Warner, Charles Dudley, 140, 146
Watterson, Henry, 41-42, 102 n.
Williamson, Harold, 173, 209-10
Wilt, Napier, 64
Woolson, Constance Fenimore, 103, 108-9, 153, 180, 184